Toni Morrison: Conversations

Edited by
Carolyn C. Denard

University Press of Mississippi
Jackson

Publication of this book is made possible in part by a gift from Peggy Whitman Prenshaw.

Books by Toni Morrison

Fiction

The Bluest Eye. New York: Holt, Rinehart, & Winston, 1970.
Sula. New York: Knopf, 1973.
Song of Solomon. New York: Knopf, 1977.
Tar Baby. New York: Knopf, 1981.
Beloved. New York: Knopf, 1987.
Jazz. New York: Knopf, 1992.
Paradise. New York: Knopf, 1998.
Love. New York: Knopf, 2003.

Nonfiction

Playing in the Dark: Whiteness and the Literary Imagination.
    Cambridge: Harvard University Press, 1992.
Remember: The Journey to School Integration. New York: Houghton Mifflin, 2004.

Edited Books

Race-ing Justice, En-gendering Power: Essays on Anita Hill, Clarence Thomas,
    and the Construction of Social Reality. New York: Pantheon Books, 1992.

With Claudia Brodsky Lacour:
Birth of a Nation'hood: Gaze, Script, and Spectacle in the O. J. Simpson Case. New York:
    Pantheon Books, 1997.

www.upress.state.ms.us

The University Press of Mississippi is a member of the Association of American University Presses.

First printing 2008
∞
Library of Congress Cataloging-in-Publication Data

Toni Morrison : conversations / edited by Carolyn C. Denard.
    p. cm. — (Literary conversations series)
    Includes index.
    ISBN 978-1-60473-018-0 (alk. paper) — ISBN 978-1-60473-019-7 (pbk. : alk. paper)
1. Morrison, Toni—Interviews. 2. Authors, American—20th century—Interviews.
3. African American authors—Interviews. I. Morrison, Toni. II. Denard, Carolyn C.
    PS3563.O8749Z46 2008
    813'.54—dc22

                                                                2008003697

British Library Cataloging-in-Publication Data available

Contents

Acknowledgments

Many individuals and institutions contributed to the completion of this volume. I am grateful for the assistance of Rosemary Cullen, Scholarly Resource Librarian at Brown University; Alex Harris at the Center for Documentary Studies at Duke University; Frankie Anderson, Reference Librarian at Wells College; and Jennifer Sandoval, my student assistant at Wells. They all provided knowledgeable and timely assistance when I was in the retrieval stage of this project.

I am especially grateful to the interviewers who have had such wonderful conversations with Toni Morrison over the years and who granted me permission to include them in this volume.

I would also like to thank my colleagues in the Office of the Dean of the College at Brown University for their support, especially my assistant Arlene Sena, whose interest in the project and whose kind encouragement sustained me. I would also like to offer my thanks and appreciation to Seetha Srinivasan, director at the University Press of Mississippi, for her enthusiastic support of this volume.

My gratitude to all of my friends and family for their support of me personally and professionally throughout the completion of this project is immeasurable. I would especially like to thank Kristine Yohe at Northern Kentucky University, who read drafts of the introduction and provided invaluable assistance with the chronology, and Janet Gabler-Hover at Georgia State University, who supported me at every stage of this project. I would also like to thank my daughter Miriam, who transcribed the Michael Silverblatt interviews with such care, and my husband Don, who is always my best reader and who supports me in countless ways in all that I do in the academy.

Finally, and most importantly, I would like to thank Toni Morrison, who approved the interviews collected in this volume and encouraged me in its publication. Her wisdom and wit, her insight and artistry, and her willingness to engage, again and again, in important conversations of our time are truly gifts to us all.

Introduction

This collection represents nearly thirty years of Toni Morrison talking about her life, her work, African American history and culture, and American society. Included here are twenty-five conversations that Morrison has had with journalists, scholars, and novelists in the United States and abroad. They are all newly collected interviews not published before in a single volume. Scholars and teachers who have appreciated Danille Taylor-Guthrie's first collection of interviews, *Conversations with Toni Morrison* (University Press of Mississippi, 1994), should find this new collection a great addition to the continuing conversation that Morrison has been having with the nation and the world now for over three decades.

Because Toni Morrison has such a broad profile—having spent nearly twenty years as a senior editor at Random House, taught and written about literature as a college professor, published eight highly acclaimed novels, and stayed actively engaged in the political and social changes in American society for more than thirty years—there is much to learn from reading these interviews. Topics range from her personal and professional involvement in literature—as a working mother, as editor, as teacher, and as writer—to national and global issues, including slavery, racism, art, politics, the Civil Rights movement, the Women's Movement, capitalism, jazz, the Nobel Prize, and the role of the artist in society. In each interview we are reminded of the great courage and depth of experience that Toni Morrison brings to the world of literature and of how committed she has been to her craft throughout her life.

"The literary interview," as Dianne Vipond points out in her own introduction to *Conversations with John Fowles*, "is a hybrid critical genre which blurs the boundaries of everyday conversation, journalism, literary criticism, and scholarship, its multiple nature providing a unique prism through which to view the artist. The facets of the prism—artistic process and conviction, philosophy, political orientation, biography, as well as personal interest—

serve as useful reference points in any reading or re-reading of the writer's work and expand the context in which it may be considered, yielding perspectives that may lead to new critical insights."[1] Certainly that is the case with this volume of interviews with Toni Morrison. Having been editor, teacher, and literary scholar, Morrison brings an incredible meta-consciousness to her own writing process and to the place her work holds in the literary canon. William Wimsatt's and Monroe Beardsley's caution regarding the "intentional fallacy"[2]— believing entirely what the writer says about the intentions of his or her own work—is well respected in literary criticism. In Morrison's case, however, because of her broad knowledge of literary history and criticism and her very deliberate construction and analysis of the literary artifice through teaching, editing, and writing, Wimsatt's and Beardsley's caution is less warranted. Moreover, if there is also qualitative value in knowing an individual's own perception of the meaning of his or her actions, then hearing Morrison talk about her work as a novelist in this self-reflective way has a particular scholarly merit. Such is the exciting challenge that the literary interview offers, and readers and scholars of Morrison's fiction should find these interviews especially rewarding.

The collection opens with Jessica Harris's 1976 interview essay, "I Will Always Be a Writer." Harris's profile gives a wonderful portrait of Morrison at the beginning of her writing career, when she was a senior editor at Random House, raising two small children, teaching part-time, and writing novels in the evening. We have often read those biographical entries about Morrison's "twenty years as an editor at Random House," but rarely do we get a glimpse of her in her office at Random House, working as an editor. Harris provides that view in this essay and talks with Morrison specifically about how she approaches her work as an editor: "When I edit somebody else's book," Morrison explains, "no vanity is involved. I simply want the writer to do the very best work he can do. Now if that means letting him alone, I'll do that. If it means holding hands, I'll hold hands. If it means fussing, I'll fuss."

During her years at Random House, Morrison was the editor for quite an impressive group of writers, and she seems to have had a close and admiring relationship with all of them. Of Muhammad Ali, she says, "he's absolutely as fascinating as he says he is," of Angela Davis, "very coherent, bright, very loving woman . . . She's the genuine article." And Morrison knows without hesitation their strengths: Gayl Jones's rich imagination, Toni Cade Bambara's reliable ear, and Lucille Clifton's poetic prose. We are not used to getting this kind of detailed information about Morrison as an editor, and readers and scholars who have an increasing interest in Morrison's biography should find the Harris interview essay a great introduction to this phase of Morrison's life.

What is also interesting in these early interviews is the nearly prophetic way that they sometimes forecast the future direction of her fiction. When Morrison tells Paula Giddings in 1977 about how important memory is to her work, we can't help but think of *Beloved*, a novel that would not be published until ten years later: "the memory is long, beyond the parameters of cognition. I don't want to sound too mystical about it, but I feel like a conduit, I really do. I'm fascinated by what it means to make somebody remember what I don't even know." Later in the interview, she foretells what will become the kernel story of *Jazz*, fifteen years before its publication, when she talks to Paula Giddings about the James Van Der Zee photograph of the young girl whose lover shot her at a party with a silencer and her refusal, as she was dying, to tell who had done it. Morrison was intrigued by the story accompanying that photo even then: "Who loves that intensely anymore?" She insists with interviewers that the sources—history or folklore—that work best for her are those that come out of an African or African American cultural matrix, providing context not just for *Song of Solomon*, which was being celebrated in the interview with Giddings, but for all of the novels that will follow. And she tells nearly every interviewer, long before the publication of *Love* in 2003, that all of her novels are really about love.

It is clear in these interviews that Morrison is also deeply grounded in the lessons and traditions of her family. Morrison's mother and father gave her a sense of wholeness and self-possession that sustains her even today. In her interview with Claudia Dreifus, where she laments not having her first novel published under her given name, Chloe Wofford, she explains the legacy that her parents passed on to her: "Growing up in Lorain, my parents made us all feel as though there were these extraordinary deserving people within us. I felt like an aristocrat—or what I think an aristocrat is. I always knew we were very poor. But that was never degrading." Hers was a house filled with song, and stories, and reading. Her mother used part of her "hard earned money," she tells Dreifus, to join a book club, and Morrison as a young girl read those books eagerly.

In my interview, "Blacks, Modernism, and the American South," Morrison explains that her mother and father had both migrated from the South, but they had "diametrically opposed positions" about the region. Her mother was often nostalgic about the Black community life of her Alabama childhood, but she never went back. Her father thought Georgia was "the most racist state in the Union," but he went back regularly. Morrison has, as a result, a complex understanding of the South. Both the terrible memories of racial subjugation and the fond memories of the language, the food, and the manners of the Black South were very much a part of her family history. In her novels, she regularly explores this larger, more complex understanding of the South in African American life. "You see my struggle with the South is to keep it from being just the old place. What Black people did in this country was brand new. These people were very inventive, very creative, and that was a very modern situation .... Out of thrown things, they invented everything."

In her interviews with other fiction writers, Morrison talks more specifically about her own works. With Salman Rushdie, an interview that appeared in the London literary monthly *Brick* after the publication of *Jazz* in 1992, she shares the challenges and the rewards of having a novel where the title worked on so many levels: as theme, structure, and setting. "What I was interested in was the concept of jazz, the jazz era, what all of that meant before it became appropriated and redistributed as music throughout the world. What was jazz when it was just music for the people and what were those people like?" With A. J. Verdelle, on the occasion of the publication of *Paradise* in 1998, she talks about the central question that informed the writing of the novel. She was interested, she explains to Verdelle, in exploring the "differences among Black people .... I'm interested to know whether [race] matters to the reader. I'm interested to know when does it stop mattering? ... And I was mightily interested in the language you have to create in order to *not* signal race. ... To refuse to do that was in some ways daunting for me, ... but I couldn't take those short cuts anymore." Diane McKinney-Whetstone, like Verdelle, was also intrigued by Morrison's desire that each of her novels address a central question. In her interview, McKinney-Whetstone wants to know the question Morrison was trying to explore in *Love*: "I was interested," Morrison explains, "in the way in which sexual love and other kinds of love lend themselves to betrayal. How do ordinary people end up ruining the thing they most want to protect?" In her conversations with Angels Carabi, Pepsi Charles, Eugene Redmond, Donald Suggs, and Sheldon Hackney,

Morrison provides other interesting insights on her writing strategies and reading and teaching her novels.

In a provocative interview with novelist Cecil Brown, Morrison talks about the relationship between Black men and women writers and the race and gender implications of the characters they create in their fiction. Black men, she says, have seemed more interested, historically, in confronting the "White gaze." Black women writers "seem to be less interested in this confrontation." She points out to Brown, however, that this should not create a necessarily adversarial relationship. "There are many ways," she tells him, "to destabilize racism, and protest novels are only one way." In addition to the broad discussions about political implications of the strategies used by men and women writers, Brown is also interested more specifically in the multi-dimensional characters that Morrison creates in her fiction and her sources for those characterizations. "How do you create somebody like Son," Brown asks, "a Black man who comes out of the sea?" Understanding fully the cultural implications of the kind of man that "comes out of the sea," Morrison answers confidently: "I know Black men like that! My father was like that! My uncle was like that! And I don't have those who are not like that. If they are not like that, I don't have them." She clearly enjoys the highly charged gender conversation that she has with Brown: "Most interviewers don't ask me questions like the ones you have put to me that would lead me to say personally what my own version is about my regard, my fascination, and my awe, as well as love for Black people."

Morrison also talks in these conversations about her role as a teacher and what she thinks is required to be successful in the classroom. "Good teachers," she tells Ann Hostetler in 2002, "need both research and experience, both analysis and intuition." As a professor at Princeton for nearly twenty years, Morrison taught creative writing courses and a course she designed on American Africanism, lectures from which she later delivered at Harvard and published as *Playing in the Dark: Whiteness and the Literary Imagination* in 1992. Teaching the novel, she explains to Hostetler, should be an exploration, "it should be about asking your students how they occupy the space of the world the writer has created." At Princeton, she also founded and directed the Princeton Atelier, a studio arts performance course where undergraduates work directly with a practicing artist. Students in the arts, Morrison insists, must understand the hard work necessary to be good at what they do. "It is really hard," she tells Pam Houston, "and I thought that if someone came and worked them to death then, they would figure it out, and they do."

As a teacher, editor, writer, and as one deeply interested in the way in which the social and political changes of the last fifty years have affected Black life in America, Morrison has a clear understanding of the role of the novel in African American life in the post–Civil Rights era. The massive move of many Blacks into the middle class as a result of integration was accompanied by a loss of the kind of cohesive cultural knowledge that sustained Blacks during segregation, the knowledge that was passed down in stories, in conversations, and in music. Because of the changes in those communities that necessarily came with integration, Morrison believes that the novel must now serve the role for Blacks that it has served for the middle class of every culture: "the novel exists," she tells Audrey McCluskey in 1986, "as it always has, to inform a class about how it ought to behave and what it ought to know." "Where," she asks McCluskey, "do you find information about how to hang onto what it is that is important and how to give up things that are not? I think in a real political sense, novels function for Black people now in a way that they may not have in 1930 when there was still enormous separation."

Morrison is quick to point out that she is not criticizing the Civil Rights struggle. It's just that "there was a price." Forgetfulness, she believes, is that price. Her novels have become a way to help her readers remember an earlier time—whether it was life during segregation (*Sula, Song of Solomon,* and *Love*), during periods of migration (*The Bluest Eye, Jazz,* and *Paradise*) or during slavery (*Beloved*). In the question-and-answer session after her lecture in 1988 when she accepted the Frederic G. Melcher Book Award ("A Bench by the Road"), Morrison explains to her audience why she wrote *Beloved*: "There is no place that you or I can go, to think about or not think about, to summon the presences of, or recollect the absences of slaves; nothing that reminds us of the ones who made the journey and of those who did not make it. There is no suitable memorial or wreath or wall or park or skyscraper lobby. There's no 300-foot tower. There's no small bench by the road. There is not even a tree scored, an initial that I can visit or you can visit in Charleston or Savannah or New York or Providence or, better still on the banks of the Mississippi. And because such a place did not exist (that I know of), the book had to."

In addition to the conversations that are mostly about literature and history and culture, Morrison also has informal, around-the-kitchen-table conversations with interviewers in this collection, like the one she has with Zia Jaffrey after the publication of *Paradise*. Their conversation covers everything from Morrison's opinions about the early reviews of *Paradise* to raising Black sons in the U.S., to the O. J. Simpson trial, to the fiction she reads, to her house fire in 1993, to the lessons of her divorce, to her desire to travel to Africa, and finally to her changing perspectives on life as she grows older. She tells Jaffrey that she doesn't get angry anymore; she experiences something closer to what she calls melancholy: "It's overload. You sort of struggle to do four good things when you're my age, and then not deal. I tell my students that: four good things. Make a difference about something other than yourselves." Jaffrey's interview is one of the more personally reflective conversations that Morrison has in this collection, and it provides an interesting window into dimensions of her life that we don't often see.

Perhaps the most intriguing conversations in this collection are those where Morrison talks about her own process as a writer. As she tells Elissa Schappell in the riveting interview in *Paris Review*, "Writers always devise ways to approach that space where they expect to make the contact, where they become the conduit, or where they engage in this mysterious process. For me light is the signal in the transition. It's not being in the light, its being there before it arrives. It enables me in some sense." She still prefers number two pencils and yellow legal pads. She goes to the computer eventually she says, but "I have to start with the old legal pads and pencils, because I don't like the act of writing—you know, the formation of letters, so I tend to be crisper and more economical, with the pencil." After writing, before she revises, she tells Pam Houston later in an equally riveting interview, she lets "it steep. If you've got it, you've got it. If you don't you don't. There is something called *novel time*. If you lay it down too clearly then you are just following a map and you're are not letting it—you just have to let it go, wait for it to be there."

Morrison's interviews with Michael Silverblatt, host of *Bookworm*, the highly respected literary arts program on KCRW radio in Los Angeles, about the language and the internal construction of *Beloved* and *Love* are also fascinating additions to this collection. Morrison calls Silverblatt a "first-rate reader," and these interviews show why he gets that description. In their conversations, Morrison and Silverblatt talk in great detail about the intricacies of the language and crafting of these two novels. In his October 1998 interview about *Beloved*, Silverblatt points out that it was important for him to talk to Morrison about the novel *before* the film was released. "It's my sense," he explains, "that after a movie hits the public, a book is altered by it and that there are things we find in language, in the shaping and writing of literature that a movie cannot touch. Not because it doesn't want to or because it's inadequate, but because they're different art forms, because it can't." The interview is a revealing conversation about the differences that the nuanced language of the novel can effect by allowing readers to process the images according to their own imaginations and associations as opposed to the fixed images of the movie.

In their second interview in 2004, Silverblatt shows again his deep understanding of Morrison's use of language in the multilayered structuring of *Love*. Silverblatt and Morrison engage in near symbiotic discussion. "The book," he says, "seems to be about the way love is a collection of the pieces that people can assemble even when they can't speak to one another, the reader assembles love." The "collection of pieces" that Silverblatt describes leads Morrison into her own metaphor for explaining the construction of the novel: "What came to mind as you were talking was the idea I had of the way crystal forms. You know you have a small piece and then it expands to another. And another layer comes on in different shape, but it's all the same material. And when you get finished it's different faces, different light looking at one simple thing." Sparks of discovery are everywhere in this interview—for Silverblatt and for Morrison. He is such a close reader. He understands perfectly Morrison's role as narrator in *Love*: "It's almost as if the Toni Morrison, implied by this book," he explains, "is a vast staff of arrangers whose job it is to get everything immaculately in place and then disappear!" He also picks up on the subtle irony of a character using "Mood Indigo" to help set the rhythm of his strokes in a late night swim. "If one's listening to the words," Silverblatt points out, "then it seems like a song that would *impede* passage." Morrison clearly enjoys and affirms the depth of Silverblatt's engagement in the novel and responds to his questions with her own profound observations about her goals in its construction. This interview will be a real treat for those who want to understand better the construction of *Love* and enjoy the discovery and engagement shared between this "first-rate reader" (her words) and "this truly extraordinary novelist" (his words).

An understated refrain in all of these interviews, which Morrison brings finally to the forefront in her interview with Michael Saur, is her claim that she "wants to write like a good jazz musician." The music becomes the metaphor for Morrison—whether it is in explaining the visceral experience of re-reading a book, or in structuring *Jazz*, or privileging in-group knowledge and not adhering to what she calls "the White gaze"— jazz is the central metaphor that governs what she wants to achieve in her novels. She echoes with Saur what she tells Claudia Dreifus in an earlier interview, "I would like for my work to do two things: be as demanding and sophisticated as I want it to be, and at the same time be accessible in a sort of emotional way to lots of people just like jazz. That's a hard task but that's what I want my work to do."

Adam Langer's interview essay, "Star Power," written shortly before the publication of *Love*, has the glow of a limelight tribute to a writer at the "top of her game." It's an easy, laughter-filled conversation about her latest novel *Love* in 2003, but also about her life. Langer calls her the "high priestess of American Literature," and as in Jessica Harris's early interview essay, you get setting and gesture and sound in this essay as well. There is the joy of a new publication, there is the fretting about eyesight and aging, and even a little of Morrison's dreams about seeing the stars again that she remembers from her childhood: "I suppose if I were really an adventuresome person, I would just say 'Look, I want to know where the stars are,' and I would go on a ship and I would just follow the stars. . . . There are probably generations that don't remember seeing the stars, and I think if somebody ripped away whatever it is that's blocking them, and the stars were out, there'd be a massive shift. All the kids would run out into the streets. Instead of fireworks, there would be this thing in your life, these stars. . . . Oh you've got me going now," she says with a laugh, "I'm going on a star trek. That's just what I'm going to do."

All of the conversations in this volume teach and delight. The side joke, the sharp wit, and the laugh-out-loud response to a myriad of large and small absurdities—from the would-be shoe bomber, to hit-me-but-don't-quit-me lyrics of the blues, to the nicknames of her father's friends—punctuate the instructive and revealing responses that Morrison gives in all of these interviews. Sometimes all of these qualities come together perfectly in a single phrase. When McCluskey asks "how has she been able to bridge that ever present gap between popular and serious fiction," Morrison responds without hesitation: "I'm smart!" Nearly every interviewer comments on the marvelous range of her voice, the twinkle in her eyes, the infectious laughter that accompany her always insightful comments about life and literature. The engagement and generosity she shows is remarkable. In the end, however, it's not only about fulfilling yet another request from an interviewer. Morrison believes that these kinds of conversations are also her way of bearing witness: "I think about it in a large sense. I use the phrase 'bear witness' to explain what my work is for. . . . Somebody has to tell somebody something."

Pam Houston's reflection on her interview with Toni Morrison in 2005 sums up what I am sure every interviewer in this collection must have felt at some point and what I believe those who read the conversations in this collection will feel as well: "Ms. Morrison is a person who gives you her full attention, who wants, even in the context of an interview, to have a conversation, who is entirely self-possessed without being the least bit self-obsessed, who is at every minute teaching and every minute eager to learn. She is soft-spoken and regal, except at the odd moment when she erupts into raucous laughter and throws herself sideways into an overstuffed chair. . . . She is young in spirit, long in wisdom, as dedicated as ever to her craft."

As customary with all books in this series, the interviews herein have not been edited from the form of their initial publication. Consequently the reader will at times encounter repetitions of both questions and answers, but it is the feeling that the significance of the same questions being asked and the consistency (or inconsistency) of responses will prove of value to readers in their unexpurgated form.

CCD

Notes

1. From *Conversations with John Fowles*, published by University Press of Mississippi in 1999.
2. From "The Intentional Fallacy" by William K. Wimsatt and Monroe C. Beardsley in *Sewanee Review*, vol. 54 (1946): 468–88.

Chronology

1931	Born February 18 in Lorain, Ohio, to George and Ella Ramah Wofford.
1949	Graduates from Lorain High School.
1953	Receives B.A. in English and a Classics minor from Howard University.
1955	Receives M.A. in English from Cornell University. Morrison's master's thesis is "The Treatment of the Alienated in Virginia Woolf and William Faulkner."
1955–57	Teaches at Texas Southern University.
1957	Teaches at Howard University.
1958	Marries Harold Morrison, a Jamaican architect. The couple has two sons, Harold Ford and Slade Kevin.
1963	Joins writers' groups at Howard University.
1965	Is hired as senior editor with textbook publisher L. W. Singer (a subsidiary of Random House) in Syracuse, New York.
1968	Moves to Random House's New York City headquarters as senior editor.
1970	*The Bluest Eye* is published by Holt, Rhinehart, Winston.
1973	*Sula* is published by Knopf.
1974	*Sula* is nominated for the American Book Award. Morrison receives the Ohioana Book Award for *Sula*.
1977	*Song of Solomon* is published by Knopf and is chosen as a Book-of-the-Month-Club selection, the first by an African American author since Richard Wright's *Native Son*.
1978	Receives the National Book Critics' Circle Award and the American Academy and Institute of Arts and Letters Award, the Oscar Micheaux Award, Friends of Writers Award, and the Cleveland Arts Prize for Literature for *Song of Solomon*. Is named distinguished writer by the American Academy and Institute of Arts and Letters.

1980   Is appointed to the National Council on the Arts.
1981   *Tar Baby* is published by Knopf. Morrison is elected to the
            American Academy and Institute of Arts and Letters. Appears
            on the cover of March issue of *Newsweek* magazine.
1983   Publishes "Recitatif," a short story, in *Confirmations: An
            Anthology of African American Women Writers,* edited by Amiri
            Baraka and Amina Baraka. Resigns from Random House after
            eighteen-year career.
1984   Is named Albert Schweitzer Professor of the Humanities at the
            College of the Humanities and Fine Arts at the State University
            of New York, Albany.
1986   Writes *Dreaming Emmett,* an unpublished play directed by
            Gilbert Moses and performed at the Marketplace Capitol
            Repertory Theater of Albany. The play, commissioned by the
            New York State Writers Institute, wins the New York State
            Governor's Award.
1987   *Beloved* is published by Knopf. It wins the Anisfield Wolf Book
            Award in Race Relations.
1988   Receives Pulitzer Prize, the Melcher Book Award, the Robert F.
            Kennedy Book Award, and the Elmer Holmes Bobst Award for
            Fiction for *Beloved.* Is inducted into the American Academy and
            Institute of Arts and Letters. Delivers Robert C. Tanner Lecture
            at the University of Michigan. Receives City of New York
            Mayor's Award of Honor for Art and Culture and the Ohioana
            Career Medal Award.
1989   Is appointed Robert Goheen Chair in the Council of the
            Humanities at Princeton University. Receives Modern Language
            Association of America Commonwealth Award in Literature
            and the Sara Lee Corporation Front Runner Award in the Arts.
1990   Delivers Massey Lectures at Harvard University, the first Chazen
            Lecture at the University of Wisconsin, the Charter Lecture at
            the University of Georgia, and the Clark Lectures at Trinity
            College in Cambridge, England. Is awarded Chianti Ruffino
            Antico Fattore International Literary Prize. Receives the Chubb
            Fellowship at Yale University.
1992   *Playing in the Dark: Essays on Whiteness and the Literary
            Imagination* (critical essays on American Literature) is published

by Harvard University Press. *Jazz* is published by Knopf.
Morrison edits *Race-ing Justice, En-Gendering Power: Essays on Anita Hill, Clarence Thomas, and the Construction of Social Reality*, which is published by Pantheon.

1993   Is awarded the Nobel Prize for Literature and the Commander of the Order of Arts and Letters (Paris, France). Writes lyrics for *Honey and Rue*, a cycle of six songs commissioned by Carnegie Hall for soprano Kathleen Battle, with composer Andre Previn. Founds the Princeton Atelier, a studio arts program at Princeton University that brings together students, faculty, and visiting artists to explore the collaborative creative process in visual arts, literature, dance, film, theater, and music.

1994   Receives Pearl Buck Award from the Pearl Buck Foundation; Premio Internazionale "Citta dello Stretto," Rhegium Julii, Reggio Calabria, Italy; and the Condorcet Medal. Is awarded the International Condorcet Chair at Ecole Normale Superieure and College de France. Delivers Condorcet Lecture at College de France. Writes lyrics for "Four Songs" with composer Andre Previn; "Four Songs" is performed by Sylvia McNair at Carnegie Hall.

1996   Is named Jefferson Lecturer in the Humanities by the National Endowment for the Humanities. Is awarded the National Book Foundation Medal for Distinguished Contribution to American Letters. *The Dancing Mind*, National Book Foundation Lecture, is published by Knopf.

1997   Edits with Claudia Brodsky Lacour *Birth of a Nation'hood: Gaze, Script, and Spectacle in the O. J. Simpson Case*, a collection of essays on the O. J. Simpson case, which is published by Pantheon. Writes lyrics for "Sweet Talk" with composer Richard Danielpour; "Sweet Talk" is performed by Jessye Norman at Carnegie Hall.

1998   *Paradise* is published by Knopf. Morrison writes lyrics for "Spirits in the Well" with composer Richard Danielpour; "Spirits in the Well" is performed by Jessye Norman at Avery Fisher Hall. Receives the Medal of Honor for Literature by the National Arts Club, New York. Is named A. D. White Professor-at-Large at Cornell University. Delivers Moffitt

	Lecture at Princeton University and Berliner Lektionen at Theater Berlin. *Beloved,* the movie starring Oprah Winfrey and directed by Jonathan Demme, premieres. Morrison receives Grammy nomination for Best Spoken Word Album, for *Beloved.*
1999	Receives Ohioana Book Award for Fiction; Oklahoma Book Award; *Ladies Home Journal* Woman of the Year Award; and Orange Prize Nomination (London, England). *The Big Box* (children's book), co-authored with Slade Morrison, is published by Hyperion.
2000	Writes lyrics for *Woman.Mind.Song,* which is composed by Judith Wier; *Woman.Mind.Song* is performed by Jessye Norman at Carnegie Hall. Morrison is awarded the National Humanities Medal.
2001	Receives Pell Award for Lifetime Achievement in the Arts, Jean Kennedy Smith NYU Creative Writing Award, and the Enoch Pratt Free Library Lifetime Literary Achievement Award. Is awarded the Cavore Prize in Turin, Italy. Is honored at Fête du Livre, the Cité du Livre, and Les Écritures Croisées, Aix-en-Provence, France.
2002	Delivers the University of Toronto Alexander Lecture and the United Nations Secretary General's Lecture Series. Writes libretto for *Margaret Garner* with composer Richard Danielpour. The opera is co-commissioned by the Michigan Opera Theatre, the Cincinnati Opera, and the Opera Company of Philadelphia. *The Book of Mean People,* with Slade Morrison, is published by Hyperion.
2003–05	*Who's Got Game Series: The Ant or the Grasshopper?* (2003); *The Lion or the Mouse?* (2003); *The Poppy or the Snake?* (2004); *The Mirror or the Glass?* (2005), all with Slade Morrison, are published by Scribners.
2003	*Love* is published by Knopf. Morrison receives Docteures Honoris Causa from the Ecole Normale Superieure in Paris, France.
2004	*Remember: The Journey to School Integration* is published by Houghton Mifflin. Morrison delivers the Amnesty International Lecture in Edinburgh, Scotland. Receives the Academy of Culture "Arts and Communities" Award in Paris, France.

Receives NAACP Image Award for Outstanding Literary Work, Fiction.

2005   Receives Coretta Scott King Award from the American Library Association. The world premiere of *Margaret Garner* at the Michigan Opera Theater in Detroit. Cincinnati, Ohio, premiere of *Margaret Garner* at the Cincinnati Opera. Morrison is awarded a Doctor of Letters Degree from Oxford University. Delivers the Leon Forrest Lecture at Northwestern University.

2006   Philadelphia premiere of *Margaret Garner* at the Opera Company of Philadelphia. Charlotte premiere of *Margaret Garner* at Opera Carolina. Morrison is awarded Honorary Doctorate of Letters from the Sorbonne. *Beloved* is chosen as the Best Work of American Fiction of the Last 25 Years by the *New York Times.* Morrison retires from seventeen-year career at Princeton. Salute to Toni Morrison is held at Lincoln Center in New York. Morrison curates "A Foreigner's Home" exhibit at the Louvre Museum in Paris.

2007   Curates "Art Is Otherwise" Humanities Programs, sponsored by the French Alliance, in New York City. Receives the Ellie Charles Artist Award from African Voices at Columbia University. Is named Radcliffe Medalist by the Radcliffe Institute at Harvard University. New York premiere of *Margaret Garner* at the New York City Opera. Morrison receives Lifetime Achievement award and is named one of 21 Women of the Year by *Glamour* magazine.

Toni Morrison: Conversations

"I Will Always Be a Writer"
Jessica Harris / 1976

From *Essence* (December 1976). Reprinted by permission of Jessica Harris.

It is paradoxical that Toni Morrison who at Random House edits and nurtures the works of authors such as Toni Cade Bambara, Muhammad Ali, Angela Davis, and Lucille Clifton then goes upstairs to Alfred Knopf and has her own work edited. The biography that appears at the back of Ms. Morrison's most recent book, *Sula,* is brief and not at all revelatory. It informs readers that Toni Morrison was born in Lorain, Ohio, graduated from Howard University, and received her master's from Cornell. *Sula,* it adds, is her second novel following *The Bluest Eye* and states that Toni Morrison has been a frequent contributor to *The New York Times.* We're told that she taught English and the humanities at Texas Southern University and Howard for nine years. This biography closes with the fact that Ms. Morrison has two sons.

To anyone who has met Toni Morrison the inadequacy of this biography is laughable, for she is much more than that. She is one of the most respected Black women writers in the literary world, and her novels, *The Bluest Eye* and *Sula,* have become contemporary classics. She is one of Random House's top editors and was instrumental in compiling, editing and publishing *The Black Book.* This work, a compendium of historical as well as contemporary information about Black Americans, was well received by the Black community and highly praised by critics. Along with all this she is the mother of two young men, Dino, eleven, and Slade, fifteen.

From her office she looks out at the world of New York skyscrapers through a veil of green plants, yet the book-lined walls and the manuscript-covered desk remind one of the office's true purpose. Both restful and functional it is the office of a woman whose five senses are always at work.

Laughter signals Ms. Morrison's arrival, and she enters the office and completes it. Although her smile remains as magnetic as ever, a new haircut has changed her appearance, softening her face, highlighting her eyes and giving her a new intensity. One feels the vitality that enables her to carry on the fantastic daily juggling of her several lives. Ms. Morrison sits down, lights the ubiquitous cigarette and begins to talk about the career triptych that is her life.

"Today women who work and take care of children can't have primary and secondary jobs as they used to. All of the three things I am, mother, editor, and writer, are primary to me. I couldn't live without any one. In order to take care of my responsibilities I have to have a job. I have one that I am suited for and it doesn't conflict in any way with writing; this is unusual—most jobs do. Obviously I could write while teaching or waiting tables, but editing keeps me in the literary world—a good place to be."

Toni Morrison will say that her first responsibility is as a mother to Dino and Slade. It is a doubly difficult task. She is a single parent. "I'm not going to talk about my ex-husband because I can't be honest without causing somebody some pain, mostly my children." But she is very open in talking about the difficulties that a single woman has raising two male children, "initially you're afraid that you're going to give your children, whether they're girls or boys, a one-sided education because you can't be that other parent. Then after a little bit, it occurs to you that it wouldn't make any difference. All you can be in any case is the most complete human being possible, and that not only must suffice, it does. Children are resilient, and they take what they need from the world and from anyone else they know." Smiling as though at some private joke, she continues. "A long time ago it occured to me that I had never been a little boy, so I could never know what that meant, ever. Certainly I could not be a father, for I had no idea what that meant either. So my best shot was to be a person, and then they'd have to take it from there."

Obviously there are sacrifices to be made in order for Toni Morrison to write with two young men around the house. "I rarely have more than three or four hours as a block of time. Usually at the end of the fourth hour somebody wants lunch, or it's 'Take me to the. . . .' It was easier when the children used to go to my parents' home in Ohio during the summer. They spend less time there now. I've cut out lots of things in order to have them with me. I'm not entertained nor do I entertain often. I don't see the plays I want to or do a lot of other things I like. Still, there's that terrible feeling that hits everybody at some point. You know your children aren't you.

"I don't know how valuable it is to spend as much time as I do with the children. It's valuable to me but is it to them? I don't think about it a lot, but it certainly is part of what one thinks when overwhelmed with enormous and varied responsibilities." She laughs, "But I haven't changed in fifteen years."

For nine of those fifteen years Toni Morrison has been an editor at Random House and the major force behind many of the Black books that they have published. Editing is Toni Morrison's bread and butter and she enjoys it immensely.

"When I describe the editor's job, it will sound simple but very packed. An editor's functions vary from house to house. One thing that we all have in common is editing manuscripts and seeking work we'd like to buy. I look for manuscripts from agents and/or people. Then I talk to the writer or the agent. If that works out and there's a manuscript or an idea available, I have to convince my editor-in-chief that it's a good idea to buy and publish it. Then we negotiate the contract and work with the author. When that's done, we turn it over to the many people inside the company: the copy editors, the design department, the subsidiary rights people, printers and book binders, and so on. Once the book is completed one waits to see what the response will be." At this point, Ms. Morrison explains, the editor's job is to get as much attention paid to the work as possible. "If you've published the author's work before, you try to direct his or her career, pace them; build it; help them."

The editor's relationship with the author is a close one and compatibility is essential. Naturally with such a close working relationship the editor is bound to have favorite works and authors. Although she published most of Henry Dumas's work posthumously, she says he is "the best naturally talented, no-holds-barred writer I have ever published. I'm always aggrieved because he is no longer alive. But he left a good deal of material. I'm under contract to do another book of his short stories.

"Working with Muhammad Ali, of course, is very exciting and electric, and I think that Richard Durham is probably the best biographer around. Obviously Muhammad Ali has his own major excitement; he's absolutely as fascinating as he says he is. I was always amazed at what Durham was able to do with those tons and tons of tapes, giving the book an immediacy that was unbelievable. He could write anything; he has a fantastic dramatic sense of power and an ear for dialogue. It's really beautiful.

"Then there are other editing situations that, because you're involved with a particular kind of perception, have no peer. Working with Angela Davis—a very coherent, bright, very loving woman—was like that. She is very committed and selfless but without that abrasive quality that many committed people have. She's the genuine article.

"I've had extremely varied experiences with Black women writers: Gayl Jones has a very fecund imagination; Toni Cade Bambara has a totally reliable ear, and Lucille Clifton is able to do something difficult: take the strengths of poetry and apply them in such a way that you have first-rate prose. I wish that Toni Cade Bambara would write a novel, and that Lucille Clifton would write a sustained one. Not that what they do isn't marvelous, it's just that I would be able to make more money for them in other forms. Poetry and short pieces have always been extremely difficult to sell."

Ms. Morrison was the editor of *Corregidora* and *Eva's Man*, two novels by Gayl Jones that received a good deal of critical acclaim and aroused an equal amount of Black controversy and discussion. Of that controversey she says, "Some women's literature is very aggressive and sometimes hostile in what it says about men. Gayl Jones's writing has enormous range, and it's unfair for conclusions to be drawn about her from these books. Although there was a lot of other Gayl Jones material from which to select. I chose to publish *Corregidora* and *Eva's Man* because I thought that they would receive an enormous amount of notice and I wanted that for her. But the men come off badly in *Corregidora*. They are violent, insensitive, greedy, selfish, and mean. Men don't like to be portrayed that way. There was no grandeur, no magic, none of the magnificence that men have. Many young women, in spite of their attraction to men, feel a lot of deep-seated hostility toward this person who has picked you. And if they have been hurt by a man—and all women have or believe they have—then they want him to get his comeuppance. Any rejection creates its own quality of vengeance. It's human nature. It's hard to understand when somebody doesn't love you.

"Of course, there are women who write for women, and then there are women who just write out of the matrix of what they know as women. But the others, like Eudora Welty and Flannery O'Connor, have just written as people. Sometimes it's about men. Sometimes not."

Ms. Morrison's editing experience has been as varied as her authors' talents. Before coming to Random House, she had been a textbook editor, which gave her still another perspective on the subject. Yet when she talks about her favorite works, most that she mentions are works by Black authors or about Black subjects. It would be incorrect, however, to infer that she is solely an editor of Black books. She has edited books covering everything from the women's movement to railroads.

When asked if there was a particular relationship between a Black writer and a Black editor, she replied. "I don't know. I think that a good editor can get it out, period. I may have a certain edge in a way. There are things that Black authors don't have to explain to me and therefore a certain immediate comfort in terms of communications. But I really don't think it's true that Black editors edit Black writers better, and I don't think that white editors edit white writers better. I think it's a question of how good an editor you are or, more important, that you choose the books in which you have certain strengths. I'm not the best person to edit some books because either I don't have the specialized expertise they call for, or I don't have the enthusiasm for them.

"My own editor is not Black. I think what Black writers complain about when they don't want a white editor is the ignorance, not the color of their skin—an inability to grasp a cultural thought or experience—not the lack of intelligence. When an editor is able to do that there are no complaints. Maya Angelou has a white editor. Ishmael Reed has a white editor. Alice Walker has a white editor. There are many instances of that, and I don't think that those people are unhappy."

While some editors may write occasionally for periodicals or newspapers, it's unusual to find one who is a writer of Toni Morrison's caliber. "I didn't want to be a writer; I wanted to be a reader. If I had chosen an art form, it would have been dance. I danced a lot." She continues, "My first book began as a short story a long time ago when I joined a little writer's group that met once a month. I had run out of those silly little poems and short stories I'd written. I had to write something new, and I wrote what became part of *The Bluest Eye*. Years later when I lived in Syracuse and didn't have anyone to talk to, I wrote it as a way to talk. I could have been there ten years later or ten years earlier and I wouldn't have felt that. You write when your back is pressed against the wall. There's nobody around, and you must trust your own instincts, rely on your resources and declare yourself competent whether you are or not. I wasn't thinking about being a writer. But a friend suggested I write to his editor, and I did, sending fifty pages of my story. He liked and eventually published it. By that time I had a contract, and so it had become work to do it well. But I was determined not to make it a job. I wanted to write my kind of novel. I realized in the process of *The Bluest Eye* that writing had become a compulsion so I became a writer. I write, that's what I do. I will always be a writer."

She goes on, "When I edit somebody else's book no vanity is involved. I simply want the writer to do the very best work he can do. Now if that means letting him alone, I'll do that. If it means holding hands, I'll hold hands. If it means fussing, I'll fuss."

Toni Morrison is a meticulous writer who admits to "rewriting a lot." Well aware of the perils of overwriting, she insists that "the whole point is that writing appear effortless. The easiest sentences are the most labored ones." Part of the rewriting comes from the fact that she is writing fiction and so must deal with conveying the feelings and perceptions of others. "When I write for magazines it's just me talking; the way I write and the way I see things. But none of that is operable in fiction. I must write dialogue the way those people speak it and, more important, see the world the way they see it. So what they choose to notice out of the infinite possibilities are not necessarily the things I personally choose to notice. The problem is to surrender one's own perceptions and to hang onto one's intelligence. It's really very split and difficult to do. I think actors also experience that in a different way. It's total possession and total aloofness at the same time. It is very draining. The third burden is to make all of that manifest with language. How do you describe all of that using ninety words (instead of nine hundred) and make it seem part and parcel, warp and woof, of the character? It's much like *Rashomon*. Four people looking at one incident can see different things. The writer must become all of those people. Truth varies when you have any complicated situation or characters. That is what is most challenging and painful about writing. At the same time there are enormous rewards in seeing new or different perspectives because your characters are new or different."

Combining a very demanding schedule as an editor and the different needs of being a writer with the other necessities of being a single parent have made Toni Morrison very adept at "juggling" things. "When I'm writing in stride, almost every thing else I do is distant from me. It gives other matters the look of being under water. When I'm not talking or working, I'm with the book. If I'm washing dishes, it's still there, and I think about it all of the time. It's never really gone."

Writing is a crazy world: not only is intense concentration and single-minded focus necessary to produce the book, one must also "hawk" it. Television guest spots, autographing tours, and all of the other involvements often get in the author's way. While Toni Morrison has been extremely willing to do these things to promote books that she has edited, like *The Black*

Book, she is reluctant to do them to promote her own works. She admits, however, that "I can really haul it up and get it together if I have something to say." While she herself is reluctant to do many of these things, she does not recommend that kind of behavior to any aspiring author.

"I have seen 'media madness' become a disease. If I expect to write true books, I must have true feelings and perceptions of things. If I lose a part of myself to the press or the public, then I've lost a lot of myself. You can feel it. You become your name in caps. In the late sixties we had marvelous political people who just lived for the crowds that they could command, the press conferences that they could have. It became necessary for them to have something to say, even when they didn't have anything to say. They became the media's creatures. It is possible as a writer to do that: it's less likely to happen to writers, but it certainly can.

"I take my responsibilities very, very seriously. I want to do good work. I want to be involved in other people's doing good work. I don't lie. I don't mislead. I don't cater to the whole media thing."

She continues, "I have a very uneventful life; I wish I had an eventful one. I'm a very solitary person. I like to talk and I'm very social. I like to be in a party or a dinner situation . . . but not a lot, not very much." She pauses. "I'm very good company to myself because I'm very much interested in what I think, how I feel. Yet my life does not interest me in terms of writing about it. But I am very stimulated by other people." It is just this quality that makes Toni Morrison such good company and that makes her writing so special. It has also helped to sustain her.

Another sustaining force has been humor "because it keeps one from dramatizing and overreacting: it keeps you from romanticizing yourself. It's the most important thing in the world, particularly in parenting and writing because delusions are destructive. Humor provides a frame and a distance and a kind of stability. It keeps me concerned about my work as an editor but not the job. It keeps me concerned about my children's growth as separate people from me, as opposed to my excellence as a mother. But the point is that you need the proscenium, the distance. High tragedy is not possible, the only other recourse is irony or that sardonic quality that makes it possible to see things clearly."

That delicate balance between wonder and irony, between surprise and sardony, between innocence and knowledge is achieved in all that Toni Morrison touches, be it mothering, editing or writing.

The Triumphant Song of Toni Morrison

Paula Giddings / 1977

From *Encore American and Worldwide News* (December 12, 1977). Reprinted by permission of Paula Giddings.

In her relatively short career at Random House, Toni Morrison has done what few have been able to do throughout the history of publishing: to be a successful editor—Angela Davis, Muhammad Ali, Gayl Jones, and Toni Cade Bambara are among her authors—and a highly acclaimed novelist as well. It is an extraordinary accomplishment—especially in this mercurial profession where there are few successful Black authors, and even fewer Black editors.

A forty-six-year-old divorcee, mother of two energetic teenage sons, a part-time professor at Yale, she will tell you that she doesn't have much time "to brood" in front of a typewriter. Although her latest novel, *Song of Solomon*, will earn her both the reputation and the dividends to write full-time, she wants to remain at her teaching position because she likes students and it stimulates her mind. She will come into her Random House office only once a week in order to devote more time to her writing. (She is already at work on a new novel, *Tar Baby*.) But she will also continue to shepherd her author's books through publication, and look for more Black writers. Toni Morrison is as dedicated to the publication of good literature as she is about perfecting her own work. "Wouldn't it be great if there were *six* big Black books a year?" she says.

Her accomplishment as a writer is all the more extraordinary because in a profession filled with prodigies she began relatively late in her life. Her first "serious" and sustained writing was *The Bluest Eye* published in 1970, followed by the highly acclaimed *Sula* in 1974. But it is *Song of Solomon* that has established her name as a major American talent.

John Leonard, probably the country's most influential critic, rated *Solomon* in the same class with Nabokov's *Lolita*, Heller's *Catch 22*, Lessing's *The Golden Notebook*, Grass's *The Tin Drum*, and Marquez's *One Hundred*

Years of Solitude. The lead review of the prestigious *New Yorker* hailed the
novel as a "rhapsodic work, demonstrating the virtues of the spoken word
and the abiding presence in certain corners of the world of a lively oral tradition." Mordecai Richler, calling *Solomon* a "cause for celebration," continued,
"from the opening pages I sat bolt upright, aware that I was in the presence
of a major talent."

Song of Solomon is the first book by a Black author to be a main selection
of the Book-of-the-Month Club since Richard Wright's *Native Son* (1940).
First serial rights have been sold to *Redbook Magazine*. Hardcover sales are
expected to reach about 50,000 and paperback rights have been sold. All in all
the book should bring Morrison dividends in the upper range of six figures.
Such success, beyond the over-the-counter sales, have been particularly elusive to Black writers.

It is difficult to describe this book which has earned Morrison so much
attention. The opening pages that so startled Richler contain a cryptic letter:

> At 3:00 p.m. on Wednesday the 18th of February 1931, 1 will take off from Mercy
> and fly away on my own wings. Please forgive me. I loved you all.

The letter is like a flare, preparing the reader for an odyssey of myth and
allegory, flight without fantasy—and a world as real as dirt. Such is the
alchemy, it seems, needed to explore the book's subject: Black men.

The protagonist, Milkman Dead, seems destined to live his life passive and
uncomprehending of the intense world that swarms around him. Hearing of
a cache of gold hidden in the Virginia mountains, he leaves his Detroit home
to embark on both a real and symbolic search to find the valuable metal of
his history and thus his emotional redemption.

The novel contains a number of extraordinary characters. There is
Milkman's father, Macon, who is ruthlessly possessive; his eccentric mother,
Ruth, who like Millay's tepid pool, is drying inwardly from the emotional
edge; two sullen sisters who threaten to slip into madness; and his lover, peri-
odically compelled to try and kill him. There is also his best friend Guitar, a
revolutionary bent on fanatic revenge who becomes his worst enemy. And
then there is his Aunt Pilate, excused from the proprieties of this world by
being born "with a stomach as naked as a knee." She alone understands the
richness of the earth; and she wears a brass box for an earring, carries a bag
of human bones, and eventually becomes Milkman's redeemer.

Like her novels, there is a lustiness about Toni Morrison, whose voice can caress a "honeychild" or a "gi-r-1" as easily as it glides over literary talk. And when she talks about *her* writing—the search for the word, the expression, the right image—her mouth will moisten with a gourmet's anticipation: "What harm did I do you on my knee?" Ruth implores Milkman. "The 'on my knee' makes you *see* it, doesn't it? Wonderful," she says unselfconsciously.

Morrison will tell you that the writing of *Song of Solomon* was more difficult than her previous books. "I believe in writing from the inside of character," she commented. "So I had to get excited about things that are alien to me—like being excited in the presence of women or relishing the male sense of dominion. Also, the structure was more demanding. I wanted to pull the reader in and close the door, but instead of closing the door to a house—like I could with *Sula* and *The Bluest Eye*, which are about women—it had to move like a train."

Solomon also represented a part of her own personal history. There was such a song about her family, and the myth of the flying African is a part of her folklore. But the book would not flow. "I was unable to finish the novel until my father died," she commented. "I was very depressed afterward— I knew that I no longer had a life that way: the way I lived in his mind.

"I remember being filled with melancholy. I was sitting at my desk, my children were in the room. Suddenly I got this incredible feeling of exhilaration and serenity at the same time. I think because I was so depressed, my defenses were down, I wasn't fighting anything. And it was like a gate that opened in me. I began to envision the things in the book. I started writing and writing—I think I wrote thirty pages that night."

She saw the colors in the first chapter—the blue silk wings, the red velvet flowers—before she saw the characters. She recognized what made those Virginia women that Milkman encounters so different: they walked down the street with nothing in their hands—no purses, no small paper bags. For the woods scene, she searched to remember what gave the hunting trips with her brother a special aura. "It was the way he talked to the dogs," she said. "He would cluck at them and they would respond. They communicated—he could tell by listening to them in the distance if they had caught the game or lost it. Now there is a lot of prelanguage there—not just before the printed word, but before words, period. It was what made me feel comfortable there."

Like any good wordsmith, Morrison works hard at the technical execution of her work. She will write passages again and again until they ring true. She will tell you how exhilarating it is to understand when to let the language billow and when one must draw back. Morrison knows how to make her prose sound like poetry, and to arouse by subliminal manipulation. Her selection of words are precise yet invoke several shades of meaning. If she sees a painting, she says, and it can "say" something to her, then she in turn can string words together to form a vivid picture. And though Morrison will say that she refuses to be seduced by music, she understands how to make its properties surrender to the written word.

Besides craftsmanship there is another dimension to her work. It is that same preconscious quality she experienced in the woods. "The memory is long," she observed, "beyond the parameters of cognition. I don't want to sound too mystical about it, but I feel like a conduit, I really do. I'm fascinated by what it means to make somebody remember what I don't even know."

Although several critics have compared her to authors like William Faulkner, it is the Latin American writers like Gabriel Garcia Marquez who inspire her. "They have an aura of magic," she said excitedly. "They can pull out of you dreams, nightmares, recollections, memories you didn't even know you had. In my writing I know I've hit it when I have the sound and the picture, the recollection and the anticipation of something either you may have seen, never saw—or sorry that you forgot."

One thing she regrets as being almost forgotten was an amber time when "passions were deeper," says Morrison. It is a time often invoked in her work, where the drama is spurred by the excess of passion rather than its absence.

"I saw some old James Van der Zee photographs recently," she said. "They were pictures of funerals. Among them was a lovely young girl who was at a party when her lover shot her with a gun that had a silencer on it. No one knew what had happened until she fell to the floor. Her friends asked her who had done it. 'I'll tell you tomorrow,' she replied. Of course tomorrow never came.

"Now the feminists may not like that, but you know that woman wanted him to escape. Who loves *that* intensely anymore?"

What has changed? "I think what we really want is to be *held*," she replied. "But we don't know that so we surround ourselves with material things—and they become substitutes for a lack of feeling, of caring.

"These things become symbols of success. And success means something else now than it used to. You know people will kill you for those little jobs in those little impersonal offices. And the jobs aren't something you do for fulfillment, or because you *like* it . . . My father used to be a welder in the shipyards," she recalled. "He told me once that when he made a perfect seam on a ship, he used to solder his name on it. No one else saw it or really even cared. But *he* cared, and that is all that mattered. Who has pride in their work like that anymore? If you have a real life, you don't need those other things."

Toni Morrison's success has made her keenly aware of its pitfalls. "You can begin to talk about things you know nothing about," she said after completing a nationwide promotion tour. "Remember the sixties? Also, I don't like being lionized. You really can't use it and it doesn't mean a thing when you're sitting in front of that typewriter, trying to think what comes after *The*.

"Of course my family is *immune* to all that," she continues. "I mean, they share all my joys, but all those other things stop when I walk through the door." Born in a small town, Lorain, Ohio, not everyone has reacted so casually. "It's awful when you go home and those women who all your life told you what to do, what to eat, what not to eat—just look at you."

Being in the limelight can also make one see herself differently. "Being a writer I'm used to being the observer, not the other way around," she said. "I've never developed a persona, so all of this is new to me. Referring to a *New York Times* article on her she said, "When I read that article—it was amazing—it was like reading about a good friend, someone I liked. You know," she said laughingly, "she sounded so-o-o interesting!"

But Toni Morrison and *Song of Solomon* have not been without their detractors. Diane Johnson, in *The New York Review of Books*, assessing three Black authors—Gayl Jones, Toni Morrison, and James Alan McPherson—asks which one portrays the truest image of Blacks. Since she felt that the work of Jones and Morrison "is more painful than the gloomiest impressions encouraged by either stereotype or sociology," Johnson asks the question if Black people *ought* to be that way. Evidently her answer was no, because she concluded that McPherson's characters "are what more people are really like."

"She is saying that there is only one notion of Black life," Morrison responded. "I'm not *allowed* to have a different Black life than Gayl Jones or James McPherson. But there is as much variety in our lives as there is skin color. In *Solomon* itself the difference between Pilate and Milkman's sister, First Corinthians, is as different as between night and day.

"And *we* are all those women. We *are* those educated women who had to marry beneath us or had the very good fortune to find a man, period. We are those women who would do anything for those children. We are those women who lived in those quiet little rich houses, rode in those cars, and didn't know which end was up. And we are those women who had the occasional opportunities to be glorious in the face of death."

The review raises a persistent dilemma of the Black writer in America. For whom should he write? "I always wanted to read Black books in which I was enlightened, I as a Black person," Morrison commented. "There are not many books like that. Even the best of them are explaining something to White people. And of course there are a lot of critics who believe that our books are there to tell them what our lives are all about.

"There are certain things I don't want to expose, not because Whites shouldn't know, but they are not who I'm addressing the book to. The Black people who never pick up a book—the Black people in *my* books who don't read books—are the people who authenticate that book for me. If Pilate put down that geography book and picked up *Solomon*, would she say, 'uh, huh,' or not? If it's alright with her, it's alright with me."

Another question raised, particularly in the Black novel, is its ultimate objective in its portrayal of Black characters. If they are interpreted in a negative way, often the charges of stereotype and gloom are heard.

"Gloom?" said Morrison, "I thought *Song of Solomon* was jubilant! Not because everyone is happy, I'm not interested in happiness in my work. I'm interested in survival—who survives and why they survive. Therefore I have to put my characters under duress.

"It is interesting to me that massive bestial treatment did not create a race of beasts. Even the most racist Whites, if they could afford it, let Blacks take care of their children. You don't let 'beasts' take care of your children. Black people managed even to *civilize* slavery!

"Who are the people who go under, and why do they go under? Look at Pilate and Eva, the grandmother in *Sula*. There is little difference between them except Pilate had the benefit of a loving father, and a brother who carried her on his back. Then she gets cut off, but she has something to work with. She is *alive* and there is a quality of magic in her life. Eva had no constructive, male presence. Like Pilate she is fierce and fearless, but lacks her compassion. She set fire to her own son because his life wasn't livable to *her*! Pilate could never have done that."

Absence of a "constructive male presence" has become more and more of a controversial issue—both socially and sociologically. "There *are*, for all kinds of reasons, a lot of Black men who split, leave, fly—they are all over the air," Morrison says with a sweeping gesture. "But, as someone said, that's a reality half in accusation and half in glory. For it also symbolizes men leaving the nest, becoming complete humans. Ulysses left for twenty years, returned, and then went again. When that happens, someone always gets left behind.

"Of course the ideal situation is to have a mother and father in the home. But if that doesn't happen, there's no reason to get bitter about it. Take the poison out of it.

"I used to hate to have to fix things myself. But after I fixed it, I said, hey, *I* fixed that. What I'm trying to say is that I like myself better for having to take hold of my life, alone. I had to grow up, be a competent human being. My kids have absolutely no use for a neurotic mother. And that independence accounts largely for the ability that Black women have."

Probably no other writer has so aptly explored the relationship between women (and particularly Black women) in their work as Toni Morrison has. "We read about Ajax and Achilles willing to die for each other, but very little about the friendship of women," she observed. "People talk about the friendship of women, and them having respect for each other, like it's something new. But Black women have always had that, they always have been emotional life supports for each other.

"That's what I was trying to say in *Sula*, when Nel discovers that it was not her husband that she had missed all those years, but her friend Sula. Because when you don't have a woman to talk to, really talk to, whether it be an aunt or a sister or a friend, that is the real loneliness. That is devastating. And it is the same with men needing the company of other men. Remember when Sula says to Nel that she thought that she shouldn't have to explain, that she never had to explain anything to her before? Honey, that is *home*. That is what women provide for each other. You know if Anna Karenina had just one female friend who would say, 'Don't throw yourself under that train, over that man—that's crazy,' her life may have been very different."

That Toni Morrison has achieved such a tremendous success with an important book *is* a cause for celebration. That she has done it largely on her own terms is a watershed. And one believes that Aunt Pilate with that brass box for an earring would probably say "uh, huh," in her way like John Leonard said it in his. For the rest of us, perhaps Toni Cade Bambara expressed the warmth toward her book best: "Now I know how to read Toni Morrison. I send my kids down the street for the neighbors to take care of them for awhile. I light some candles, fry some fish, and put about nine cushions on my sofa. Then I sit back and read."

An Interview with Toni Morrison

Pepsi Charles / 1977

From *Nimrod International Journal of Prose and Poetry* (vol. 21, no. 1, 1977).
Reprinted by permission of *Nimrod International Journal of Prose and Poetry.*

Toni Morrison is a senior editor at Random House in New York, the author of three novels—*The Bluest Eye, Sula,* and recently released, *Song of Solomon*—a lecturer at Yale University, and the mother of two sons. In the past three years I have interviewed Toni on two different occasions, hoping to illuminate for myself and our listeners the process through which she discovers the distinctive nouns and verbs that comprise what John A. Williams has called "the freshest, most precise language I've run across in years." Our meetings have taken place on my program, *Nuances,* which is heard over WBAI-Pacifica Radio in New York City. Toni's voice and the imagery that she conjures up, even in conversation, have provided my audience with a rare glimpse of the author's "nuances" and life force. Her earnest attempt to explain the constant evolution of self-exploration is, quite evidently, the center of her wizardry and her humanness. P.C.

PC: When I read one of your books I always enter another world, and each experience changes my life a little. Your characters—their names alone are intriguing—Sula, Pecola Breedlove, Milkman . . . . Where would I find these people if I went out looking for them?

TM: I don't know that much about the neighborhoods of New York, but I can't imagine that they're not here. I can't imagine that because, with some exceptions, most of us who are here came from somewhere else. They are in the mid-west, and they are in the south, in Chicago, and in Lorain, Ohio. We are all over this country. The names that I've chosen for people in the books are very often real names of real people. Breedlove is a very common name among Black people, so is Sula Mae. And I know names of friends of my father's, and my mother's, and my brother's that are far stranger than the ones I included in my books. To name a child a color, Green—some of it is affection, some of it is a gesture. The names are just labels to some people, but they're real symbols in another sense. The magic starts with a name. There are reasons for naming people things that have to do with the child himself, as well as the family. But for Black people in a kind of large orphan sense, in the sense of looking for the parent, for the ancestor, it has even more significance.

PC: You always seem to exclude white people from your books. Your novels always focus on how Black people deal with each other, why?

TM: That's much more important to me than a posture that we may or may not take against "the oppressor," or white people who give us jobs or not. That situation can be complex, but what one does with one's own life under the given situation, and how one comes to terms with one's own life under the given situation is what is fascinating to me. Whatever the onus is, whatever the plague is, what that individual does out of those circumstances. It is very curious to me that people create slavery, and they create concentration camps, and they create walks for Indians—and all of that treatment, treating people like beasts, never seemed to produce beasts. It has never made large-scale herds of bestial people. And that is what interests me: how under the most inconceivable abuse, there is this grace, there is this power, and there is this tenacity.

PC: Where does it come from?

TM: I don't always know where it comes from. Some of it is just bullheaded-ness, like Pilate (in *Song of Solomon*), who just backs up and starts from zero again when she doesn't understand. All she knows is, whatever it is, it isn't working for her. So she's fearless in that sense. She's willing to stop and say, I don't know anything, let me go all the way back and start again and see what it is I like.

PC: You gave a different look at men this time. In your two previous novels you were much less subjective, although empathetic.

TM: I got interested in men as main characters in this book, initially, because I wanted to talk about something that I hadn't talked about before. Some idea which was a combination of surrender and dominion at the same time. I think I was compelled to do it because my father died when I was writing the book. I, at some point, remember asking myself, I wonder what he knew that I don't know—about his comrades and about his life? There is a kind of intimacy that one establishes with a parent or friend who dies that does not exist when they are alive, because the persona can sometimes interfere. And it broke then, it was like a door that opened when I began to think about the world he lived in through his point of view. I had no way of knowing whether that was accurate. It's just a shift for me to see how it must have been, not only in the main character (Milkman), but how it must have been to be a man, and think about those things, and worry about that thing. And who were the men he respected and why? And what about that combination? My father had that wholeness. He was able to command enormous respect from all sorts of people, though he was quite gentle. But he could walk in the midst of the wildest fights and people might put their guns down while he cracked a joke. But at the same time, if you were ill, young, old, chick, or child, he knew what to do. There was in him that combination that I didn't know at the time was rare. But it is, and he was whole. And so I got interested in how it might happen that a human being could become complete. That seemed to lean me towards the problems of being a male in this society as opposed to being a female, because those are a different set of problems. We are maybe a couple of jumps ahead of them in certain ways.

PC: What ways?

TM: Well, we can rely on ourselves, our inself, faster. There isn't anything else. So you get it together a little bit faster. I don't mean it's painless or easy. I'm saying that the Black women in the book don't have any back-up. There's nobody back there, and there's no place to go to get that information. The men have their masculinity to fall back on, they can always be that. So sometimes it's a little harder for them because they can hide.

PC: I learned what you just said from a man. He told me he thought that came from having to know, most of our adult life, where the ground is, and quickly, because we might conceive a life. But it's very rare to get a woman writer's view of a male through the eyes of the main character.

TM: It's not very popular these days. It used to be quite common a long time ago, before women were writing as females. Now, I think there is an enormous curiosity on the part of women writers and readers, and perhaps men as well who are reading it, to start to find out who and what they are, independent of all that. And so, therefore, most of the writing is from a woman's point of view, which is a perfectly legitimate and necessary exploration. I had concentrated on that sense of a woman's self in *Sula*. Then I was finished, in my own mind, having wrestled with something that was challenging and interesting to me. I don't mean that the subject is closed, but I had done that and I needed another kind of thing. So I tried to have most of the women in *Song of Solomon*—I did not succeed mind you—subsidiary to Milkman. But Pilate kind of leaped away from me a little bit.

PC: Can you explain who Pilate is in the novel.

TM: Pilate is Milkman's aunt. Milkman's father is the second Macon Dead, who is far along on his road to acquiring things, wealth and property, and moving into a middle-class existence which is secure for him. It gives him a sense of power. His sister, Pilate, who has moved well into the opposite direction of securing herself in a kind of tranquility that has to do with love and serenity. She lives with absolutely nothing. They're just two opposite ends of the pole. The son, the man who the book is about, has both of these things to deal with. And he has to learn a lot. He learns very slowly. Pilate is a kind of *original*. She's like the beginning. I was reading a book that a friend had given me about African cosmology. In it I came across the most marvelous story about the origin of the earth. In African terms females created life. And men did not know for a long, long time, around 10,000 B.C., that they, in fact, impregnated women, because there was a big time gap between the act and the child. So they thought that women just produced life. But by the time they got around to herding sheep, domesticating sheep, then they began domesticating women. Then they could make the connection. That's when you got a male religion, that a male-God was the creator of life. Before that, everywhere the religious centered on women. So the center of the earth, the caves, this was the womb. You saw the center of the earth as a warm, black, fertile place out of which all life sprang. After the men got hold of it, the center of the earth was no longer this wonderful womb; it became hell, chaos, danger, death. But the men began to describe the name by which these creator women were called. The most common name for these women was "Ma." I got a big charge out of that, the name you hear every twenty minutes during a day, "Ma," "Ma." Pilate is a kind of "Ma." I don't know why she came to me with no navel, but I knew that that was so. It was a given in the book that this woman had no navel, and that would set her apart from people and give her a reason for being different. Not just because she was eccentric, but

because there had to be a reason, and that was it. And of course, she was literally born after her mother died. So she's self-invented, self-created,
metaphorically, and in fact. Because of this flat stomach that looks like a
back, people are very curious and frightened of her.

PC: How do you know when you've created a real character?
TM: When I fall in love. Sometimes they say something, then I'll know.
I don't always approve of them, but I love them.

PC: There is a legend among us that Black people once could fly; you
included this legend in *Song of Solomon*. Where did you first hear it?
TM: Everybody told me, my grandmother, all of them. They never said to
me, "Did you know Black people could fly?" They'd say, "You know, during
the days when Black people could fly . . . ." It was a given. But they always
talked about it. When I grew up I didn't think about it that much. Then I
began to read slave narratives. They always talk about it. They all either knew
somebody who flew, or they saw somebody who flew, or they knew somebody who said they saw somebody who flew. It's all over the stories, everywhere. Somebody whirls around, whirls around when he gets fed up, and flies
away. They say, "Where did he go? Back to Africa." So I decided figuratively
you have death maybe, or collective wish fulfillment or something. What got
me excited about the book was precisely that. Suppose it were literally so,
what would it take to fly? If you swim you'd have to trust the water and work
with it. But suppose you could just move one step up and fly? What would
you have to be, and feel, and know, and do, in order to do that?

PC: Okay, answer that.
TM: You would have to be able to surrender, give up all of the weights, all of
the vanities, all of the ignorances. And you'd have to trust and have faith in
the harmony of your body. You would also have to have perfect control.

PC: I asked you once, in relation to *Sula*, about the voices of characters you
may, or may not, hear in the process of creating them. You told me then that
your characters are always looking over your shoulders.
TM: They check up. I begin with a character that is there. Sometimes I learn
more about them. Then sometimes, when I'm inside them, they say extraordinary things that I hear. Sometimes they are phrases that I have heard
elsewhere, that I just pick up and use, a phrase that says everything to me

about a relationship or about a point of view, limited or expansive. But it has to have the sound. And then the people, once they are created, are sort of there—and they say yes to some things, or no to others. Those are the people I check against. It's straight up fiction. But that's irrelevant when you're writing whether they're real people or not to me. I have a visceral response to them.

PC: The idea is real.
TM: That's right. Absolutely!

PC: Does *Song of Solomon* have what you consider to be a happy ending?
TM: Happy ending? I thought it was a book of absolute triumph!

PC: Why?
TM: Because a man learns the only important lesson there is to learn. And he wins himself, he wins himself. And the quality of his life improves immeasurably. Whether its length improves or lengthens is irrelevant. And his friend knows he has improved. His friend knows that, and the two of them know it. I was thrilled with that.

PC: You wear a double hat professionally. I don't know of any other major writer who is also a senior editor at a major publishing house. Does that influence your creative process?
TM: I suppose it's the same industry, but the worlds are so different. The way I think when I write is totally unlike the way I think when I'm editing. There are people who are excellent fishermen who cannot cook. And there are marvelous cooks who can't fish. Even though it's all about fish. The processes are very different to me. I don't find any overlap in terms of work. When I go to my editor, I go not as a colleague; I go as an author: ready to fight, ready to give in, eager to know, defensive about some things. My editing doesn't help me as a writer. I don't think my writing helps me as an editor. It may give me some sympathy for writers in a general sense, but sometimes it doesn't do that.

PC: Do your books help you as a woman?
TM: I'm not sure that they do help me as a woman. They certainly help me as a person.

PC: Why the distinction?

TM: I think of helping me as a woman as having something to do with the complicated levels of one's sexuality. But the books emanate out of where I am as a Toni Morrison, as opposed to as a woman, or a Black, or an editor, or any of these other words. But they enhance my life. Immeasurably.

Faulkner and Women
Faulkner and Yoknapatawpha Conference / 1985

From *Faulkner and Women,* edited by Doreen Fowler and Ann J. Abadie (Jackson: University Press of Mississippi, 1986). Reprinted by permission of University Press of Mississippi.

I'm ambivalent about what I'm about to do. On the one hand, I want to do what every writer wants to do, which is to explain everything to the reader first so that, when you read it, there will be no problems. My other inclination is to run out here and read it; then run off so that there would be no necessity to frame it. I have read from this manuscript three or four times before, and each time I learned something in the process of reading it, which was never true with any other book that I wrote. And so when I was invited to come to Oxford and speak to this conference about some aspect of "Faulkner and Women," I declined, saying that I really couldn't concentrate enough to collect remarks on "Faulkner and Women" because I was deeply involved in writing a book myself and I didn't want any distractions whatsoever. And then very nicely the conference directors invited me to read from this manuscript that had me so obsessed, so that I could both attend the conference and associate myself in some real way with the Center for the Study of Southern Culture and also visit Mississippi and "spend the night," as they say. So, on the one hand, I apologize for reading something that is not finished but is in process; but this was a way to satisfy my eagerness to visit the campus of the University of Mississippi; and I hope there will be some satisfaction rippling through the audience once I have finished. My other hesitation is simply because some of what I read may not appear in print, as a developing manuscript is constantly changing. Before reading to a group gathered to discuss "Faulkner and Women," I would also like to add that in 1956 I spent a great deal of time thinking about Mr. Faulkner because he was the subject of a thesis that I wrote at Cornell. Such an exhaustive treatment of an author makes it impossible for a writer to go back to that author for sometime afterwards until the energy has dissipated itself in some other form. But I have to say, even before I begin to read, that there was for me not only an academic interest in Faulkner, but in a very, very personal way, in a very personal way as a reader, William Faulkner had an enormous effect on me, an enormous effect.

The title of the book is *Beloved,* and this is the way it begins: . . . .

(The author read from her work-in-progress and then answered questions from the audience.)

Morrison: I am interested in answering questions from those of you who may have them. And if you'll stand up and let me identify you before you ask a question, I'll do the best I can.

Question: Ms. Morrison, you mentioned that you wrote a thesis on Faulkner. What effect did Faulkner have on your literary career?

Morrison: Well, I'm not sure that he had any effect on my work. I am typical, I think, of all writers who are convinced that they are wholly original and that if they recognized an influence they would abandon it as quickly as possible. But as a reader in the '50s and later, of course (I said 1956 because that's when I was working on a thesis that had to do with him), I was concentrating on Faulkner. I don't think that my response was any different from any other student at that time, inasmuch as there was in Faulkner this power and courage—the courage of a writer, a special kind of courage. My reasons, I think, for being interested and deeply moved by all his subjects had something to do with my desire to find out something about this country and that artistic articulation of its past that was not available in history, which is what art and fiction can do but sometimes history refuses to do. I suppose history can humanize the past also, but it frequently refuses to do so for perfectly logically good reasons. But there was an articulate investigation of an era that one or two authors provided and Faulkner was certainly at the apex of that investigation. And there was something else about Faulkner which I can only call "gaze." He had a gaze that was different. It appeared, at that time, to be similar to a look, even a sort of staring, a refusal-to-look-away approach in his writing that I found admirable. At that time, in the '50s or the '60s, it never crossed my mind to write books. But then I did it, and I was very surprised myself that I was doing it, and I knew that I was doing it for some reasons that are not writerly ones. I don't really find strong connections between my work and Faulkner's. In an extraordinary kind of memorable way there are

literary watersheds in one's life. In mine, there are four or five, and I hope
they are all ones that meet everybody's criteria of who should be read, but
some of them don't. Some books are just awful in terms of technique but
nevertheless they are terrific: they are too good to be correct. With Faulkner
there was always something to surface. Besides, he could infuriate you in such
wonderful ways. It wasn't just complete delight—there was also that other
quality that is just as important as devotion: outrage. The point is that with
Faulkner one was never indifferent.

Question: Ms. Morrison, would you talk a little bit about the creation of
your character Sula?
Morrison: She came as many characters do—all of them don't—rather full-
fleshed and complete almost immediately, including her name. I felt this
enormous intimacy. I mean, I knew exactly who she was, but I had trouble
trying to make her. I mean, I felt troubled trying to make her into the kind of
person that would upset everybody, the kind of person that sets your teeth on
edge; and yet not to make her so repulsive that you could not find her attractive at the same time—a nature that was seductive but offputting. And playing back and forth with that was difficult for me because I wanted to describe
the qualities of certain personalities that can be exploited by conventional
people. The outlaw and the adventuress, not in the sense of somebody going
out to find a fortune, but in the way a woman is an adventuress; which has to
do with her imagination. And people such as those are always memorable
and generally attractive. But she's troublesome. And, by the time I finished
the book, *Sula*, I missed her. I know the feeling of missing characters who are
in fact, by that time, much more real than real people.

Question: Ms. Morrison, you said earlier that reading a work-in-progress is
helpful to you as a writer. Could you explain how reading helps you?
Morrison: This whole business of reading my own manuscript for information is quite new for me. As I write I don't imagine a reader or listener, ever. I
am the reader and the listener myself, and I think I am an excellent reader. I
read very well. I mean I really know what's going on. The problem in the
beginning was to be as good a writer as I was a reader. But I have to assume
that I not only write books, I read them. And I don't mean I look to see what
I have written; I mean I can maintain the distance between myself the writer
and what is on the page. Some people have it, and some people have to learn

it. And some people don't have it; you can tell because if they had read their work, they never would have written it that way. The process is revision. It's a long sort of reading process, and I have to assume that I am also this very critical, very fastidious and not-easily-taken-in reader who is smart enough to participate in the text a lot. I don't like to read books when all the work is done and there's no place for me there. So the effort is to write so that there is something that's going on between myself and myself—myself as writer and myself as reader. Now, in some instances, I feel content in doing certain kinds of books without reading them to an audience. But there are others where I have felt—this one in particular because it's different—that what I, as a reader, am feeling is not enough, and I needed a wider slice, so to speak, because the possibilities are infinite. I'm not interested in anybody's help in writing technique—not that. I'm just talking about shades of meaning, not the score but the emphasis here and there. It's that kind of thing that I want to discover, whether or not my ear on this book is as reliable as I have always believed it to be with the others. Therefore, I agree quickly to reading portions of this manuscript. Every other book I wrote I didn't even negotiate a contract until it was almost finished because I didn't want the feeling that it belonged to somebody else. For this book I negotiated a contract at a very early stage. So, I think, probably some of the business of reading is a sort of repossession from the publisher. It has to be mine, and I have to be willing to not do it or burn it, or do it, as the case might be. But I do assume that I am the reader, and, in the past, when I was in doubt, if I had some problems, the people I would call on to help me to verify some phrase or some word or something would be the people in the book. I mean I would just conjure them up and ask them, you know, about one thing or another. And they are usually very cooperative if they are fully realized and if you know their name. And if you don't know their names, they don't talk much.

Question: Ms. Morrison, could you discuss the use of myth and folklore in your fiction?

Morrison: This is not going to sound right, but I have to say it anyway. There is infinitely more past than there is future. Maybe not in chronological time, but in terms of data there certainly is. So in each step back there is another world, and another world. The past in infinite. I don't know if the future is, but I know the past is. The legends—so many of them—are not just about the past. They also indicate how to function in contemporary times and they

hint about the future. So that for me they were not ever simple, never simple. I try to incorporate those mythic characteristics which for me are very strong characteristics of black art everywhere, whether it was in music or stories or paintings or what have you. It just seemed to me that those characteristics ought to be incorporated into black literature if it was to remain that. It wasn't enough just to write about black people, because anybody can do that. But it was important to me as a writer to try finally to reach a point where they could say "it's all right. It's okay," The community says it's okay. Your husband says it's okay. Your children say it's okay. Your mother says it's okay. Eventually everybody says it's okay, and then you have all the okays. It happened to me: even I found a moment after I'd written the third book when I could actually say it. So you go through passport and customs and somebody asks, "what do you do?" And you print it out:
W R I T E.

Interview with Toni Morrison

Eugene Redmond / 1985

From *River Styx* (no. 19, 1986). Conducted on 27 October 1985, St. Louis. Transcribed by Jan Garden Castro. Reprinted by permission of Eugene Redmond and *River Styx*.

Eugene Redmond: Welcome to St. Louis and East St. Louis. I've taught your work at the University of Wisconsin. The students experience many different emotions, including fear and terror. Could you talk about the reactions you've gotten to what you say about sexuality, race, and gender?

Toni Morrison: I assumed there would be some terror since it caused me some terror to write them. The shadows cast over our interior lives as a race, as women, as young people. This kind of information was available only in new music but was inarticulate. It once seemed important in literature to make the best presentation of ourselves so that they, the other, would see us in our best light. For me, it made the literature different, in a way. The emotional landscape could not exist if I had in mind as I wrote presenting the best possible front to a mainstream civilization. I was not interested in the perceptions of the mainstream because I knew what they were. What was interesting to me were the things that were hidden, interiorized, private— having it read by people like me. The risk is that there may not be any people like me. The responses to the books are frequently severe. No one is indifferent.

Redmond: At Wisconsin, my system started to race, teaching the rape scene in *The Bluest Eye.* I started to curse, I was so angry.

Morrison: One of the major characteristics one can identify in black art has always been a gaze that's quite steady, never blinking. The idea of knowing exactly what it was.

Redmond: That's another tributary. Is there a progression, an evolution, that you're aiming at? I'm thinking of *Beloved* coming.

Morrison: I don't deny a pattern, but it was hindsight for me that I began to talk about innocence and victimization of black, poor girls, and then, in the

29

second volume, to see what their relationship was. My reliance on forces that were pressing out, on magic, as in *Song of Solomon*, was about soaring, flight—the folkloric idea that is prophesy as well as history. When I got to *Tar Baby*, I wanted to take this theme all the way out. The metaphors were more ancient and prehistoric but the levels were located in historical events.

Beloved, from which I will read tonight, uses a story that nagged or haunted me as its code of departure. It concerns another level of spiritual experience that, I think, came out of my fear, as a child, of that tar baby story. My periodic alarm about that Margaret Garner story—a poor woman who ran away from Kentucky with her four children and killed them rather than return to slavery. So what I'm interested in are the wonderful artistic questions that shoot up from that. It has to do with the imagination of what was slavery really like in her day—that it was so terrible she thought it would be better for her children to die, although she loved her children. What did she think death was? Those children were the best part of her—she did not want them sullied, dirtied. Women transfer the best part of themselves into the *beloved*—the children, the husband. . . . The point is reclamation. The point is not enough that it is there; the point is to reclaim it.

Redmond: This is yet another wing. I'm interested in your plans for a movie, and I read about a musical. I'm curious about what happened to these projects. And, does the attention that you're getting affect your work, your love life, and other relationships? What is happening in the Morrison constellation?
Morrison: I quit Random House. I thought, if I don't do it now, I will always wonder if I could have. I was at Random House for twenty years. I wrote a musical, *New Orleans*, now on hold. I wrote a play that is going to be produced in January in Albany. When I get back Tuesday, the final casting will be done. *Beloved* I started two or three years ago. The contract calls for it to be finished by 1986. I have four hundred pages of manuscript.

Redmond: You astounded me in *Song of Solomon* with the way you characterized men. In your return or reincarnation, would you like to be a man?
Morrison: I think I would not like to come back as a man, but I would like to have more access to what men have, whatever that means. I think part of that means my relationship to danger. And I think I would like their social origin, relation to space. I wish I knew more about it. Being a man is a very scary thing; I don't have the emotional arsenal for it.

Redmond: You have helped humanize the writing arena, but your works terrify many male writers and critics.

Morrison: What is problematic is that I'm not certain that the best young black minds are even interested in writing. They don't see it as the powerful gleaming thing, the absolute, total engagement of the mind.

Redmond: One of my main interests in your work is that your prose is quite poetic. Should your work be read aloud? Do you read and write poetry?

Morrison: I used to get very annoyed at people who said there were poetic things in my writing. Good prose is poetic. I have recently written a poem because I was annoyed deeply at a situation in a book I was writing. I don't write it and I don't want to write it, but my notion of good prose is that it has to have this underground life. The metaphor is a way of energizing it. And absolutely— absolutely—the sounds of the sentence, the choice of words. Aural literature leans heavily on oral traditional ways. The audience can participate in the book. For me, that's what musicians are doing, part of what I want the reader to feel.

Redmond: In writing about black women, what specific and general materials figure profoundly in your grasp and control of your work?

Morrison: The shape of writing about black women, for me, is compulsive. Any black woman who has achieved international fame or awards makes everything possible. I had an interview with Gloria Naylor in *Southern Review*, and in that interview I said I clean one facet of this stone that seems to be like this incredible diamond. Another writer is on another side feeling another face. All of this is about this incredible gem. I refuse, categorically, to be involved in any ladder, any pyramid. I am truly egalitarian. I am not to be seduced by capitalistic pyramids. I will not fight other people's fights. I also feel the same way about men and women. Love is still pervasive for me.

Redmond: Would you repeat what you said earlier about racism?

Morrison: Racism is a scientific, scholarly pursuit. Beginning with Malthus, it's a specific, examined, learned, recorded body of study. Whether it's I.Q. testing or the size of one's brain, it's all a systematized study. Racists always try to make you think they are the majority, but they never are. It's always the minority against all of the poor, all of the women, or all of the blacks.

Interview with Toni Morrison

Donald Suggs / 1985

From *River Styx* (no. 19, 1986). Reprinted by permission of Donald Suggs and *River Styx*.

Donald Suggs: Your first novel, *The Bluest Eye*, deals with the destruction of a young black girl at the hands of a black community that had adopted white standards of beauty. How did you develop your own literary values in the academic and publishing worlds, both dominated by white standards of excellence?

Toni Morrison: I think that when I was writing *The Bluest Eye* that idea was uppermost in my mind even in attempting it. It was my desire to read such a book, one that had its own aesthetic integrity. I didn't phrase it that way. What I thought was that I would like to write a book that didn't try to explain everything to white people or take as its point of departure that I was addressing white people, that the audience for it would be somebody like me. And when that happened certain things just fell away: certain kinds of editorializing, certain kinds of definitions, and to think about the subject matter— those girls—their interior life, my interior life, to do, I suppose, what black musicians have done which is to make judgments myself about what was valuable, what was not valuable, and what was worth saving. That was the impetus for writing it, because I had read a lot of very powerful black literature by men, but I had the feeling that they were talking about somebody else. It was not for my enlightenment. It was for clarification . . . It was extremely important for them to do this, for Richard Wright to say, "let me show *you* America."

Suggs: Could you elaborate on how the process you've described extends to teaching black students?

Morrison: That's very difficult because I've done it with mixed classes, but never to an all-black class. It might be interesting to see how that works. But in

mixed classes you have an obligation to everyone in the class. So the important thing is not to start with white value systems and then see how blacks
reflect off them. The problem has been to start with a black value system and
how the texts connect with it or reject it. That was the pedagogical problem,
for me to draw up what I think are the characteristics of all black art, the given
reality of the black world, which even some black people don't articulate, and
the perceived reality. Identify them and then we can go to the books.

Suggs: Teaching white students must present special problems. How do you
approach realities of the black experience which might be commonly
accepted in an all-black class?

Morrison: You start by saying, in the beginning was dispossession and violence. Then you look at what happened, what positive things came out of
that, what black people were able to do with the forms of reclamation and
dignity, the forms of that resistance and so on. I take a lot for granted, I used
to, rather, and I thought that everybody knew what I meant. But they don't,
so I try and say what does it mean to have no self? When the "other" denies
it, which is what slavery is, and what do you have to do to reclaim the self or
status, and what it means to have no art that you can claim. I just bring in all
these quotes from everybody in the world, from then to now, in which it's
clear in the criticism that what they're saying is that black Americans don't
have anything.

Suggs: What about black schools? Teaching in that setting is the task any
easier?

Morrison: It should be. I don't know that it is. Because as a student and
teacher there, those years were the pre–Civil Rights years, I left in 1964, were
years when the measure of excellence was to outstrip the white schools at one
thing or another. Presumably, after Civil Rights curriculum changes were
made that were significant and the emphasis was on interior study. I don't
know how that turned out. I hear interesting things. I think, for example, that
Howard is supposed to be one of the best schools for child development. I
don't know what happened to liberal arts. In addition, it was an unfair situation that they were placed in because the hoped-for consequences of Civil
Rights were that students could go anywhere. They didn't have to go to
Howard for the so-called best education. They could go to other schools,
and so could the faculty. They lost the creme de la creme, or whatever the

mythological pull was in the '60s when the established, superior white schools started recruiting black kids who didn't have to go to Howard or Fisk or those schools. There were always some who didn't, but I mean in large numbers. And also to attract the faculty, so you lost some of the faculty. So they were in a very difficult position because Howard was always at the forefront of the integrationist fight. And then when that happened you got white kids coming to Howard. You know, the medical school down there is almost two-thirds white.

Suggs: In your novel, *Sula*, you explore a friendship between two black women, set entirely in the black community. If a woman like Sula were alive today and writing books, how might she reconcile her emphatically black female sensibility with a more mainstream, feminist view of relationships and gender?

Morrison: It would be a little problematic for her. Clearing the field for some intelligent discussion of gender, and say, feminist problems are important. It's not a cul-de-sac. It's not an aim in itself. And a world deprived of male sensibilities is an incomplete world. So it's very delicate. It's not a line. It's where two things come together and touch. Each one, hopefully, is enhanced by its relationship to the other. What I'm trying to say is that white feminist views are in some areas so problematic for me, since I'm going to assume that I can do what Sula would do. If she was unorthodox enough, she probably would be interested in unorthodox, or at least non-mainstream solutions. But then she might not.

The divisiveness is unfortunate, that we have words like "either/or" in the vocabulary that are taken too seriously. I think that forced to make a choice between my sons and the feminists. . . If I do, it will not be with the latter. But I don't know why I have to make that choice, and I refuse to. It's like abortion and right to life, as though there were an inevitable conflict there. There isn't. But it's being drawn up as a battle ground when it doesn't exist. Nobody is saying you have to do this.

The idea of conflicting modes of life existing in the same place has always been a troublesome thing in this country. People are always drawing up sides and battle grounds. And the other side should be killed. It can't contain two points of view in a harmonious society. That is just the way we are educated toward conflict and destruction. Because if you're proven right and the other person is wrong, then wrong means death. You can't exist. As a woman with

X and Y chromosomes, it seems to me that what women ought to be able to do is make reconciliations among these various types. The idea of ideological slaughter of the other is chewing up everybody's intelligence. People are making the most unbelievable statements about the other based on that kind of insistence that the person who disagrees with you fundamentally can't exist. These are political statements as well as biological and everything else. The hierarchy being established is what's problematic. So there are those who want to accommodate themselves into a man's world, those who want to take over the freedom and access of a man's world, and those who want to exclude men entirely from the world that they live in. They run the gamut, it seems to me, all based on some hostility. Not that they're not legitimate complaints. The enemy is not men. The enemy is the concept of patriarchy, the concept of patriarchy as the way to run the world or do things is the enemy, patriarchy in medicine, patriarchy in schools, or in literature.

Suggs: You've said that you feel that questions about the role of black women are best examined in the context of the black experience. How do you respond to criticism of what is sometimes seen as an unfair portrayal of black men in the world of black women writers?

Morrison: Women writers, some of them, are very sensitive to the special considerations of black males in white, patriarchal society. Because of the intimacy, they understand the nature of racism and they do not lump black men in the category of simply alien men. Others of them seem to, but I don't find it as strident among black women as I do among white women. When you see a very militant white feminist, it's very exclusive. They tend not to permit male sensibilities in their world. I don't find that as strong among black women. Although people tell me, and I guess that perhaps they're right, because I'm not familiar with all of it, that black men complain about the kind of men in the literature that black women write. Nobody's tender and nobody's reasonable. But I think that they're mistaken. I think that Paule Marshall doesn't write about men that way. I certainly don't. Some of them are terrible and some of them are nice. Toni Cade Bambara doesn't write about men that way. Gloria Naylor doesn't write about men that way. So I think that they're misinformed, because there are those who—whenever they see that men are not wonderful—get alarmed. Their sensitivity is real. They should be sensitive, because no one should take the easy route when describing male characters. There are some books in which black men are just foils for the women's growth. And you don't believe in them for a minute. It may be useful for your story, but I don't believe it. So men have a right to be alert and sensitive to that problem, just as we have a right to be sensitive to the opposite problem, of how black women are treated in the books of black men.

Suggs: An interviewer once asked you about the effect of the number of one-parent families on the black community. Could you expand on your answer that black women could use the absence of a man as a resource for independence?

Morrison: I believe that suggesting that a one-parent family is crippled in some way is somebody else's notion. I do know that no one parent can raise a child completely. But it is also true that two parents can't do it either. You need everybody. You need the whole community to raise a child. And one parent can get that community. You have to work at it. You have to decide. I mean community, not meaning neighborhood the way it was meant when I was a little girl. There was a street and a block. That doesn't exist now for most of us, particularly if you're a single working parent. You have to collect around you the people who can serve that function for you, and provide multiple kinds of resources for your children. I have women friends who raise their children alone and are working, whose children relate to her friends like family members. They call on one another in times of crisis and duress. They really use each other as a kind of life-support system, so that you don't have this kind of single, one-on-one relationship that is too tense for the child and too tense for the parent. Nobody can deliver that much. The parent can't and the child can't, so you do need these other people. You need a tribe. I don't care what you call it, extended family, large family. That's what one needs.

Suggs: Alice Walker has criticized books which she felt had "white folks on the brain." What effect might it have on the works of black women writers who have been commercially successful largely due to whites at the bookstore cash register?

Morrison: There is an advantage to having a wide readership, both black and white, which is that it makes it possible for lots of other writers to get published. Once there's a market—and you have to remember that the whole system is controlled by whites—once that readership exists, then it's likely that other black writing will be purchased by companies and distributed and sold.

That is important. As far as it affects the writings, it can't. I suppose one could let it. Writing for the gallery is something that a writer must resist no matter who he is. You know the writers that are writing for their audience because they write the same book over and over again with the sort of cute things that their readership likes. Serious writers write things that compel them, new challenges, new situations, and a new landscape that they have not been in before. But I had always made sure from the beginning that the address of the novel would be interior, that I would write for a reader who wanted what I wanted, and I could put myself up as a person whose demands were at least different and then would be higher and higher. But paradoxically, what happens is that the more specific one is, the more specificity there is in the writing, the more accessible it is. Tolstoy was not writing for little colored girls in Ohio. He was writing Russian, specifically upper class things about a certain situation and so on. And so was everybody who was of any interest. That subtle racist argument about how universal art works better than any other is fraudulent entirely. Anybody who sets out and writes a universal novel has written nothing. The more concentrated it is in terms of its culture the more revealing you find it, because you make those connections. You see, there are more connections among us than differences, and that is the point. You don't wipe out a culture. You don't wipe out the ethnic quality. You certainly don't address yourself to a parallel or dominant culture. Some black writers did. Much of what was written during the Harlem Renaissance was written with white readers in view, very sort of "let me show you how exotic I am." You can always hear that voice. That may be what she meant. There are contemporary writers who do it still. I don't think that readership has anything to do with it. I suppose there may be black writers who have a large white readership who write for that readership, but I can't imagine it. That only happens on television. You have these little comic book things. You try and straddle some line where it's this, but it's really that. It's black face really. It may be in different dress, but that's what it is, black people playing black people. It's interesting though that there are a lot of women who write books with an audience of men in mind. I can feel when they're getting over on some man. He looms too large. What is this? The wilder they get in their approbation, the more important he must have been. That's a mighty big gun, isn't it, for just that little character over there? A big Gatlin gun they used to call it, just to blow this little man away. So he really must have been important. The gun's too big.

A Conversation with Toni Morrison

Audrey T. McCluskey / 1986

From *Women in the Arts: A Celebration*, in the Occasional Papers Series (vol. 2, 1986), published by the Women's Studies Program at Indiana University. Reprinted by permission of Audrey T. McCluskey.

The following interview with Toni Morrison was conducted by Audrey T. McCluskey during an informal gathering of Women's Studies students on the Bloomington campus. The interview, which orginally appeared in *Women's Studies in Indiana*, has been updated and edited.

Q: Your work has such musical intonation and character . . . when you write do you have specific songs or genres in mind—the blues, for instance?

TM: Some of them are bluesie, some of them are more gospelly, but it's a flavor that you want . . . an atmosphere that informs some of the sentences because they have a blues beat. I don't analyze it from a musician's point of view because there is some danger for a writer who's dealing with words, with the assumption that the words are strong enough and that music is somehow overwhelming it . . . But there has to be a relish for language, of its possibilites, of its inventiveness and what it can do among black people. This is almost never explored in literature. (It is important for me as a writer) to break the language open with a heavy reliance on the Bible, parables and various kinds of repetitions. If a mother says to her son, "All I ever did was pray for you." She says, "on my knees." She wants the picture in his mind. The last three words are unnecessary in a clear sentence, but she has given him a picture of herself in solitude, in private . . . "so whatever else you've got to say about me is irrelevant." And that's the kind of searching of the visual image that Pilate [*Song of Solomon*] can do in her son and just say "mercy" four different ways . . .

Q: And I think that's the quality that makes it possible, even desirable, to go back and re-read your novels again and again even though you know the ending—like replaying a favorite song.

TM: That's right; if it's done right. It's like Greek drama—you can always go back and look at it one more time. But that's the nature of the stature of tragedy, which people who don't read my books are just not interested in. They say, "What about the happy ending?" I'm so bored with this phoney optimism . . . why don't you ever write stories that end happily? What!? If you value what in the old days used to be called tragic stature, it is about epiphany and knowledge as more important than that other feeling. If you can, as somebody says, "Look what it could have been, look how nice this was . . ." and that's the way it is in life. It doesn't really matter and that's part of what was going on. You could work all your life to make your farm and get blown away—and it's living with that and knowing that and not being afraid to say that.

Q: Which is another way that music—especially the blues functions in your work—it becomes a kind of worldview, a fortifying force in some of your characters . . .
TM: Absolutely, that's exactly what I mean. It's not just the sound of it—it's what is being said, it's things that are really still almost indescribable . . . And I think maybe they should remain indescribable, because you see these very subtle reductivist solutions—what blues is, what jazz is, and you're always annoyed because there is anger in it, there is freedom in it, there is contempt in it, there is, all of this stuff is there. There is never any whining. That's all I know about it. Nobody is whining. They may be upset, they may be tragic, they may be this, but they don't whine.

Q: What was your reaction to the interpretation of Nell and Sula's relationship as lesbian?
TM: The first time I heard that and read Barbara Smith's article it was sort of interesting. I thought at the time that I was writing *Sula*, that this was this extraordinary new thing that I was doing and that I would do it in such a way that nothing else would matter in that book except the relationship between those two women. It would have to be about their friendship so it was an easy shot to make them homosexual because friendship among women is so discredited. And always subordinate. One of the ways to discredit it is to say that they had no choice. So to give it homosexual color or thrust—I'm not making any statements about homosexuality—but it was again to detract from the ability [of women to have real friendships]. However, I like the *fact* of that kind of effort—to make something out of black feminist criticism.

I don't know if it'll ever become, but I like the arrogance. I love the feistiness of those women.

Q: Are you concerned that the effort to define a black feminist criticism may become too narrow or doctrinaire?
TM: Oh sure. It always does. The people who are doing it hook their careers on it, you see. Therefore, they can't really change their minds as [Amiri] Baraka does but each one opens another little path. If Black women's criticism ever emerges, something will have to be done with the definition of lesbian, stretching it to encompass everything or narrow it. That's a problem about definition. I like the notion, however, of its extension of that call and response thing and the place of the story teller in the community. I love the notion of the controversy that emanates from anything I write . . . I like the fact that no one is indifferent to it. People say, "I HATE it!" or "I really liked it." Nobody says, "Enh . . ." If that's going on you know there's life. But the risks are exactly there. You take your womb, and then after your children are born you just stretch it to include the house, then the neighborhood, then the town . . . 'til the whole world becomes part of that.

Q: What do you see as the role of black writers and black literature today?
TM: I was talking to a woman writer a couple of years ago and she said that all her hopes in her work were in the future. And I said that all mine were in the past, meaning that it was just a different way of looking at the world or maybe having lived long enough or remembering something. There were things that were already there that had either been buried, discredited, or never looked at and I feel it particularly strongly with black literature because it really is new; I know that there have been black writers since, I don't know—whatever the current discovery is—but the point is that it's just like the tip of the iceberg. I don't care if you've got fifty books, they're still fifty. But the examination of it, the experimentation within it, the information that has to surface from it, the play in it—it's still very, very young and new and that's all right because I think it's only been very recently that it was important to have black novels really, for black people at large, because they had something else—they had music, and now it's not theirs anymore. It used to be a very personal, private thing and now it's not. It belongs to anybody who can play it. They used to have ceremonies, gossip, storytelling, all of that—I don't mean it's gone, in the sense that you can't find it, but it used to be something that sustained the culture,

and now when the village confronts the city that disperses, because you're making these other contacts, so now black children have to be pulled off somewhere, in order to know what that is. That's what I meant by preservation. If I were going to do anything, it would have to be about making sure that this existed. What I miss now is something that I took for granted for the first twenty years of my life which was I used to hear people sing all over the house, all over the street, wherever they were. When my mother would get up on Saturday and spend the *whole* day doing that [singing], whatever else she was doing, she was doing that. It was her novel. It was something that was holding her . . . So, the novel exists as it always has, to inform a class about how it ought to behave and what it ought to know.

Q: So for black people novels are filling a cultural void?
TM: Where do you find information about how to hang onto what it is that is important and how to give up things that are not? I think in a real political sense, novels function for black people in a way that they may not have in 1930, when there was still enormous separation, culture separation.

Q: How have you been able to bridge that everpresent gap between what is termed "popular" and "serious" fiction?
TM: I'm smart! Well, I do cut corners a little bit because all of us go through those channels. I went to all those schools. It's like we were saying, if I am as intimate with Aeschylus as I am with gospel, then I can do that. And I want the people who talk about it [my work] to have the same breadth as I do. I really do feel that much control, exercising the reins in that fashion. It never just comes off exactly the way I would like it to—which is why I do a novel—it's gonna be real, this is the real—

Q: So if you ever write the perfect novel, you stop . . . ?
TM: I tell you. This is IT! This is the one!

Q: That brings me to your women characters. Some critics have called them "superwomen" and larger than life. Although to me, there is a comforting reality about women like Pilate.
TM: I feel like that. It's all larger than life. All the people who are not larger than life are dead. I am amazed at the things that my grandmother did. I'm absolutely staggered. And I thought, "Well, surely I can go to Cornell if she

could do that. What is that? That's nothing." I mean, people were in really life-threatening circumstances—all of the time. And when I said the other night: the quality of their lives was really fantastic. I don't know what it all looked like to other people, but it was unbelievable. And they were not heroic, in the sense of what people did. You think of emigrant women or women out on those ranges—if you ever penetrated that veil and got away from the routine, larger-than-life activities of such people. So my question is how on earth did they remain that coherent? And I don't feel like apologizing for them. I don't care—all those little articles about the super this—I don't even know what that means! That was the way it was.

Q: What do you most remember about your foremothers?
TM: I remember one of the most overwhelming experiences of my life was to be in the same room (with three generations of women in my family) my great grandmother, my grandmother, and my mother. I stood there speechless looking from one face to the other—observing the interactions between them. I'll never forget that!

Q: Your writing captures that awe you describe, but at the same time you're not "in awe" of your characters. What they do and say is on their own terms. There is a lot of respect there but no sentimentality.
TM: I didn't want to come in there empty-handed. I owe a debt and I will pay off. The reason for the debt is that I know what just moving from Alabama to Ohio entailed with seven children and fifteen dollars and don't know where you're going but life back there is death. It's not like it wasn't a good life. It was death. But they managed to get out and when that migration happened it was not playful. Those stories were not the backdrop—it was real life and they have managed to survive it with an incredible amount of grace. There was no reason for that kind of joy and sanity unless there was something else operating. And that's what I meant when I said I'm not telling you that these were flawless, wonderful people—some of them were so mean you wouldn't believe it—but you pick from that which you can use in order to go forward and give your own children, or your friends. That's how one bears a culture—that's b-e-a-r-s.

Q: Isn't that a heavy load?
TM: Oh, indeed. Oh, it's terrible! You just do what you do. I don't—I can't worry about failing now. I don't have another life and I'm not sure how much

time I have left in the one I have. I have to take risks and that means that you have to be willing to have it all fall like a plate . . . So, when I say I want to be cool—what is it that makes it possible to make a life of quality and when is it just too much? I mean I know who Pecola is. I have seen it and I know about it and I know when it doesn't work and I know in some instances why. When you haven't got the resources to get through it—it is not an easy life—it is NOT an easy life. So that it's not that I'm looking for recipes for survivals—I also have to find out what the dangers are—where you sink—and that's what most of the conflict and tension in the books are. When is it just not worthwhile for a self-invented, self-exploratory woman to want to go on another minute. What does she need in her life? And when she loses that, she's quite content to die—except that she can be curious even about her death. So, I dwell, because I need to, on the resources that come from those people, but I also can dwell in a very painful way on the things that I know about in which those things just did not work. When people were crushed and they never, ever made it through and that is part of the past as well.

Q: In an article you wrote back in 1971, "What Black Women Think of Women's Liberation," one of the points you made was while black women may envy some of the material comforts of white women, they do not respect them in terms of how they function in the world. How do you feel about that today? **TM:** I don't have any evidence to change my mind on that subject. It seems that there is always some expectation of maturity and adulthood that black women, at least of a certain age, expect of white women, organizationally speaking, to do something really politically powerful and really non-racist and directed toward the sorority of women—they frequently turn away from that opportunity and rest again on the class distinctions or the race distinctions. I find it sometimes in their writing, and I wonder how can a writer live in that world and not mention the woman who's cleaning her house or do it in such an odd way. I think I have seen *some* changes in some of the scholarship of white feminists. For example, you see the women's article by a black or Third World woman in it and, then you'll see anthologies which still tip their hats, but that has come, I think, because of the *battering* done by the black women. It's very difficult for them to touch us in their minds. The racism that is in them is simply a barrier and I just don't feel it's my job to fix that for them. That racism is something that white women have got to address directly to themselves—that is their problem and until they look at it right in the eye, it will always separate us.

A Bench by the Road: *Beloved* by Toni Morrison

The World: The Journal of the Unitarian Universalist Association / 1988

From *The World: The Journal of the Unitarian Universalist Association* (January/February 1989). Reprinted by permission of the Unitarian Universalist Association.

When a writer begins to think about value and worth it usually means dwelling on a moment after publication, after the work is done—a period which I can call "after *Beloved*" now.

It's that post-publication period when one can assess what was done as well as why. Outside of its novelistic or literary merit, even outside of the reader confronting the transfiguration of the page, what is it for? It's almost as though the novel substitutes for something, that it exists instead of something else. I have to think about what drove me to do it.

The primary conviction one has when one begins is that it is absolutely necessary. The secondary certainty is that I alone am the one who can do it. How delusional. It's a strong feeling, but is it also the necessary fiction one needs to construct in order to do the work? The work which takes so long, which one has to feel one would have been just as driven to write without readers, without publishers? And my answer's always, "Oh yes. Yes." The question I'm putting to myself now is Why? Well, it has become a little bit more clear to me, a year after *Beloved*, what perhaps, in very personal terms, the book has substituted for.

There is no place you or I can go, to think about or not think about, to summon the presences of, or recollect the absences of slaves; nothing that reminds us of the ones who made the journey and of those who did not make it. There is no suitable memorial or plaque or wreath or wall or park or skyscraper lobby. There's no three-hundred-foot tower. There's no small bench by the road. There is not even a tree scored, an initial that I can visit or you can visit in Charleston or Savannah or New York or Providence or, better still, on the banks of the Mississippi. And because such a place doesn't exist (that I know of), the book had to. But I didn't know that before or while I wrote it. I can see now what I was doing on the last page. I was finishing the story, transfiguring and disseminating the haunting with which the book begins. Yes, I was doing that; but I was also doing something more. I think I was pleading. I think I was pleading for that wall or that bench or that tower or that tree when I wrote the final words.

Q: When I read *Beloved* I found myself stopping because I was scared and felt threatened. Did you feel the same way?
A: I didn't feel threatened. I felt a lot of melancholy, sometimes fury, a lot of affection. But none of that was of any use. Love, fury, melancholy, joy—all of these profound feelings are the reasons that you write, but none of them is useful when you do it, because if you write out of that, you don't have control.

I meant it to be real. To look at it with a prolonged gaze seemed to me to be constructive. One comes out in a better position than one was in without that information. I wanted that sudden feeling of being snatched up and thrown into that house, precisely the way they were. They were picked up from any-where, at any time, and removed without resources, without defenses, without anything. Naked. They had each other, they had a little music, and they had the urgency of the task at hand. So that's what the reader has.

Q: I think that everybody that reads your work feels like you're writing directly to them, right to their soul. How do you do it?
A: You can connect with other people, on a very personal level, in a number of ways. You don't give them everything; you open spaces where they can come in. I never describe the characters a great deal—just a mark, an odor, something peculiar to them. I also leave spaces in scenes, particularly sensual scenes. You have to assume that the reader's sensuality is more sensual than your own. Therefore, you just provide the way in which they can step in.

In *Beloved*, this child just appeared. I knew that the mother, Sethe, would believe that she was her daughter, that she would need to believe it, and that her daughter, Denver, would need it. But I also knew that I was doing some-thing that might not work—having a ghost who may not be a ghost. So how do I get the readers to go along with me on that? Those who read it anyway know that anything might happen at any moment, but it still has to have some basis, though not necessarily in fact. Ghosts are not difficult because everybody believes in them, even those of us who don't believe in them, because we don't put our hands outside the bed when we sleep. We're convinced that there's something underneath.

So if you know that somewhere in the heart, there's still this little voice that says, "Ah no, but . . . just in case," then you can move with that. You can use that remembrance that's in me, in you, in everybody.

Q: In the section of *Beloved* which concerns Sethe's story, do you or does the novel take a moral position on the infanticide?
A: The novel admits that it cannot negotiate the morality of that act, that there's no one qualified who can, except the dead child. That is why her presence, or the belief in her presence, is so important. She alone can ask that question with any hope of a meaningful answer. I personally don't know. I can't think of anything worse than to kill one's children. On the other hand, I can't think of anything worse than to turn them over to a living death. It was that question which destroyed Baby Suggs.

Q: When did you first know that you wanted to be a writer?
A: I didn't think about being a writer as a young person. I was content to be a reader, an editor, a teacher. I thought that everything that was worth reading had probably been written, and if it hadn't somebody would write it eventually. I didn't become interested in writing until I was about thirty years old. I didn't really regard it as writing then, although I was putting words on paper. I thought of it as a very long, sustained reading process—except that I was the one producing the words. It doesn't sound very ambitious or even sensible now. But I'm very happy with that attitude. The complicated way in which I try to bring the reader in as co-author or a complicitous person really stems from my desire to be engaged as a reader myself.

After I wrote *Song of Solomon* I began to think of myself legally as a writer. Up until that time I had another job; I never put "writer" on my tax return. I put something that I thought the income tax people would respect. But after that book was published I remember someone saying to me, "This is probably what you do." I said, "You mean this is what I'm going to be when I grow up?" They said, "Yeah." And I quit work.

Q: Recently many black female authors have been receiving some criticism for the lack of positive black characters in their work, especially male characters. Do you see this as a real concern?

A: It's true that when I first began to write, my work was much criticized—even despised I think—because I was not writing happy stories, about people who were able to put it all together in spite of difficulties, about people who had risen to a certain status. I realized that it was a problem, and I realized how important positive images could be, but I thought that nobody intelligent would take that seriously as criticism of a writer. If the critics felt that they could force me to "write positive images," then clearly they assumed that I was writing for white people. It was a demand that I create an image for the "other" as opposed to my making an intimate and direct account to the people in the book and to black people. I thought the complaint was just headline stuff: things to say to reporters.

I have persisted in letting the characters manifest the idea. I don't choose them for their category: *Song of Solomon* is loaded with a whole realm of positions: physicians, well educated doctors, entepreneur husbands, and so on. Milkman is not, you know, barefoot. I have used what seemed to me to be necessary for the explication of the idea, pulling from the whole range of the available. It's humiliating to be asked to write propaganda. That's not literature.

Q: What writers do you read, and who do you turn to for inspiration?
A: As a publisher, as an editor, you get a little stupid because you read what's submitted and you have to keep on top of that. You don't have a lot of free time; it's a twenty-four-hour job. But there are people whom I read religiously, and people whom I read over and over again. Sometimes it's just technique. I regularly read all of Marguerite Duras for example. I like the way she writes in French and English. I read a lot of Latin American novels—almost all that I can get. But I've also been reading fewer and fewer novels and more and more biography for some reason.

With regard to inspiration, I have to tell you that I was so self-conscious about developing a style of my own, about going to a place that I thought was virgin territory, that I was terrified of reading. Most writers don't read anybody while they are writing, because they don't want anything to rub off. I was very concerned about developing this sound that I thought would be my own. I was not convinced I had done it until *Sula.* That book seemed to suggest that I had hit on a voice that was mine, that I didn't write like anybody else.

I do know that I'm often dependent on painting for what one means literally by inspiration. I find literary solutions in paintings sometimes. It's not just the action and the characters. You have to have a subtext, something underneath—image or scene or color—that is making contact with the reader.

Q: What do you think of grouping yourself, Alice Walker, Zora Neale Hurston, and others under the title of "black women writers"? Is there some benefit in teaching all of your works together?
A: It can't hurt. I don't mind being taught with Alice Walker, William Shakespeare, Milton, Marguerite Duras, or anybody. In some quarters, contemporary black women's literature has been perceived as secondary or tertiary, a kind of limited ghettoization. But that's only if I accept that definition. And I don't.

Q: Writing is my love. I'm young and I know there's a lot I haven't seen yet. How much living is necessary to tell a good story or to write a good book?
A: I think it differs with people. Experience just for the sake of it is almost pointless. If you can't make anything coherent out of it then it's not information. It's not knowledge. And it certainly may not be creatively handled. Some people sit on the edge of the bank and fish all day. They don't even talk and yet they're complex and fascinating. You have to work within your own life.

My life now is as uneventful as you can imagine. And that's just the way I like it. I'm interested in what I think. I'm interested in what I imagine. I am not fascinated with my autobiography however. I'm reminded of a number of biographies about the wives of great writers that I've just been reading. It's amazing how the fecund imagination of certain powerful gentlemen has been in fact almost a theft of the fecund existence of the mate. So I don't have an answer for you. If you find that your work is mediocre it may not be because you haven't lived. It may be because you have not learned enough about the craft.

Q: After reading your books, I always feel so drained. I see my mother there. I see my grandmother there. I see my aunts there. It's absolutely overwhelming. After you've finished such a work, do you feel drained?
A: The draining you should feel only for a little while. Don't you feel nurtured and full later on?

Q: I feel glad that it's there on paper. But I was wondering how you felt after you'd written it.

A: Well, this book was difficult for me because I had done different things with other books, and posed certain technical obstacles for myself in order to stay interested in the writing in a way other than "how does it all turn out?" The process itself is extremely interesting to me. And from one book to the next I learned a lot about how to do certain things.

For *Beloved* though, there was almost nothing that I knew that I seemed sure of, nothing I could really use. All of my books have been different for me, but *Beloved* was like I'd never written a book before. It was brand new. And I knew that I was in the company of people whom I absolutely adored, in a situation which I absolutely abhorred. To stay in their company, to listen, to imagine, to invent—and not to write—was exhausting.

I thought, more than I've thought about any book, "I cannot do this." I thought that a lot. And I stopped for long, long, long periods of time and said, "I know I've never read a book like this because who can write it?" But then I decided that was a very selfish way to think. After all, these people had lived that life. This book was only a tiny little part of what some of that life had been. If all I had to do was sit in a room and look at paper and imagine it, then it seemed a little vain and adolescent for me to complain about the difficulty of that work. I was also pricked by the notion that the institution, which had been so organized and had lasted so long, was beyond art. And that depressed me so much that I would just write some more.

Q: I can see that you could have been really caught up because I could not put the book down. What was your family doing while you were haunted by these characters?

A: Writing is always a displacement. It's like walking underwater. And everything else looks a little dim and a little far away. It can last for a long time. You miss things, and friends who don't understand get mad at you. Friends who know that you're really not responsible during those times come back. But children make you pay. You have to pay them for that neglect.

Q: I was very moved by your opening remarks about creating a memorial through art for those who have no memorial. Who do you see as your models for that sort of effort?

A: I guess I'm just beginning to think of it in terms of a three-dimensional thing. I've always had a very close, rather intimate family relationship, because my parents do, and their parents did. I never felt that distance from history. I do all sorts of things because I'm embarrassed to think that my great-grandmother would laugh at me. And she's been dead a long time.

But somebody told me that there's a gentleman in Washington who makes his living by taking busloads of people around to see the monuments of the city. He has complained because there is never anything there about black people that he can show. And he's black. I can't explain to you why I think it's important but I really do . . . I think it would refresh. Not only that, not only for black people. It could suggest the moral clarity among white people when they were at their best, when they risked something, when they didn't have to risk and could have chosen to be silent; there's no monument for that either.

I don't have any model in mind, or any person, or even any art form. I just have the hunger for a permanent place. It doesn't have to be a huge, monumental face cut into a mountain. It can be small, some place where you can go put your feet up. It can be a tree. It doesn't have to be a statue of liberty.

An Interview with Toni Morrison

Salman Rushdie / 1992

From *Brick: A Literary Magazine* (Summer 1992). Reprinted by permission of Salman Rushdie and the Wylie Agency, Inc. Originally telecast on BBC's *The Late Show* in June 1992.

Rushdie: Toni Morrison, hello. Your novel *Jazz*—it's interesting because it's deceptively simple, the given of the novel is deceptively simple. You've got this middle-aged man; he's got a young girl who is his lover; he murders her because she's going to leave him; his wife goes to the funeral to slash the dead girl's face and then you have an extraordinary image—the idea that the only thing that would come out of the face is straw. You set this up, and yet these people are not musicians, they're not involved in the world of music. Although there is music in the novel, it's peripheral, there aren't big musical scenes. Yet the novel's called *Jazz*. Why the title, why *Jazz*?

Morrison: I lucked out this time with a working title that actually was usable as a title. But what I was interested in was the concept of jazz, the jazz era, what all of that meant before it became appropriated and redistributed as music throughout the world. What was jazz when it was just music for the people, and what were those people like? That subject is highly contested—its origins, what it means, what the word's etymology is, and so on. The only thing that's consistent in the debate is the nature of improvisation—that one works very hard in order to be able to invent. It was that quality in these people's lives that I wanted to capture, moving from the South on into a city, where there were endless possibilities, of both security and danger.

Rushdie: Trying to improvise life—
Morrison: Exactly.

51

Rushdie: That's very interesting, because it's like what you do in the book—as Antonia Byatt [British writer and literary critic] said in her little piece—you tell the story in more or less the first paragraph.
Morrison: Exactly.

Rushdie: And then you tell it from every which way, the music goes round and round.
Morrison: Right. The plot is just the melody—not *just* the melody, but it's the familiar, predictable story or story that the voice thinks it can predict. Then you begin to play off of it, and to hear it afresh from somebody else's point of view.

Rushdie: Just like Miles Davis starting off by playing "Bye Bye Blackbird," and then it goes off into almost anything.
Morrison: Exactly.

Rushdie: I wondered if that's technique—the novel is very worked, it's very crafted, like all your writing, but in the making of it are there passages of improvisations, other passages where you just let it go, and see what happens?
Morrison: There are passages where I wanted the reader to feel as though I had let it go, and that it was loose and didn't know quite where it was going, and it sort of was in love with itself. But some of those passages took so much rewriting in order to make them look as though they were loose! I like what you said about the contrivance, though, the artifice. Even though one's working for a kind of freedom and escape, in a sense, from the novel itself, one has to accept the fact that art is contrivance.

Rushdie: Of course.
Morrison: Surprise has to be planned. If the novel seems not to know quite where it's going and the narrator is dumbfounded by what it has imagined and has to keep recreating itself, the working of that takes a lot of contrivance and artifice.

Rushdie: I think quite often the bits that read like you just did them like that, are the hardest bits. And the other bits, the ones which you actually did do like that, people read as if they're very stuttering and faltering. That's

happened to me a lot, as well, and I'm sure to all writers . . . I wondered about another aspect of jazz, which is this idea of performance. That's to say, one of the meanings of improvisation is that you don't have what you have in classical music, which is a text—
Morrison: A script.

Rushdie: —which is then performed. The performer is also the creator.
Morrison: Exactly.

Rushdie: That's something which I suspect is why, back in the sixties, there were attempts to make Indo-jazz fusions. Because in Indian music it's the same thing. You have the sitarist, who improvises. There's a kind of great affinity, I've felt, in that sense.
Morrison: Yes.

Rushdie: This led me to the idea of writing in a way which enjoyed the performance, something that in England might be called showing off.
Morrison: *(laughs)* Deliberately!

Rushdie: *(laughs)* Is that something you do?
Morrison: Oh yes. In this book, deliberately. The voice starts out believing it is totally knowledgeable. It knows everything or says it does, and begins to love its language and love its point of view and likes to sort of dwell and relish its own—

Rushdie: Yes, it goes off into long riffs about stuff—
Morrison: That's right!

Rushdie: Which isn't really to do with the story, it just wants to tell you about things.
Morrison: And then a character's own aria, or own soliloquy or own interior thoughts surrounded in quotes can object to what the book-voice has said, disagree with it, or even ignore it, so that along with the major sound of the voice, there are these other instruments that comment on that narrative.

Rushdie: Yes. I'd like to circle around a bit and come back to this question of the relationship of the voice, which, as you say, is in fact the voice of the book.

Morrison: Yes.

Rushdie: And the thing it writes about. If we could just go for a little trip and come back to this. There's a thing here about this novel, which is the most obvious thing about it—it's a big city novel. It's about a capitalized City—the novel makes no attempt to conceal that it's Harlem. It uses lots of identifying names—

Morrison: Right. Yes.

Rushdie: —but it's called "the City." It contrasts that urban present moment—which is, so to speak, the jazz age—

Morrison: Yes.

Rushdie: —with a historical, more rural, slavery-ridden past.

Morrison: Yes.

Rushdie: One thing that's really interesting to me, about the characterization of the city, in the novel—you could characterize the city as being jazz. If the countryside is blues, the city is jazz. That's to say, the city is energy and possibility—

Morrison: And danger.

Rushdie: It's the place where you can renew and make yourself.

Morrison: Exactly.

Rushdie: That's clearly a sense of the city which many American writers have had, but here you're applying it specifically to Black experience in the aftermath of slavery.

Morrison: I wanted to recreate a migratory experience, an immigrant's experience of movement to cities, when they were the places to go, when there were, as you say, infinite possibilities. Seeing oneself in numbers, so that you felt the security of one's own family or kind. At the same time—I use the word danger, not so much in its bloodletting sense, but you can't be urbane outside the city. You can be clever and brilliant and shrewd and a guru, but you can't be sophisticated and urbane, unless you confront the variety of difference, strong difference, the mix in a city.

Rushdie: Yes. I remember writing in a novel—which I don't want to talk about!—about how the city was a place where incompatible realities collided.
Morrison: Exactly.

Rushdie: And sometimes they collide a bit too much and then boom!
Morrison: Yes, but it's there.

Rushdie: But it's there. I wanted to remind you of when we last met, which was when we were on a panel discussion at a PEN conference in New York. The subject there was the imagination of the state, and how it differed from that of the writer's. I remember you said that you didn't feel American. I may be slightly misquoting, but you said words to the effect that you had never felt American.
Morrison: Exactly.

Rushdie: I know in the essays, you talk about how the problem with the word American is that it means White American.
Morrison: Yes. As a writer (if we think of novels historically as the building of a nation, actually constructing it, making it original) I felt very strongly identified by my culture, which is to say my race, but not by the state, not by the country. I wanted, very very much as a child, to *be* American, to *feel* that way. Everything was designed to prevent me from that. Because of my race there were parts of the lake I could not enter. There were shops I couldn't go to. I was always a marginalized person within the context of the mainstream, the major civilization. I began to value more the marginality, the sort of peripheral existence, because it seemed to offer so much more. It was deeper, more complex, it had a tension, it related to the centre but it wasn't the centre. So of that sense of feeling American, I was deprived. I was deprived of that, and I felt bereft. Now, of course, I take it as a position of far more interesting possibilities.

Rushdie: You have a very telling phrase, somewhere in the essays, which I'll misquote, where you talk about how America has, so to speak, an ideology of freedom and a mechanism of oppression.
Morrison: Exactly.

Rushdie: And that's the contradiction your writing comes out of. Let's turn a little bit to that part of the novel and to your writing in general, which has to do with that mechanism of oppression, that is to say, the central concern of slavery which is there in this novel and was there in *Beloved* as well. Let's turn to that section in the novel, the long riff which goes back, in *Jazz*, into the countryside, where you have the story of the half-breed, Golden Grey, and the discovery of the wild woman living in the wild, literally, who turns out to be the mother of one of the characters. There are some quite striking similarities with this novel and *Beloved*, in its structure. For a start, there's this crisscross we've talked about, between the city now and the slave-world then. In both books we have the death of the beloved, the murder of the beloved, by somebody who loves her. In that novel, the mother kills the daughter to save her from slavery. In this novel the lover kills the young girl really because he's jealous, to keep her away from another man. So what's that about?

Morrison: How to own your own body and love somebody else. Under historical duress, where one fights for agency, the problem is how to be an individual, how to exert individual agency under this huge umbrella of determined historical life. In the case of Sethe, the story was based on the real story of a slave woman who did indeed kill her children rather than have them go back to slavery. Her claim is grotesque, but it comes out of a determination to nurture and to be a parent. So the beloved for her was the best thing she was, which were her children. In the jazz age, in the large city, where people now were in a position *not* to marry who was next to them, who lived next door, or to whom they had been given, but to actually choose to fall in love, it's an overwhelming passion. It's a wonderful expression of how one inhabits the flesh that now is yours. Therefore it becomes, again, excessive. I like to look at what happens at the outside, pushing characters.

Rushdie: Yours to kill. That's a very strange idea, isn't it! It's that very dark thing that is a kind of engine in both these books.

Morrison: Exactly.

Rushdie: Let's talk about that violence a little bit. One of the things that's interesting in *Jazz*—There have been a number of books, by yourself, by other Black American women writers, talking about the violence of Black

men, and that's been controversial sometimes. For example, Alice Walker's
novel, *The Color Purple*, was criticized for that.
Morrison: Yes, I remember.

Rushdie: What's interesting in this book is . . . one of your voice's long riffs is
about the violence of women. It talks about how women are armed these
days. If the men have guns, the women have knives. One of the most
memorable characters in the book is this wild woman, who is very
dangerous, who lives in the cornfields. What are you saying here? That it's
war? People coming at each other with weaponry?
Morrison: *(laughs)* Our lives have been lived in what has got to be one of the
world's most violent countries. Everyday violence is apple-pie in the United
States, an everyday possibility. How people respond to that would, in many
instances, be with peace, love, religion, or defence, or attack. What was interesting to me about the women was—in these days of focus on battered
women and how helpless women are before the strength of men, it occurred
to me that in my own recollection of the way people talked about themselves,
Black women always felt themselves to be the most vulnerable in that society,
and some of them prepared themselves and refused to be lightly attacked,
refused to be—I think the word in the book is "easy prey." It may happen
because rape, abuse, sexual assault was understood to be the *menu* of Black
women, in particularly a slave or post-reconstruction society. There was no
protection. Black men who wanted to protect them were all strung from
trees, so you have to make decisions about these things. People understand
that. Black women took it upon themselves, and therefore not be easy, easy
prey.

Rushdie: Let's talk about this refusal to be the victim. No just in the case of
the women characters, but broadly speaking in the case of the whole world
you depict. There are those who have criticized your work for saying that it
doesn't do that, for saying that it presents Blacks as victims, for saying that all
the things that are wrong with Black culture are external to it. But what about
what's wrong inside it, not just in terms of between men and women but the
various corruptions inside Black history as well as culture, for example, the
accusation that it was Blacks who helped Whites make people slaves. Do you
not turn away from that, whereas you should be looking at it? What do you
say to that?

Morrison: That's a little simplified notion of the past, I think, that there was a sort of "good old days," when people understood what slavery was and were complicit in it. But the lived life of a slave had a certain amount of determinism in it. It *was* determined from outside, but there was a lot of agency too. What I think is true, really, about the characters, is that you can't pity them. They are not available for the reader's pity. They are not available for easy answers.

Rushdie: That's true.

Morrison: They are not available for uncomplicated responses. Even a woman who is running away from slavery exerts agency over her children and her children's future. The same thing is true with Joe. He is moving because of his past. He does not understand who he is hunting, but he understands what is in his hand.

Rushdie: . . . In *Jazz*, as in *Beloved*, there's no real, serious, true interaction, other than the power relationship of slavery, between a White or a Black character. Even the creation of children is a kind of power relationship in that world. *Beloved* is set fifty years before *Jazz*, and *Jazz* is set more than sixty years before the present. It seems to me, rereading a lot of your books at speed, there's an absence there. Do you feel that as a deliberate absence, or is it something you haven't. . . .

Morrison: Oh, it's calculated. I think I was very much aware of the gaze of white people, in a lot of books written by African-Americans. They always—frequently, not always—seemed to be addressed to a white person's readership, talking just over my shoulder and not really to me. When I first began to write, I didn't want to clear away those things, but I certainly wanted the book to be free of major white characters, and that confrontation which destabilizes the narrative I wanted to tell. I *was* interested more in black people's reality.

Rushdie: So that's a deliberate omission.

Morrison: Absolutely.

Rushdie: Is that something you think you might change around sometime? Do you think you might actually look at what happens between a white and black character in a different way other than rape?

Morrison: *(laughs)* Interesting you should say that! I'm not so sure that I will. But I do remember—at least in *Beloved*—I had a white character touch a black person with some motive other than rape or violence, and I thought that was quite radical!

Rushdie: Yes. I want to take you away from a kind of social look at your books into what I think for most readers is the thing that makes your work different, which is its language, its linguistic enterprise. The first of your books I read, years ago, was *Song of Solomon*, and it came as an explosion because of that linguistic force. It's impossible, and very wrong, to ask a writer what it is that creates that energy in the language, but clearly it's something that you work at, a kind of compression, an almost operatic concentration in your writing. There's a danger there, isn't there? A danger of it going over the edge. I think you almost never do it—
Morrison: *(laughs)* Almost!

Rushdie: Nobody's perfect!
Morrison: That's true!

Rushdie: In *Jazz* there are some passages when that narrative voice seems to universalize completely, seems to not talk about these people in this place doing these things, but to talk about a black Everywoman or Everyman. There's a danger there, isn't there, of wafting off and not coming back down to earth? I'll put this to you straightforwardly, there's a danger of becoming a wise woman, you sit there and tell the world how it is.
Morrison: Oh yes, that is the ultimate danger.

Rushdie: There's the use of biblical language in your writing—
Morrison: My effort in writing in a language which, in the United States, is wholly coded and highly racialized . . . is to liberate myself, as a writer, from these codes. I want to merge vernacular with the lyric, with the standard, and with the biblical, because it was part of the linguistic heritage of my family, moving up and down the scale, across it, in between it. On some occasions, when they were saying something very very serious, they were sermonic, rhetorical. And sometimes they invented words and sometimes they simply used the current street language. All of that was an enhancement for me, not a restriction. It made me feel as though there was an enormous power in the

way in which language could be handled and was understood. There are all sorts of *double entendres*, all sorts of associations that standard English, or even lyrical language, did not provide me with. I was interested in that linguistic play always. Also it was the language that could restrain me, because I'm bound by those twenty-six letters, but at the same time there were doors that I could open and open for the reader to step through onto nothing, to sort of float free there and not know what the visceral or the intellectual response should be. It operated both as a rein and as a kind of Pandora's box.

Rushdie: I think that enterprise has been central in what happens in your work. As well as that purely linguistic side, there's also the use of certain intensifiers of image, what could be called surrealism. The way in which, in *Beloved*, the house is malevolent and throws the sideboard across the sitting-room. Image, like Milkman Dead in *Song of Solomon*, who's been suckled by his mother till he was grown up, or the wild woman in *Jazz*. I go into some of this myself, and the attack that's used against that kind of writing is usually that it's too easy, it's whimsical, you can make anything happen. It seems to me that that's not so, that what you're making happen is driven by the situation the people are in. Perhaps you could talk about why you use imagery like that, that nonrealistic stuff.

Morrison: Part of it is because life is not as small as many people think it is, it's not completely repressed, it's not wholly scientific. A human being understands why he can't sleep with his hand outside the bed. It doesn't make any difference how old you are, we all know there may be something underneath the bed! We may jettison some of that, but it still lives there. To look at the world as though, in addition to being very shrewd about it, you see an enchanted world, extraordinary things, odd coincidences—that's what makes life original. That part of it seemed to me absolutely part of the warp and woof of African-American life.

Rushdie: Let me ask you, finally, a kind of double question. Ralph Ellison once wrote—roughly speaking—that it was his great desire, as a black American writer, to connect all the things that he loved inside what he would have called the Negro community, and everything in the world that he perceived that lay beyond. I wanted to ask you firstly, is that how you would see it, or is that not a view that you would take? And secondly, it seems to me that in *Beloved* and *Jazz* there is a continuous work going on. I read an

interview in which you said that earlier on you thought *Beloved* might actually not be finished, and this might be a continuation of it. So is there more to come? Is this an alternative history of America?
Morrison: *(laughs)* In a way it's a little archaeological exploration. Ralph Ellison is clearer about things than I am. He really could project a Negro. He knew what that was. He knew what was valuable in it. He could also figure out what was *not* a Negro. I can't do that, I'm not sure what that word "Negro" means, which is why I write books. What is a black child/woman/ friend/mother? What is a black person? It seems to me that there are so many things that inform blackness. One of the modern qualities of being an African-American is the flux, is the fluidity, the contradictions, is being Miles Davis *and* Louis Armstrong *and* Bessie Smith *and* Kathleen Battle. All of those things are encompassed in what it means to be black. It's that excitement, I think, that makes me want to do this sort of archaeology about the history of black people in the United States.

Rushdie: If we've gone from the 1870s to the 1920s, do we now have a fifty-year leap into the seventies?
Morrison: Yes, we do.

Rushdie: We do? Oh! Well, you're obviously not going to tell me anything about it at all! So, Toni Morrison, thank you very much.

Toni Morrison: The Art of Fiction

Elissa Schappell / 1992

With additional material from Claudia Brodsky Lacour. "Toni Morrison: The Art of Fiction" was first published in *The Paris Review*. Reprinted by permission of Elissa Schappell and *The Paris Review*.

Toni Morrison detests being called a "poetic writer." She seems to think that the attention that has been paid to the lyricism of her work marginalizes her talent and denies her stories their power and resonance. As one of the few novelists whose work is both popular and critically acclaimed, she can afford the luxury of choosing what praise to accept. But she does not reject all classifications, and in fact, embraces the title "black woman writer." Her ability to transform individuals into forces and idiosyncrasies into inevitabilities has led some critics to call her the "D. H. Lawrence of the black psyche." She is also a master of the public novel, examining the relationships between the races and sexes and the struggle between civilization and nature, while at the same time combining myth and the fantastic with a deep political sensitivity.

Born Chloe Wofford in 1931 in Lorain, Ohio, a steel town on the banks of Lake Erie, Morrison sets many of her novels in the Midwest, in part because it is what she knows, but, more importantly, because the black experience she wants to dramatize is neither stereotypically inner-city ghetto nor deep-South plantation. It was in Lorain that she learned the importance of community, which she has described as being "both a support system and a hammer." She grew up hearing folk tales of the supernatural, and her own grandmother kept a dream book she believed enabled her to foretell the future. But it was Morrison's father who taught her to look at the world critically and question white standards of beauty and success. He worked three jobs during the Depression and distrusted "every word and every gesture of every white man on earth."

After graduating from Howard University, where she acquired the nickname Toni, she went on to get a master's degree in English at Cornell

University. She then taught at Texas Southern University and Howard University. While at Howard she joined an informal writer's workshop to which she took "the old junk" she'd written in high school until her stockpile was depleted, and she was forced to compose a new story, a tale of a black girl who dreams of having blue eyes. This would become Morrison's first novel, *The Bluest Eye*, which was published in 1969. By the time her first book was published, Morrison was thirty-eight, divorced, and had left Howard for a job as a textbook editor at Random House. Later she became an editor in the trade book division concentrating on bringing in books by black Americans like Toni Cade Bambara, Gayl Jones, Angela Davis, and Muhammed Ali. At the same time she found time to write essays, criticism, and two novels. In 1977, her third novel, *Song of Solomon*, was chosen as a Book-of-the-Month Club selection (the first novel by a black writer to be chosen since Richard Wright's *Native Son* in 1940) and won the National Book Critics' Circle Award. It was only then that she decided to quit her day job and make a "genuine commitment" to writing. In 1988 her fifth novel, *Beloved*, won the Pulitzer Prize. Her most recent novel, *Jazz*, is a literary improvisation which has received great critical praise. Ms. Morrison, who has been teaching American literature and creative writing at Princeton University for the last four years, learned, just as this issue was going to press, that she had been named the recipient of the 1993 Nobel Prize for literature.

We talked with Ms. Morrison one summer Sunday afternoon on the lush campus of Princeton University. The interview took place in Ms. Morrison's office, which is decorated with a large Helen Frankenthaler print, pen and ink drawings an architect did of all the houses that appear in her work, photographs, a few framed book-jacket covers, and an apology note to her from Hemingway—a forgery meant as a joke. On her desk is a blue glass tea cup emblazoned with the likeness of Shirley Temple filled with the number two pencils that she uses to write her first drafts. Pots of jade sit in a window and a few more plants hang above. A coffeemaker and cups are at the ready. Despite the high ceilings, the big desk, and the high-backed black rocking chairs, the room had the warm feeling of a kitchen, maybe because talking to Morrison about writing is the intimate kind of conversation that often seems to happen in kitchens; or perhaps it was the fact that as our energy started flagging she magically produced mugs of cranberry juice. We felt that she had allowed us to enter into a sanctuary, and that, however subtly, she was completely in control of the situation.

Outside, high canopies of oak leaves filtered the sunlight, dappling her white office with pools of yellowy light. Morrison sat behind her big desk, which, despite her apologies for the "disorder," appeared well organized. Stacks of books and piles of paper resided on a painted bench set against the wall. She is smaller than one might imagine, and her hair, gray and silver, is woven into thin steel-colored braids that hang just at shoulder length. Occasionally during the interview Morrison let her sonorous, deep voice break into rumbling laughter and punctuated certain statements with a flat smack of her hand on the desktop. At a moment's notice she can switch from raging about violence in the United States to joyfully skewering the hosts of the trash TV talk shows through which she confesses to channel-surfing late in the afternoon, assuming her work is done.

Interviewer: You have said that you begin to write before dawn. Did this habit begin for practical reasons, or was the early morning an especially fruitful time for you?

Toni Morrison: Writing before dawn began as a necessity—I had small children when I first began to write, and I needed to use the time before they said, "Mama"—and that was always around five in the morning. Many years later, after I stopped working at Random House, I just stayed at home for a couple of years. I discovered things about myself I had never thought about before. At first I didn't know when I wanted to eat, because I had always eaten when it was lunchtime or dinnertime or breakfast-time. Work and the children had driven all of my habits . . . I didn't know the weekday sounds of my own house; it all made me feel a little giddy.

I was involved in writing *Beloved* at that time—this was in 1983—and eventually I realized that I was clearer-headed, more confident, and generally more intelligent in the morning. The habit of getting up early, which I had formed when the children were young, now became my choice. I am not very bright or very witty or very inventive after the sun goes down.

Recently I was talking to a writer who described something she did whenever she moved to her writing table. I don't remember exactly what the gesture was—there is something on her desk that she touches before she hit the computer keyboard—but we began to talk about little rituals that one goes through before beginning to write. I, at first, thought I didn't have a ritual, but then I remembered that I always get up and make a cup of coffee while it is still dark—it must be dark—and then I drink the coffee and watch the light come. And she said, well, that's a ritual. And I realized that for me this ritual comprises my preparation to enter a space that I can only call non-secular. . . . Writers all devise ways to approach that place where they expect to make the contact, where they become the conduit, or where they engage in this mysterious process. For me, light is the signal in the transition. It's not being *in* the light, it's being there *before it arrives.* It enables me, in some sense.

I tell my students one of the most important things they need to know is when they are their best, creatively. They need to ask themselves, What does the ideal room look like? Is there music? Is there silence? Is there chaos outside or is there serenity outside? What do I need in order to release my imagination?

Interviewer: What about your writing routine?

Morrison: I have an ideal writing routine that I've never experienced, which is to have, say, nine uninterrupted days when I wouldn't have to leave the house or take phone calls. And to have the space: a space where I have huge tables. I end up with this much space (*she indicates a small square spot on her desk*) everywhere I am, and I can't beat my way out of it. I am reminded of that tiny desk that Emily Dickinson wrote on, and I chuckle when I think, "Sweet thing, there she was." But that is all any of us have—just this small space and no matter what the filing system or how often you clear it out, life, documents, letters, requests, invitations, invoices just keep going back in. I am not able to write regularly. I have never been able to do that—mostly because I have always had a nine-to-five job. I had to write either in between those hours, hurriedly, or spend a lot of weekend and predawn time.

Interviewer: Could you write after work?

Morrison: That was difficult. I've tried to overcome not having orderly spaces by substituting compulsion for discipline, so that when something is urgently there, urgently seen or understood, or the metaphor was powerful enough, then I would move everything aside and write for sustained periods of time. I'm talking to you about getting the first draft.

Interviewer: You have to do it straight through?

Morrison: *I* do. I don't think it's a law.

Interviewer: Could you write on the bottom of a shoe while riding on a train like Robert Frost? Could you write on an airplane?

Morrison: Sometimes something that I was having some trouble with falls into place, a word sequence, say, so I've written on scraps of paper, in hotels on hotel stationery, in automobiles. *If* it arrives you *know*. If you know it *really* has come then you *have* to put it down.

Interviewer: What is the physical act of writing like for you?
Morrison: I write with a pencil.

Interviewer: Would you ever work on a word processor?
Morrison: Oh I do that also, but that is much later when everything is put together. I type that into a computer, and then I begin to revise. But everything I write for the first time is written with a pencil, maybe a ball point if I don't have a pencil. I'm not picky, but my preference is for yellow legal pads and a nice number two pencil.

Interviewer: Dixon Ticonderoga number two soft?
Morrison: Exactly. I remember once trying to use a tape recorder, but it doesn't work.

Interviewer: Did you actually dictate a story into the machine?
Morrison: Not the whole thing, but just a bit. For instance, when two or three sentences seemed to fall into place, I thought I would carry a tape recorder in the car, particularly when I was working at Random House going back and forth every day. It occurred to me that I could just record it. It was a disaster. I don't trust my writing that is not written, although I work very hard in subsequent revisions to remove the writerliness from it, to give it a combination of lyrical, standard, and colloquial language. To pull all these things together into something that I think is much more alive, and representative. But I don't trust something that occurs to me, and then is spoken and transferred immediately to the page.

Interviewer: Do you ever read your work out loud while you are working on it?
Morrison: Not until it's published. I don't trust a performance. I could get a response that might make me think it was successful when it wasn't at all. The difficulty for me in writing—*among* the difficulties—is to write language that can work quietly on a page for a reader who doesn't hear anything. Now

for that, one has to work very carefully with what is *in between* the words. What is not said. Which is measure, which is rhythm and so on. So, it is what you don't write that frequently gives what you do write its power.

Interviewer: How many times would you say you have to write a paragraph over to reach this standard?
Morrison: Well, those that need reworking I do as long as I can. I mean I've revised six times, seven times, thirteen times. But there's a line between revision and fretting, just working it to death. It is important to know when you are fretting it; when you are fretting it because it is not working, it needs to be scrapped.

Interviewer: Do you ever go back over what has been published and wish you had fretted more over something?
Morrison: A lot. Everything.

Interviewer: Do you ever rework passages that have already been published before reading them to an audience?
Morrison: I don't change it for the audience, but I know what it ought to be and isn't. After twenty some years you can figure it out; I know more about it now than I did then. It is not so much that it would have been different or even better; it is just that, taken into context with what I was trying to effect, or what consequence I wanted it to have on the reader, years later the picture is clearer to me.

Interviewer: How do you think being an editor for twenty years affected you as a writer?
Morrison: I am not sure. It lessened my awe of the publishing industry. I understood the adversarial relationship that sometimes exists between writers and publishers, but I learned how important, how critical an editor was, which I don't think I would have known before.

Interviewer: Are there editors who are helpful critically?
Morrison: Oh yes. The good ones make all the difference. It is like a priest or a psychiatrist; if you get the wrong one then you are better off alone. But there are editors so rare and so important that they are worth searching for, and you always know when you have one.

Interviewer: Who was the most instrumental editor you've ever worked with?

Morrison: I had a very good editor, superlative for me—Bob Gottlieb. What made him good for me was a number of things: knowing what not to touch; asking all the questions you probably would have asked yourself had there been the time. Good editors are really the third eye. Cool. Dispassionate. They don't love you or your work; for me that is what is valuable—not compliments. Sometimes it's uncanny: the editor puts his or her finger on exactly the place the writer knows is weak but just couldn't do any better at the time. Or perhaps the writer thought it might fly, but wasn't sure. Good editors identify that place, and sometimes make suggestions. Some suggestions are not useful because you can't explain everything to an editor about what you are trying to do. I couldn't possibly explain all of those things to an editor, because what I do has to work on so many levels. But within the relationship if there is some trust, some willingness to listen, remarkable things can happen. I read books all the time that I know would have profited from, not a copy editor, but somebody just talking through it. And it is important to get a great editor at a certain time, because if you don't have one in the beginning, you almost can't have one later. If you work well without an editor, and your books are well received for five or ten years, and then you write another one, which is successful but not very good, why should you then listen to an editor?

Interviewer: You have told students that they should think of the process of revision as one of the major satisfactions of writing. Do you get more pleasure out of writing the first draft, or in the actual revision of the work?

Morrison: They are different. I am profoundly excited by thinking up or having the idea in the first place . . . before I begin to write.

Interviewer: Does it come in a flash?

Morrison: No, it's a sustained thing I have to play with. I always start out with an idea, even a boring idea, that becomes a question I don't have any answers to. Specifically, since I began the *Beloved* trilogy, the last part of which I'm working on now, I have been wondering why women who are twenty, thirty years younger than I am, are no happier than women who are my age and older. What on earth is that about, when there are so many more things that they can do, so many more choices? *All right*, so this is an embarrassment of riches, but so what. Why is everybody so miserable?

Interviewer: Do you write to figure out exactly how you feel about a subject?

Morrison: No, I know how I *feel*. My feelings are the result of prejudices and convictions like everybody else's. But I am interested in the complexity, the vulnerability of an idea. It is not: "This is what I believe," because that would not be a book, just a tract. A book is: "This may be what I believe, but suppose I am wrong . . . what could it be?" Or, "I don't know what it is, but I am interested in finding out what it might mean to me, as well as to other people."

Interviewer: Did you know as a child you wanted to be a writer?

Morrison: No. I wanted to be a reader. I thought everything that needed to be written had already been written or would be. I only wrote the first book because I thought it wasn't there, and I wanted to read it when I got through. I am a pretty good reader. I love it. It is what I do, really. So, if I can read it, that is the highest compliment I can think of. People say, "I write for myself," and it sounds so awful and so narcissistic, but in a sense if you know how to read your own work—that is, with the necessary critical distance—it makes you a better writer and editor. When I teach creative writing, I always speak about how you have to learn how to read your work; I don't mean enjoy it because you wrote it. I mean, go away from it, and read it as though it is the first time you've ever seen it. Critique it that way. Don't get all involved in your thrilling sentences and all that . . .

Interviewer: Do you have your audience in mind when you sit down to write?

Morrison: Only me. If I come to a place where I am unsure, I have the characters to go to for reassurance. By that time they are friendly enough to tell me if the rendition of their lives is authentic or not. But there are so many things only I can tell. After all, this is my work. I have to take full responsibility for doing it right as well as doing it wrong. Doing it wrong isn't bad, but doing it wrong and thinking you've done it right is. I remember spending a whole summer writing something I was very impressed with, but couldn't get back to until winter. I went back confident that those fifty pages were really first-rate, but when I read them, each page of the fifty was terrible. It was really ill-conceived. I knew that I could do it over, but I just couldn't get over the fact that I thought it was so good at the time. And that is scary because then you think it means you don't know.

Interviewer: What about it was so bad?
Morrison: It was pompous. Pompous and unappetizing.

Interviewer: I read that you started writing after your divorce as a way of beating back the loneliness. Was that true, and do you write for different reasons now?
Morrison: Sort of. Sounds simpler than it was. I don't know if I was writing for that reason or some other reason, or one that I don't even suspect. I do know that I don't like it here if I don't have something to write.

Interviewer: Here, meaning where?
Morrison: Meaning out in the world. It is not possible for me to be unaware of the incredible violence, the willful ignorance, the hunger for other people's pain. I'm always conscious of that though I am less aware of it under certain circumstances—good friends at dinner, other books. Teaching makes a big difference, but that is not enough. Teaching could make me into someone who is complacent, unaware, rather than part of the solution. So what makes me feel as though I belong here, out in this world, is not the teacher, not the mother, not the lover but what goes on in my mind when I am writing. Then I belong here, and then all of the things that are disparate and irreconcilable can be useful. I can do the traditional things that writers always say they do, which is to make order out of chaos. Even if you are reproducing the disorder, you are sovereign at that point. Struggling through the work is extremely important—more important to me than publishing it.

Interviewer: If you didn't do this. Then the chaos would . . .
Morrison: Then I would be part of the chaos.

Interviewer: Wouldn't the answer to that be either to lecture about the chaos or to be in politics?
Morrison: If I had a gift for it. All I can do is read books and write books, and edit books and critique books. I don't think that I could show up on a regular basis as a politician. I would lose interest. I don't have the resources for it, the gift. There are people who can organize other people, and I cannot. I'd just get bored.

Interviewer: When did it become clear to you that your gift was to be a writer?

Morrison: It was very late. I always thought I was probably adept, because people used to say so, but their criteria might not have been mine. So, I wasn't interested in what they said. It meant nothing. It was by the time I was writing *Song of Solomon*, the third book, that I began to think that this was the central part of my life. Not to say that other women haven't said it all along, but for a woman to say, "I am a writer" is difficult.

Interviewer: Why?

Morrison: Well, it isn't so difficult *anymore*, but it certainly was for me, and for women of my generation or my class or my race. I don't know that all those things are folded into it, but the point is you're moving yourself out of the gender role. You are not saying, "I am a mother, I am a wife." Or, if you're in the labor market, "I am a teacher, I am an editor." But when you move to "writer" what is that supposed to mean? Is that a job? Is this the way you make your living? It's an intervention into terrain that you are not familiar with—where you have no provenance. At the time I certainly didn't personally know any other women writers who were successful; it looked very much like a male preserve. So you sort of hope you're going to be a little minor person around the edges. It's almost as if you needed permission to write. When I read women's biographies and autobiographies, even accounts of how they got started writing, almost every one of them had a little anecdote which told about the moment someone gave them permission to do it. A mother, a husband, a teacher . . . somebody said, "Okay, go ahead—you can do it." Which is not to say that men have never needed that; frequently when they are very young, a mentor says, "You're good," and they take off. The entitlement was something they could take for granted. I couldn't. It was all very strange. So, even though I knew that writing was central to my life, that it was where my mind was, where I was most delighted and most challenged, I couldn't say it. If someone asked me, "What do you do?" I wouldn't say, "Oh I'm a writer." I'd say, "I'm an editor, or a teacher." Because when you meet people and go to lunch, if they say, "What do you do?" and you say, "I'm a writer," they have to think about that, and then they ask, "What have you written?" Then they have to either like it, or not like it. People feel obliged to like or not like and say so. It is perfectly all right to hate my work. It really is. I have close friends whose work I loathe.

Interviewer: Did you feel you had to write in private?

Morrison: Oh yes, I wanted to make it a private thing. I wanted to own it myself. Because once you say it, then other people become involved. As a matter of fact, while I was at Random House I never said I was a writer.

Interviewer: Why not?

Morrison: Oh, it would have been awful. First of all they didn't hire me to do that. They didn't hire me to be one of *them*. Secondly, I think they would have fired me.

Interviewer: Really?

Morrison: Sure. There were no in-house editors who wrote fiction. Ed Doctorow quit. There was nobody else—no real buying, negotiating editor in trade who was also publishing her own novels.

Interviewer: Did the fact that you were a woman have anything to do with it?

Morrison: That I didn't think about too much. I was so busy. I only know that I will never again trust my life, my future, to the whims of men, in companies or out. Never again will their judgment have anything to do with what I think I can do. That was the wonderful liberation of being divorced and having children. I did not mind failure, ever, but I minded thinking that someone male knew better. Before that, all the men I knew *did* know better, they really did. My father and teachers were smart people who knew better. Then I came across a smart person who was very important to me who *didn't* know better.

Interviewer: Was this your husband?

Morrison: Yes. He knew better about his life, but not about mine. I had to stop and say, let me start again and see what it is like to be a grown-up. I decided to leave home, to take my children with me, to go into publishing and see what I could do. I was prepared for that not to work either, but I wanted to see what it was like to be a grown-up.

Interviewer: Can you talk about that moment at Random House when they suddenly realized that they had a writer in their midst?

Morrison: I published a book called *The Bluest Eye*. I didn't tell them about it. They didn't know until they read the review in the *New York Times*. It was published by Holt. Somebody had told this young guy there that I was writing something, and he had said in a very offhand way, if you ever complete something send it to me. So I did. A lot of black men were writing in 1968, 1969, and he bought it, thinking that there was a growing interest in what black people were writing, and that this book of mine would also sell. He was wrong. What was selling was, "Let me tell you how powerful I am and how horrible you are," or some version of that. For whatever reasons, he took a small risk. He didn't pay me much, so it didn't matter if the book sold or not. It got a really horrible review in the *New York Times Book Review* on Sunday and then got a very good daily review.

Interviewer: You mentioned getting permission to write. Who gave it to you?

Morrison: No one. What I needed permission to do was to succeed at it. I never signed a contract until the book was finished because I didn't want it to be homework. A contract meant somebody was waiting for it, that I *had* to do it, and they could ask me about it. They could get up in my face, and I don't like that. By not signing a contract, I do it, and if I want you to see it, I'll let you see it. It has to do with self-esteem. I am sure for years you have heard writers constructing illusions of freedom, anything in order to have the illusion that it is all mine, and only I can do it. I remember introducing Eudora Welty and saying that nobody could have written those stories but her, meaning that I have a feeling about most books that at some point somebody would have written them *anyway*. But then there are some writers without whom certain stories would never have been written. I don't mean the subject matter or the narrative but just the way in which they did it—their slant on it is truly unique.

Interviewer: Who are some of them?

Morrison: Hemingway is in that category, Flannery O'Connor. Faulkner, Fitzgerald . . .

Interviewer: Haven't you been critical of the way these authors depicted blacks?

Morrison: No! Me, critical? I have been revealing how white writers imagine black people, and some of them are brilliant at it. Faulkner was brilliant at it. Hemingway did it poorly in places and brilliantly elsewhere.

Interviewer: How so?

Morrison: In not using black characters, but using the aesthetic of blacks as anarchy, as sexual license, as deviance. In his last book, *The Garden of Eden*, Hemingway's heroine is getting blacker and blacker. The woman who is going mad tells her husband, "I want to be your little African Queen." The novel gets its charge that way: "Her white white hair and her black, black skin" . . . almost like a Man Ray photograph. Mark Twain talked about racial ideology in the most powerful, eloquent and instructive way I have ever read. Edgar Allan Poe did not. He loved white supremacy and the planter class, and he wanted to be a gentleman, and he endorsed all of that. He didn't contest it, or critique it. What is exciting about American literature is that business of how writers say things under, beneath, and around their stories. Think of *Pudd'nhead Wilson* and all these inversions of what race is, how sometimes nobody can tell, or the thrill of discovery? Faulkner in *Absalom, Absalom!* spends the entire book tracing race, and you can't find it. No one can see it, even the character who *is* black can't see it. I did this lecture for my students that took me forever, which was tracking all the moments of withheld, partial, or disinformation, when a racial fact or clue *sort* of comes out but doesn't quite arrive. I just wanted to chart it. I listed its appearance, disguise, and disappearance on every page, I mean every phrase! Everything, and I delivered this thing to my class. They all fell asleep! But I was so fascinated, technically. Do you know how hard it is to withhold that kind of information but hinting, pointing all of the time? And then to reveal it in order to say that it is *not* the point anyway? It is technically just astonishing. As a reader you have been forced to hunt for a drop of black blood that means everything and nothing. The insanity of racism. So the structure is the argument. Not what this one says, or that one says . . . it is the *structure* of the book, and you are there hunting this black thing that is nowhere to be found, and yet makes all the difference. No one has done anything quite like that ever. So, when I critique, what I am saying is, I don't care if Faulkner is a racist or not; I don't personally care, but I am fascinated by what it means to write like this.

Interviewer: What about black writers . . . how do they write in a world dominated by and informed by their relationship to a white culture?

Morrison: By trying to alter language, simply to free it up, not to repress it or confine it, but to open it up. Tease it. Blast its racist straitjacket. I wrote a story entitled "Recitatif," in which there are two little girls in an orphanage, one white and one black. But the reader doesn't know which is white and which is black. I use class codes, but no racial codes.

Interviewer: Is this meant to confuse the reader?
Morrison: Well, yes. But to provoke and enlighten. I did that as a lark. What was exciting was to be forced as a writer not to be lazy and rely on obvious codes. Soon as I say, "Black woman . . ." I can rest on or provoke predictable responses, but if I leave it out then I have to talk about her in a complicated way—as a person.

Interviewer: Why wouldn't you want to say, "The black woman came out of the store"?
Morrison: Well, you can, but it has to be important that she is black.

Interviewer: What about *The Confessions of Nat Turner?*
Morrison: Well, here we have a very self-conscious character who says things like, "I looked at my black hand." Or "I woke up and I felt black." It is very much on Bill Styron's mind. He feels charged in Nat Turner's skin . . . in this place that feels exotic to him. So it reads exotically to us, that's all.

Interviewer: There was a tremendous outcry at that time from people who felt that Styron didn't have a right to write about Nat Turner.
Morrison: He has a right to write about whatever he wants. To suggest otherwise is outrageous. What they should have criticized, and some of them did, was Styron's suggestion that Nat Turner hated black people. In the book Turner expresses his revulsion over and over again . . . he's so distant from blacks, so superior. So the fundamental question is why would anybody follow him? What kind of leader is this who has a fundamentally racist contempt that seems unreal to any black person reading it. Any white leader would have some interest and identification with the people he was asking to die. That was what these critics meant when they said Nat Turner speaks like a white man. That racial distance is strong and clear in that book.

Interviewer: You must have read a lot of slave narratives for *Beloved.*
Morrison: I wouldn't read them for information because I knew that they had to be authenticated by white patrons, that they couldn't say everything they wanted to say because they couldn't alienate their audience; they had to

be quiet about certain things. They were going to be as good as they could be under the circumstances and as revelatory, but they never say how terrible it was. They would just say, "Well, you know, it was really awful, but let's abolish slavery so life can go on." Their narratives had to be very understated. So while I looked at the documents and felt *familiar* with slavery and overwhelmed by it, I wanted it to be truly *felt*. I wanted to translate the historical into the personal. I spent a long time trying to figure out what it was about slavery that made it so repugnant, so personal, so indifferent, so intimate, and yet so public.

In reading some of the documents I noticed frequent references to something that was never properly described—*the bit*. This thing was put into the mouth of slaves to punish them and shut them up without preventing them from working. I spent a long time trying to find out what it looked like. I kept reading statements like, "I put the bit on Jenny," or, as Equiano says, "I went into a kitchen" and I saw a woman standing at the stove, and she had a brake, (b-r-a-k-e, he spells it) "in her mouth," and I said, "What is that?" and somebody told me what it was, and then I said, "I never saw anything so awful in all my life." But I really couldn't image the thing—did it look like a horse's bit or what?

Eventually I did find some sketches in one book in this country, which was the record of a man's torture of his wife. In South America, Brazil, places like that, they kept such mementos. But while I was searching, something else occurred to me, namely that this bit, this item, this personalized type of torture, was a direct descendant of the inquisition. And I realized that of course you can't buy this stuff. You can't send away for a mail-order bit for your slave. Sears doesn't carry them. So you have to make it. You have to go out in the backyard and put some stuff together and construct it and then affix it to a person. So the whole process had a very personal quality for the person who made it, as well as for the person who wore it. Then I realized that describing it would never be helpful: that the reader didn't need to *see* it so much as *feel* what it was like. I realized that it was important to imagine the bit as an active instrument, rather than simply as a curio or an historical fact. And in the same way I wanted to show the reader what slavery *felt* like, rather than how it looked.

There's a passage in which Paul D. says to Sethe, "I've never told anybody about it, I've sung about it sometimes." He tries to tell her what wearing the bit was like, but he ends up talking about a rooster that he swears smiled at him when he wore it—he felt cheapened and lessened and that he would never be worth as much as a rooster sitting on a tub in the sunlight. I make other references to the desire to spit, to sucking iron and so on; but it seemed to me that describing what it *looked* like would distract the reader from what I wanted him or her to experience, which was what it *felt* like. The kind of information you can find between the lines of history. It sort of falls off the page, or it's a glance and a reference. It's right there in the intersection where an institution becomes personal, where the historical becomes people with names.

Interviewer: When you create a character is it completely created out of your own imagination?
Morrison: I never use anyone I know. In *The Bluest Eye* I think I used some gestures and dialogue of my mother in certain places, and a little geography. I've never done that since. I really am very conscientious about that. It's never based on anyone. I don't do what many writers do.

Interviewer: Why is that?
Morrison: There is this feeling that artists have—photographers more than other people, and writers—that they are acting like a succubus . . . this process of taking from something that's alive and using it for one's own purposes. You can do it with trees, butterflies, or human beings. Making a little life for oneself by scavenging other people's lives is a big question, and it does have moral and ethical implications.

In fiction, I feel the most intelligent, and the most free, and the most excited, when my characters are fully invented people. That's part of the excitement. If they're based on somebody else, in a funny way it's an infringement of a copyright. That person *owns* his life, has a patent on it. It shouldn't be available for fiction.

Interviewer: Do you ever feel like your characters are getting away from you, out of your control?
Morrison: I take control of them. They are very carefully imagined. I feel as though I know all there is to know about them, even things I don't write—like how they part their hair. They are like ghosts. They have nothing on their minds but themselves and aren't interested in anything but themselves. So you can't let them write your book for you. I have read books in which

I know that has happened—when a novelist has been totally taken over by a character. I want to say, "You can't do that. If those people could write books they would, but they can't. *You* can." So, you have to say, "Shut up. Leave me alone. I am doing this."

Interviewer: Have you ever had to tell any of your characters to shut up?
Morrison: Pilate, I did. Therefore she doesn't speak very much. She has this long conversation with the two boys, and every now and then she'll say something, but she doesn't have the dialogue the other people have. I had to do that, otherwise she was going to overwhelm everybody. She got terribly interesting; characters can do that for a little bit. I had to take it back. It's *my* book; it's not called *Pilate*.

Interviewer: Pilate is such a strong character. It seems to me that the women in your books are almost always stronger and braver than the men. Why is that?
Morrison: That isn't true, but I hear that a lot. I think that our expectations of women are very low. If women just stand up straight for thirty days, everybody goes, "Oh! How brave!" As a matter of fact, somebody wrote about Sethe, and said she was this powerful, statuesque woman who wasn't even human. But at the end of the book, she can barely turn her head. She has been zonked; she can't even feed herself. Is that tough?

Interviewer: Maybe people read it that way because they thought Sethe made such a hard choice slashing Beloved's throat. Maybe they think that's being strong. Some would say that's just bad manners.
Morrison: Well, Beloved surely didn't think it was all that tough. She thought it was lunacy. Or, more importantly, "How do you know death is better for me? You've never died. How could you know?" But I think Paul D., Son, Stamp Paid, even Guitar, make equally difficult choices; they are principled. I do think we are too accustomed to women who don't talk back or who use the weapons of the weak.

Interviewer: What are the weapons of the weak?
Morrison: Nagging. Poison. Gossip. Sneaking around instead of confrontation.

Interviewer: There have been so few novels about women who have intense friendships with other women. Why do you think that is?

Morrison: It has been a discredited relationship. When I was writing *Sula*, I was under the impression that for a large part of the female population a woman friend was considered a secondary relationship. A man and a woman's relationship was primary. Women, your own friends, were always secondary relationships when the man was not there. Because of this, there's that whole cadre of women who don't like women and prefer men. We had to be taught to like one another. *Ms.* magazine was founded on the premise that we really have to stop complaining about one another, hating, fighting one another, and joining men in their condemnation of ourselves—a typical example of what dominated people do. That is a big education. When much of the literature was like that—when you read about women together (not lesbians, or those who have formed long relationships that are covertly lesbian, like in Virginia Woolf's work), it is an overtly male view of females together. They are usually male dominated—like some of Henry James's characters—or the women are talking about men, like Jane Austen's girl-friends . . . talking about who got married and how to get married, and are you going to lose him, and I think she wants him and so on. To have hetero-sexual women who are friends, who are talking only about themselves to each other, seemed to me a very radical thing when *Sula* was published in 1971 . . . but it is hardly radical now.

Interviewer: It is becoming acceptable.

Morrison: Yes, and it's going to get boring. It will be overdone, and as usual it will all run amok.

Interviewer: Why do writers have such a hard time writing about sex?

Morrison: Sex is difficult to write about because it's just not sexy enough. The only way to write about it is not to write much. Let the reader bring his own sexuality into the text. A writer I usually admire has written about sex in the most off-putting way. There is just too much information. If you start saying "the curve of . . ." you soon sound like a gynecologist. Only Joyce could get away with that. He said all those forbidden words. He said *cunt*, and that was shocking. The forbidden word can be provocative. But after a while it becomes monotonous rather than arousing. Less is always better. Some writers think that if they use dirty words they've done it. It can work for a short period and for a very young imagination, but after a while it doesn't deliver. When Sethe and Paul D. first see each other, in about half a page they get the sex out of the way, which isn't any good anyway—it's fast, and they're embarrassed about it—and then they're lying there trying to pretend they're not in that bed, that they haven't met, and then they begin to think different thoughts, which begin to merge so you can't tell who's thinking what. That merging to me is more tactically sensual than if I had tried to describe body parts.

Interviewer: What about plot? Do you always know where you're going? Would you write the end before you got there?
Morrison: When I really know what it is about, then I can write that end scene. I wrote the end of *Beloved* about a quarter of the way in. I wrote the end of *Jazz* very early and the end of *Song of Solomon* very early on. What I really want is for the plot to be *how* it happened. It is like a detective story in a sense. You know who is dead and you want to find out who did it. So, you put the salient elements up front, and the reader is hooked into wanting to know, How did that happen? Who did that and why? You are forced into having a certain kind of language that will keep the reader asking those questions. In *Jazz*, just as I did before with *The Bluest Eye*, I put the whole plot on the first page. In fact, in the first edition the plot was on the cover, so that a person in a bookstore could read the cover and know right away what the book was about, and could, if they wished, dismiss it and buy another book. This seemed a suitable technique for *Jazz* because I thought of the plot in that novel—the threesome—as the melody of the piece, and it is fine to follow a melody—to feel the satisfaction of recognizing a melody whenever the narrator returns to it. That was the real art of the enterprise for me: bumping up against that melody time and again, seeing it from another point of view, seeing it afresh each time, playing it back and forth.

When Keith Jarrett plays "Ol' Man River," the delight and satisfaction is not so much in the melody itself but in recognizing it when it surfaces and when it is hidden and when it goes away completely, what is put in its place. Not so much in the original line as in all the echoes and shades and turns and pivots Jarrett plays around it. I was trying to do something similar with the plot in *Jazz*. I wanted the story to be the vehicle which moved us from page one to the end, but I wanted the delight to be found in moving away from the story and coming back to it, looking around it, and through it, as though it were a prism, constantly turning.

This playful aspect of *Jazz* may well cause a great deal of dissatisfaction in readers who just want the melody, who want to know what happened, who did it and why. But the jazz-like structure wasn't a secondary thing for me— it was the raison d'être of the book. The process of trial and error by which the narrator revealed the plot was as important and exciting to me as telling the story.

Interviewer: You also divulge the plot early on in *Beloved*.

Morrison: It seemed important to me that the action in *Beloved*—the fact of infanticide—be immediately known, but deferred, unseen. I wanted to give the reader all the information and the consequences surrounding the act, while avoiding engorging myself or the reader with the violence itself. I remember writing the sentence where Sethe cuts the throat of the child very, very late in the process of writing the book. I remember getting up from the table and walking outside for a long time—walking around the yard and coming back and revising it a little bit and going back out and in and rewriting the sentence over and over again . . . each time I fixed that sentence so that it was exactly right, or so I thought, but then I would be unable to sit there and would have to go away and come back. I thought that the act itself had to be not only buried but also understated, because if the language was going to compete with the violence itself it would be obscene or pornographic.

Interviewer: Style is obviously very important to you. Can you talk about this in relation to *Jazz*?

Morrison: With *Jazz*, I wanted to convey the sense that a musician conveys— that he has more but he's not gonna give it to you. It's an exercise in restraint, a holding back—not because it's not there, or because one had exhausted it, but because of the riches, and because it can be done again. That sense of knowing when to stop is a learned thing, and I didn't always have it. It was probably not until after I wrote *Song of Solomon* that I got to feeling secure enough to experience what it meant to be thrifty with images and language and so on. I was very conscious in writing *Jazz* of trying to blend that which is contrived and artificial with improvisation. I thought of myself as like the jazz musician: someone who practices and practices and practices in order to be able to invent and to make his art look effortless and graceful. I was always conscious of the constructed aspect of the writing process, and that art

appears natural and elegant only as a result of constant practice and awareness of its formal structures. You must practice thrift in order to achieve that
luxurious quality of wastefulness—that sense that you have enough to waste,
that you are holding back—without actually wasting anything. You shouldn't
over-gratify, you should never satiate. I've always felt that that peculiar sense
of hunger at the end of a piece of art—a yearning for more—is really very,
very powerful. But there is at the same time a kind of contentment, knowing
that at some other time there will indeed be more because the artist is end-
lessly inventive.

Interviewer: Were there other . . . ingredients, structural entities?
Morrison: Well, it seems to me that migration was a major event in the cultural
history of this country. Now I'm being very speculative about all of this—I guess
that's why I write novels—but it seems to me something modern and new happened after the Civil War. Of course, a number of things changed, but the era
was most clearly marked by the disowning and dispossession of ex-slaves. These
ex-slaves were sometimes taken into their local labor markets, but they often
tried to escape their problems by migrating to the city. I was fascinated by the
thought of what the city must have meant to them, these second and third generation ex-slaves, to rural people living there in their own number. The city
must have seemed so exciting and wonderful, so much the place to be.

I was interested in how the city worked. How classes and groups and
nationalities had the security of numbers within their own turfs and territories, but also felt the thrill of knowing that there were other turfs and other
territories, and felt the real glamor and excitement of being in this throng.
I was interested in how music changed in this country. Spirituals and gospel
and blues represented one kind of response to slavery—they gave voice to the
yearning for escape, in code, literally on the underground railroad.

I was also concerned with personal life. How did people love one another?
What did they think was free? At that time, when the ex-slaves were moving
into the city, running away from something that was constricting and killing
them and dispossessing them over and over and over again, they were in a
very limiting environment. But when you listen to their music—the beginnings of jazz—you realized that they are talking about something else. They
are talking about love, about loss. But there is such grandeur, such satisfaction in those lyrics . . . they're never happy—somebody's always leaving—but
they're not whining. It's as though the whole tragedy of choosing somebody,

risking love, risking emotion, risking sensuality, and then losing it all didn't matter, since it was their choice. Exercising choice in who you love was a major, major thing. And the music reinforced the idea of love as a space where one could negotiate freedom.

Obviously, jazz was considered—as all new music is—to be devil music; too sensual and provocative, and so on. But for some black people jazz meant claiming their own bodies. You can image what that must have meant for people whose bodies had been owned, who had been slaves as children, or who remembered their parents being slaves. Blues and jazz represented ownership of one's own emotions. So of course it is excessive and overdone: tragedy in jazz is relished, almost as though a happy ending would take away some of its glamour, its flair. Now advertisers use jazz on television to communicate authenticity and modernity; to say "trust me," and to say "hip."

These days the city still retains the quality of excitement it had in the jazz age, only now we associate that excitement with a different kind of danger. We chant and scream and act alarmed about the homeless; we say we want our streets back, but it is from our awareness of homelessness and our employment of strategies to deal with it that we get our sense of the urban. Feeling as though we have the armor, the shields, the moxie, the strength, the toughness, and the smarts to be engaged and survive encounters with the unpredictable, the alien, the strange, and the violent is an intrinsic part of what it means to live in the city. When people "complain" about homelessness they are actually bragging about it: "New York has more homeless than San Francisco"—"No, no, no, San Francisco has more homeless"—"No, you haven't been to Detroit." We are almost competitive about our endurance, which I think is one of the reasons why we accept homelessness so easily.

Interviewer: So the city freed the ex-slaves from their history?
Morrison: In part, yes. The city was seductive to them because it promised forgetfulness. It offered the possibility of freedom—freedom, as you put it, from history. But although history should not become a straitjacket, which overwhelms and binds, neither should it be forgotten. One must critique it, test it, confront it, and understand it in order to achieve a freedom that is more than license, to achieve true, adult agency. If you penetrate the seduction of the city, then it becomes possible to confront your own history—to forget what ought to be forgotten and use what is useful—such true agency is made possible.

Interviewer: How do visual images influence your work?

Morrison: I was having some difficulty describing a scene in *Song of Solomon* . . . of a man running away from some obligations and himself. I used an Edvard Munch painting almost literally. He is walking, and there is nobody on his side of the street. Everybody is on the other side.

Interviewer: *Song of Solomon* is such a painted book in comparison with some of your others like *Beloved*, which is sepia toned.

Morrison: Part of that has to do with the visual images that I got being aware that in historical terms women, black people in general, were very attracted to very bright colored clothing. Most people are frightened by color anyway.

Interviewer: Why?

Morrison: They just are. In this culture quiet colors are considered elegant. Civilized western people wouldn't buy blood red sheets or dishes. There may be something more to it than what I am suggesting. But the slave population had no access even to what color there was, because they wore slave clothes, hand-me-downs, work clothes made out of burlap and sacking. For them a colored dress would be luxurious; it wouldn't matter whether it was rich or poor cloth . . . just to have a red or a yellow dress. I stripped *Beloved* of color so that there are only the small moments when Sethe runs amok buying ribbons and bows, enjoying herself the way children enjoy that kind of color. The whole business of color was why slavery was able to last such a long time. It wasn't as though you had a class of convicts who could dress themselves up and pass themselves off. No, these were people marked because of their skin color, as well as other features. So color is a signifying mark. Baby Suggs dreams of color, and says, "Bring me a little lavender. . . ." It is a kind of a luxury. We are so inundated with color and visuals. I just wanted to pull it back so that one could feel that hunger and that delight. I couldn't do that if I had made it the painterly book *Song of Solomon* was.

Interviewer: Is that what you are referring to when you speak about needing to find a controlling image?

Morrison: Sometimes, yes. There are three or four in *Song of Solomon*, I knew that I wanted it to be painterly, and I wanted the opening to be red, white, and blue. I also knew that in some sense he would have to "fly." In *Song* *of Solomon* it was the first time that I had written about a man who was the central, the driving engine of the narrative; I was a little unsure about my ability to feel comfortable inside him. I could always look at him and write from the outside, but those would have been just perceptions. I had to be able not only to look at him but to feel how it really must have felt. So in trying to think about this, the image in my mind was a train. All the previous books have been women-centered, and they have been pretty much in the neighborhood and in the yard; this was going to move out. So, I had this feeling about a train . . . sort of revving up, then moving out as he does, and then it sort of highballs at the end; it speeds up, but it doesn't brake, it just highballs and leaves you sort of suspended. So that image controlled the structure for me, although that is not something I articulate or even make reference to; it only matters that it works for me. Other books look like spirals, like *Sula*.

Interviewer: How would you describe the controlling image of *Jazz*?
Morrison: *Jazz* was very complicated because I wanted to re-represent two contradictory things—artifice and improvisation, where you have an artwork, planned, thought through, but at the same time appears invented, like jazz. I thought of the image being a book. Physically a book, but at the same time it is writing itself. Imagining itself. Talking. Aware of what it is doing. It watches itself think and imagine. That seemed to me to be a combination of artifice and improvisation—where you practice and plan in order to invent. Also the willingness to fail, to be wrong, because jazz is performance. In a performance you make mistakes, and you don't have the luxury of revision that a writer has; you have to make something out of a mistake, and if you do it well enough it will take you to another place where you never would have gone had you not made that error. So, you have to be able to risk making that error in performance. Dancers do it all the time, as well as jazz musicians. *Jazz* predicts its own story. Sometimes it is wrong because of faulty vision. It simply did not imagine those characters well enough, admits it was wrong, and the characters talk back the way jazz musicians do. It has to listen to the characters it has invented, and then learn something from them. It was the most intricate thing I had done, though I wanted to tell a very simple story about people who do not know that they are living in the jazz age, and to never use the word.

Interviewer: One way to achieve this structurally is to have several voices speaking throughout each book. Why do you do this?

Morrison: It's important not to have a totalizing view. In American literature we have been so totalized—as though there is only one version. We are not one indistinguishable block of people who always behave the same way.

Interviewer: Is that what you mean by "totalized?"
Morrison: Yes. A definitive or an authoritarian view from somebody else or someone speaking for us. No singularity and no diversity. I try to give some credibility to all sorts of voices each of which is profoundly different. Because what strikes me about African-American culture *is* its variety. In so much of contemporary music everybody sounds alike. But when you think about black music, you think about the difference between Duke Ellington and Sidney Bechet or Satchmo or Miles Davis. They don't sound anything alike, but you know that they are all black performers, because of whatever that quality is that makes you realize, "Oh yes, this is part of something called the African-American music tradition." There is no black woman popular singer, jazz singer, blues singer who sounds like any other. Billie Holiday does not sound like Aretha, doesn't sound like Nina, doesn't sound like Sarah, doesn't sound like any of them. They are really powerfully different. And they will tell you that they couldn't possibly have made it as singers if they sounded like somebody else. If someone comes along sounding like Ella Fitzgerald, they will say, "Oh we have one of those . . ." It's interesting to me how those women have this very distinct, unmistakable image. I would like to write like that. I would like to write novels that were unmistakably mine, but nevertheless fit first into African-American traditions and second of all, this whole thing called literature.

Interviewer: First African-American?
Morrison: Yes.

Interviewer: . . . rather than the whole of literature?
Morrison: Oh yes.

Interviewer: Why?
Morrison: It's richer. It has more complex sources. It pulls from something that's closer to the edge, it's much more modern. It has a human future.

Interviewer: Wouldn't you rather be known as a great exponent of literature rather than as an African-American writer?

Morrison: It's very important to me that my work be African-American; if it assimilates into a different or larger pool, so much the better. But I shouldn't be *asked* to do that. Joyce is not asked to do that. Tolstoy is not. I mean, they can all be Russian, French, Irish, or Catholic, they write out of where they come from, and I do too. It just so happens that that space for me is African-American; it could be Catholic, it could be Midwestern. I'm those things too, and they are all important.

Interviewer: Why do you think people ask, "Why don't you write something that we can understand?" Do you threaten them by not writing in the typical western, linear, chronological way?

Morrison: I don't think that they mean that. I think they mean, "Are you ever going to write a book about white people?" For them perhaps that's a kind of a compliment. They're saying, "You write well enough, I would even let you write about me." They couldn't say that to anybody else. I mean, could I have gone up to André Gide and said, "Yes, but when are you going to get serious and start writing about black people?" I don't think he would know how to answer that question. Just as I don't. He would say, "What?" "I will if I want," or "Who are you?" What is behind that question is, there's the center, which is white, and then there are these regional blacks or Asians, or any sort of marginal people. That question can only be asked from the center. Bill Moyers asked me that when-are-you-going-to-write-about question on television. I just said, "Well, maybe one day . . . " but I couldn't say to him, you know, you can only ask that question from the center. The center of the world! I mean he's a white male. He's asking a marginal person, "When are you going to get to the center? When are you going to write about white people?" I can't say, "Bill, why are you asking me that question?" or "As long as that question seems reasonable is as long as I won't, can't." The point is that he's patronizing; he's saying, "You write well enough. You could come on into the center if you wanted to. You don't have to stay out there on the margins." And I'm saying, "Yeah, well I'm gonna stay out here on the margin, and let the center look for me."

Maybe it's a false claim, but not fully. I'm sure it was true for the ones we think of as giants now. Joyce is a good example. He moved here and there, but he wrote about Ireland wherever he was, didn't care where he was. I am sure people said to him, "Why . . . ?" Maybe the French asked, "When you gonna write about Paris?"

Interviewer: What do you appreciate most in Joyce?

Morrison: It is amazing how certain kinds of irony and humor travel. Sometimes Joyce is hilarious. I read *Finnegans Wake* after graduate school, and I had the great good fortune of reading it without any help. I don't know if I read it right, but it was hilarious! I laughed constantly! I didn't know what was going on for whole blocks but it didn't matter because I wasn't going to be graded on it. I think the reason why everyone still has so much fun with Shakespeare is because he didn't have any literary critic. He was just doing it; and there were no reviews except for people throwing stuff on stage. He could just do it.

Interviewer: Do you think if he had been reviewed he would have worked less?

Morrison: Oh, if he'd cared about it, he'd have been very self-conscious. That's a hard attitude to maintain, to pretend you don't care, pretend you don't read.

Interviewer: Do you read your reviews?

Morrison: I read everything.

Interviewer: Really? You look deadly serious.

Morrison: I read everything written about me that I see.

Interviewer: Why is that?

Morrison: I have to know what's going on!

Interviewer: You want to see how you're coming across?

Morrison: No, no. It's not about me or my work, it's about what is going on. I have to get a sense, particularly of what's going on with women's work, or African-American work, contemporary work. I teach a literature course. So I read any information that's going to help me teach.

Interviewer: Are you ever really surprised when they compare you to the magic realists, such as Gabriel García Márquez?

Morrison: Yes, I used to be. It doesn't mean anything to me. Schools are only important to me when I'm teaching literature. It doesn't mean anything to me when I'm sitting here with a big pile of blank yellow paper . . . what do I say? I'm a magic realist? Each subject matter demands its own form, you know.

Interviewer: Why do you teach undergraduates?

Morrison: Here at Princeton, they really do value undergraduates, which is nice because a lot of universities value only the graduate school or the professional research schools. I like Princeton's notion. I would have loved that for my own children. I don't like freshman and sophomores being treated as the staging ground or the playground or the canvas on which graduate students learn how to teach. They need the best instruction. I've always thought the public schools needed to study the best literature. I always taught *Oedipus Rex* to all kinds of what they used to call remedial or development classes. The reason those kids are in those classes is that they're bored to death; so you can't give them boring things. You have to give them the best there is to engage them.

Interviewer: One of your sons is a musician. Were you ever musical, did you ever play the piano?

Morrison: No, but I come from a family of highly skilled musicians. Highly skilled, meaning most of them couldn't read music but they could play everything that they heard . . . instantly. They sent us, my sister and me, to music lessons. They were sending me off to learn how to do something that they could do naturally. I thought I was deficient, retarded. They didn't explain that perhaps it's more important that you learn how to *read* music . . . that it's a good thing, not a bad thing. I thought we were sort of lame people going off to learn how to walk, while, you know they all just stood up and did it naturally.

Interviewer: Do you think there is an education for becoming a writer? Reading perhaps?

Morrison: That has only limited value.

Interviewer: Travel the world? Take courses in sociology, history?

Morrison: Or stay home . . . I don't think they have to go anywhere.

Interviewer: Some people say, "Oh I can't write a book until I've lived my life, until I've had experiences."

Morrison: That may be—maybe they can't. But look at the people who never went anywhere and just thought it up. Thomas Mann. I guess he took a few little trips. . . . I think you either have or you acquire this sort of imagination. Sometimes you do need a stimulus. But I myself don't ever go anywhere for

stimulation. I don't want to go anywhere. If I could just sit in one spot
I would be happy. I don't trust the ones who say I have to go do something
before I can write. You see, I don't write autobiographically. First of all, I'm
not interested in real-life people as subjects for fiction—including myself.
If I write about somebody who's an historical figure like Margaret Garner,
I really don't know anything about her. What I knew came from reading two
interviews with her. They said, Isn't this extraordinary. Here's a woman who
escaped into Cincinnati from the horrors of slavery and was not crazy.
Though she'd killed her child, she was not foaming at the mouth. She was
very calm, she said, "I'd do it again." That was more than enough to fire my
imagination.

Interviewer: She was sort of a *cause célèbre*?
Morrison: She was. Her real life was much more awful than it's rendered in
the novel, but if I had known all there was to know about her I never would
have written it. It would have been finished, there would have been no place
in there for me. It would be like a recipe already cooked. There you are.
You're already this person. Why should I get to steal from you? I don't like
that. What I really love is the process of invention. To have characters move
from the curl all the way to a full-fledged person, that's interesting.

Interviewer: Do you ever write out of anger or any other emotion?
Morrison: No. Anger is a very intense but tiny emotion, you know. It doesn't
last. It doesn't produce anything. It's not creative . . . at least not for me. I
mean these books take at least three years!

Interviewer: That is a long time to be angry.
Morrison: Yes. I don't trust that stuff anyway. I don't like those little quick
emotions, like, "I'm lonely, *ohhh*, God . . ." I don't like those emotions as fuel.
I mean, I have them, but . . .

Interviewer: . . . they're not a good muse?
Morrison: No, and if it's not your brain thinking cold, cold thoughts, which
you can dress in any kind of mood, then it's nothing. It has to be a cold, cold
thought. I mean cold, or cool at least. Your brain. That's all there is.

Nobel Laureate Toni Morrison
Speaks about Her Novel *Jazz*

Angels Carabi / 1993

From *Belles Lettres* 10.2 (Spring 1995). Interview conducted in Barcelona in 1993. Reprinted by permission of Angels Carabi.

AC: As a general introduction to the book, I would first like to talk about the period of the 1920s, the postwar years after Reconstruction, when black people moved from rural to urban places. What did this mean from the black perspective?

TM: During Reconstruction, which occurred after 1865, two things happened. First, there was a lot of migration of black people. They built towns, and in some places—particularly the West—they were very well organized and prosperous. There were over a hundred black towns in Oklahoma, with their own banks, schools, and churches—beautiful buildings. But there was also a huge backlash during Reconstruction. Blacks were attacked by white people, including the business community, because they were making a lot of money, were self-sufficient, and were on land that other people wanted. Then the lynchings began to increase. So there was a combination of dashed hopes of freedom after the war and some successes, because of the black people in the Senate, the government, and so forth. Of course the huge repression of black people prompted many of them to move to places like New York, Chicago, and Detroit—the big industrial centers where there was safety in numbers and where they could make a good life.

World War I—like all the other wars—called black men to serve. So many young black men had gone to Europe and India, in all-black battalions, and they suffered the way all soldiers did. They fought for the country that lynched them, and when they came back and wore their uniforms in many parts of the country, they were again lynched. There were a lot of emasculations, surgical emasculations. People were snatched out of houses and burned, killed, or maimed. So the violence was particularly nasty after the war.

Somebody told me that in Tulsa (which had a well-protected, prosperous black community), a black boy was arrested on the alleged charge of rape. He was an elevator operator and a white woman claimed that he had made an indecent gesture toward her. Nothing actually happened—this is even what *she* said—and he was innocent. So the black people rescued him from prison and took him into the black neighborhood. When the authorities came to get him, the people were armed, so the police blew up the whole neighborhood with bombs. It wasn't just poverty that drove black people to the big cities. It was also success, because their success was a major threat to the white population.

But the music also began to change in the 1920s. It always changes, but this was the period of the seeds of jazz, instead of the spiritual begging for relief or the coded language of escape from slavery. Now you had musicians who played in bars, bordellos, or for entertainment. They began to express anger and yearning, but they were confident, and very seductive. So where were the areas where you could claim freedom? You got into a big city. There was the thrill of seeing yourself in large numbers, again developing a sort of black town, Harlem. There was a very successful black middle class in Brooklyn, but for everyday people, one of the most interesting things was a freedom to fall in love, to own your body, to be immoral.

As far as black people were concerned, white people always put the stamp of immorality on them, even when the women were forced to have babies. The accusation was not on the people who forced them, but on the women who were forced, you know, as usual. Anyway, some of the elements of that period seem so pervasive because I think it affected America and the world. Jazz became the sign of modernity, a license that black people would try desperately to express.

In the little short life they had, that was how they felt good about themselves, while fully aware of their difficulties. It was also a postwar period, when there's always a lot of excitement, and people want to finally be in the lead at this time of earthiness. It was that spirit that was enabled by the music. I always see background music to everything. In cultural terms, the period is identified with white people, who symbolized the period in literature.

AC: *The Great Gatsby* for instance?
TM: Yes. F. Scott Fitzgerald is typical, and early Hemingway, John Dos Passos, and Gertrude Stein. But the people who enabled the core and the shape of

that period were, of course, black people, whose culture was evolving different things and being constantly invented and improvised. You had to stay
alert to political changes, because you never knew what people were going to
do at any moment. So you had to be always on guard and be able to adjust
quickly. That ability was a double entendre: at the same time accommodating
the grief we felt and the determination not to let life beat us up completely—
you know, the instinct for survival plus "joie de vivre" was very important.
The word *jazz* seems to encompass all of that, although its etymology has
been contested. Most people agree that it is French "jism," meaning an ejacu-
lation, semen. They used to call bordellos jazz houses because they were
about sexual relations. And in these jazz houses, black musicians played. So
you can see that the word comes out of a vulgar, sexual term, which is why
many black musicians abhor the word *jazz*.

Black music's always called something—spiritual, gospel, jazz, boogie-
woogie, bop, bebop, rap—but it's never called *music*, for example, twentieth-
century music, modern music. So it's argued about in another way. White
critics, in general, claim it as American, which it is, but it's almost as though
it was made with their culture, and so black people have no part in it, except
marginally, to provide the music. To talk about it is to appropriate it. On one
hand, art that is disseminated is good, that's what it was for. But on the other
hand is the constant discrediting of the musicians and their impact: commercially, they made no money. The white people who imitated their music
made money. The "king of swing" was Benny Goodman! The jazz musicians
went to Europe for recognition and appreciation of their music, because the
Europeans in the twenties were aficionados and the white Americans were
not, except in a sort of bland or played-down reproduction of it. So the
music got a lot of security and satisfaction in Europe that it did not get in the
States until very late. The white musicians in the States were feeding off of it,
claiming it as their own, but the original musicians were unable to get aesthetic and critical acclaim there.

I believe the twenties began to be the moment when black culture, rather
than American culture, began to alter the whole country and eventually
the western world. It was an overwhelming development in terms of excitement and glamour, and the sense of individualizing ourselves swept the
world.

So that's why I used the term *jazz*, because it sums all this up. But nobody in
the book would call it that. In the States, it's always associated with something

vulgar, which is part of its anarchy. It has implications of sex, violence, and chaos, all of which I wanted in the book.

Nobody agrees on anything about jazz (except that it survived beautifully and blossomed), but everybody thinks they know all about it, anywhere in the world. There is an interesting ownership of jazz.

So, when I was thinking of who was going to tell this story, the idea of "who owns jazz," or who knows about it, came up. I was looking for a voice and having trouble figuring it out, but then I decided that the voice would be one of assumed knowledge, the voice that says "I know everything." This is a kind of dominant ownership: without sex, gender, or age. Because the voice has to actually imagine the story it's telling, using the art of imagination, it's in trouble, because if it's really involved in the process of telling the story and letting the other voices speak, the story that it thought it knew turns out to be entirely different from what it predicted because the characters will be evolving within the story, within the book.

It reminded me of a jazz performance in which the musicians are on stage. And they know what they are doing, they rehearse, but the performance is open to change, and the other musicians have to respond quickly to that change. Somebody takes off from a basic pattern, then the others have to accommodate themselves. That's the excitement, the razor's edge of a live performance of jazz. Now, in improvising on the spot in front of an audience, you find yourself in a place you could not possibly predict. But what happens when you go to this unpredictable place is that you are frequently taken into a room that you could not possibly have found if you had gone the normal way.

So, then the voice realizes, after hearing other voices, that the narrative is not going to be at all what it predicted. The more it learns about the characters (and they are not what the voice thought), it has to go on, but it goes on with more knowledge. The voice says, "Now I know. Now I know." It began to imagine another kind of life taking place. You could never imagine those two could reconcile, but they are able to—not because the voice says so, but because the voice discovers who they are. I was trying to align myself with more interesting and intricate aspects of my notion of jazz as a demanding, improvisatory art form, so I had to get rid of the conventions, which I distrust. I've done this in other places but not as radically as here. The thing is, I could not think of the voice of a person; I know everybody refers to "I" as a woman (because I'm a woman, I guess), but for me, it was very important that the "I" would say what a typical book would limit itself to, what a physical book would say. The book uses verbs—"I think," "I believe," "I wonder," "I imagine," "I know"—but it never sits down, it never walks, because it's a book. The voice is the voice of a talking book. So when the voice says, "I know what it's like to be left standing when someone promises," it talks to the reader. It sounds like a very erotic, sensual love song of a person who loves you. This is a love song of a book talking to the reader.

It's a book talking, but few people read it like that. Most reviewers said "she [I mean Toni Morrison] is pleading with the reader to forgive her."

It was interesting to me how the whole act of reading, holding, surrendering to a book, is part of that beautiful intimacy of reading. When it's tactile, your emotions are deeply involved; if it's a good book, if you're just there. I deliberately restricted myself using an "I" that was only connected to the artifact of the book as an active participant in the invention of the story of the book, as though the book were talking, writing itself, in a sense. It's an interesting and overwhelming technical idea to me. But also it gave me an opportunity to check the actor, performance, style, without knowing the play, knowing what the next movement is going to be, and then getting caught up in it, and then having to invent something new, the more you get involved in it. It's very strange, but I like it because it's risky. But jazz unsettles you. You always feel a little on edge. "Did I catch it?" Then you have to listen again. You're not in control. It was this assumption of control, the reader's control, the book's control—all of these had to be displaced, so no one's in control.

AC: Tell me about Dorcas. Initially part of her story reminds me of Sula in the sense that she learns about the unexpectedness of death, and that keeps her silent.
TM: She decides to throw herself into it.

AC: Exactly. Because she has experienced that, then she is ready to go to the limit.
TM: Dorcas is just straining at the bit the way her aunt has overprotected her. You can imagine the adoration that an older man can bring to a young girl, particularly at that age. It's so flattering and you're so empowered by it, and you can manipulate him for attention and that's terribly exciting. And then once she gets real strength from Joe, she gets an identity, she feels empowered. Then she goes to this other guy. She feels like a woman, but the source of her

feeling like that has come from Joe. Oh! That stupidness, that sort of girlish, goopy feeling. But if you look at her from Felice's point of view, she was always interested in a kind of a wanton power. She would get guys to do things for her. She was always a little bit of—not an outcast—but a little bit different from the other girls.

Felice begins to doubt whether their friendship was really true friendship. And Felice learns a great deal from exploring the relationship and talking to Joe and Violet and rethinking what is going on. Even if there was that strong affection between them, she knew that Dorcas didn't like her enough to stay alive because she let herself die. Felice gets to think back and let herself think about how she was with men and decides herself not to be like that. She's the one who has to go out and face the world and become somebody who's independent of all that. But yet she can put herself in perspective of that relationship, so in the end even the voice says, Felice is nobody's ham and she's nobody's toy. And she's walking to a new tune, she's like the future—as Denver [in *Beloved*] is the future. She says I want to be independent. I want to work. I don't want to be a prostitute. And she's looking like that experience has been good for her. Sad for her. But at the same time she has learned a lot from it, I think. And she's more likely to be a coherent personality. She will never be somebody else's side chick again.

AC: And she brings the records and the music and then Joe dances.
TM: That's right. She brings music to the awful house and they dance. So the jazz enables possibility once again. Because it's when, narratively speaking, Joe feels better. He knows that he's sort of killed Dorcas but she helped kill herself, so that lightens his load a little bit.

AC: Wild puzzles me a lot.
TM: Wild is a kind of Beloved. The dates are the same. You see a pregnant black woman naked at the end of *Beloved*. It's at the same time, you know back in the Golden Gray section of *Jazz*, there is a crazy woman out in the woods. The woman they call Wild (because she's sort of out of it from the hit on the head) could be Sethe's daughter, Beloved. When you see Beloved towards the end, you don't know; she's either a ghost who has been exorcised or she's a real person pregnant by Paul D, who runs away, ending up in Virginia, which is right next to Ohio. But I don't want to make all these connections.

AC: Are you working on another book now?

TM: Remember I was talking about those black towns? Most of them disappeared, but I'm going to project one that moved away from the collapse of an original black town and set up in Oklahoma. They went from being very rebellious, to being progressive, to stability. Then they got compromised and reactionary and were unable to adjust to new things happening. The novel is called *Paradise*.

Chloe Wofford Talks about Toni Morrison

Claudia Dreifus / 1994

From the *New York Times Magazine* (September 11, 1994). Reprinted by permission of Claudia Dreifus.

The woman breezing into a Princeton, New Jersey, restaurant in a brilliant silk caftan and with salt-and-pepper dreadlocks is Toni Morrison, sixty-three, the Robert F. Goheen Professor in the Council of the Humanities at Princeton University and the 1993 Nobel Prize winner for literature. Heads turn as she moves to a table. Princetonians in khaki stare.

Since her Grand View-on-Hudson, New York, home burned to the ground last Christmas, Morrison has been living in this very Anglo-Saxon American town. "Princeton's fine for me right now," she explains as we sit down to lunch. "I have wonderful students and good friends here. Besides, I'm in the middle of a new novel and I don't want to think about where I'm living."

The new novel is tentatively called "Paradise." In writing it, Morrison says she has been trying to imagine language to describe a place where "race exists but doesn't matter." Race has always mattered a lot in Morrison's fiction. In six previous novels, including *Beloved*, *Song of Solomon*, and *Jazz*, she has focused on the particular joys and sorrows of black American women's lives. As both a writer and editor—Morrison was at Random House for eighteen years—she has made it her mission to get African-American voices into American literature.

As a luncheon companion, she is great fun—a woman of subversive jokes, gossip, and surprising bits of self-revelation (the laureate unwinds to Court TV and soap operas). The stories Morrison likes to tell have this deadpan/astonished quality to them. Like fellow Nobel winner Gabriel García Márquez, she can recount the most atrocious tale and give horror a charming veneer. One suspects that Morrison long ago figured out how to battle the cruelties of race with her wit.

98

She grew up Chloe Anthony Wofford, in the rust-belt town of Lorain, Ohio. Her father, George, was a ship welder, her mother, Ramah, a home-maker. At Howard University, where she did undergraduate work in English, Chloe Anthony became known as Toni. After earning a master's in English literature at Cornell, she married Harold Morrison, a Washington architecture student, in 1959. But the union—from all reports—was difficult. (As open as Morrison is about most subjects, she refuses to discuss her former husband.) When the marriage ended in 1964, Morrison moved to Syracuse and then to New York with her two sons, Harold Ford, three, and Slade, three months old. She supported the family as a book editor.

Evenings, after putting her children to bed, she worked on a novel about a sad black adolescent who dreams of changing the color of her eyes. *The Bluest Eye* was published in 1970, inspiring a whole generation of African-American women to tell their own stories—women like Alice Walker, Gloria Naylor, and Toni Cade Bambara.

"I'm not pleased with all the events and accidents of my life," she says over coffee and a cigarette. "You know, life is pretty terrible and some of it has hurt me a lot. I'd say I'm proud of a third of my life, comfortable with another third and would like to redo, reconfigure, the last third."

Q: When you went to Stockholm in December to collect the Nobel Prize, did you feel a sense of triumph?
A: I felt a lot of "we" excitement. It was as if the whole category of "female writer" and "black writer" had been redeemed. I felt I represented a whole world of women who either were silenced or who had never received the imprimatur of the established literary world. I felt the way I used to feel at commencements where I'd get an honorary degree: that it was very important for young black people to see a black person do that; that there were probably young people in South-Central Los Angeles or Selma who weren't quite sure that they could do it. But seeing me up there might encourage them to write one of those books I'm desperate to read. And *that* made me happy. It gave me license to strut.

Q: You've said that even after publishing three novels, you didn't dare call yourself "a writer." How was that possible?
A: I think, at bottom, I simply was not prepared to do the adult thing, which in those days would be associated with the male thing, which was to say, "I'm a writer." I said, "I am a mother who writes" or "I am an editor who writes."

The word "writer" was hard for me to say because that's what you put on your income-tax form. I *do* now say, "I'm a writer." But it's the difference between identifying one's work and being the person who does the work. I've always been the latter. I've always thought best when I wrote. Writing is what centered me. In the act of writing, I felt most alive, most coherent, most stable and most vulnerable.

Interestingly, I've always felt deserving. Growing up in Lorain, my parents made all of us feel as though there were these rather extraordinary deserving people within us. I felt like an aristocrat—or what I think an aristocrat is. I always knew we were very poor. But that was never degrading. I remember a very important lesson that my father gave me when I was twelve or thirteen. He said, "You know, today I welded a perfect seam and I signed my name to it." And I said, "But, Daddy, no one's going to see it!" And he said, "Yeah, but I know it's there." So when I was working in kitchens, I did good work.

Q: When did you do that kind of work?
A: I started around thirteen. That was the work that was available: to go to a woman's house after school and clean for three or four hours. The normal teen-age jobs were not available. Housework always was. It wasn't uninteresting. You got to work these gadgets that I never had at home: vacuum cleaners. Some of the people were nice. Some were terrible. Years later, I used some of what I observed in my fiction. In *The Bluest Eye*, Pauline lived in this dump and hated everything in it. And then she worked for the Fishers, who had this beautiful house, and she loved it. She got a lot of respect as their maid that she didn't get anywhere else. If she went to the grocery store as a black woman from that little house and said, "I don't want this meat," she would not be heard. But if she went in as a representative of these white people and said, "This is not good enough," they'd pay attention.

Q: What role did books play in your childhood?
A: Major. A driving thing. The security I felt, the pleasure, when new books arrived was immense. My mother belonged to a book club, one of those early ones. And that was hard-earned money, you know.

Q: As a young reader, when you encountered racial stereotypes in the classics of American literature—in Ernest Hemingway or Willa Cather or William Faulkner—how did you deal with them?

A: I skipped that part. Read over it. Because I loved those books. I loved them. So when they said these things that were profoundly racist, I forgave them. As for Faulkner, I read him with enormous pleasure. He seemed to me the only writer who took black people seriously. Which is not to say he was, or was not, a bigot.

Q: It must have been fulfilling, in 1970, to see your name on the cover of *The Bluest Eye*.
A: I was upset. They had the wrong name: Toni Morrison. My name is Chloe Wofford. Toni's a nickname.

Q: Didn't you know that your publisher, Holt, was going to use the name?
A: Well, I sort of knew it was going to happen. I was in a daze. I sent it in that way because the editor knew me as Toni Morrison.

Q: So you achieved fame misnamed?
A: Tell me about it! I write all the time about being misnamed. How you got your name is very special. My mother, my sister, all my family call me Chloe. It was Chloe, by the way, who went to Stockholm last year to get the Nobel Prize.

Q: In your acceptance speech you spoke against "unyielding language content to admire its own paralysis"—language that "suppresses human potential." Some of your critics thought you were using the Nobel ceremony to advocate politically correct literature.
A: You know, the term "political correctness" has become a shorthand for discrediting ideas. I believe that powerful, sharp, incisive, critical, bloody, dramatic, theatrical language is not dependent on injurious language, on curses. Or hierarchy. You're not stripping language by requiring people to be sensitive to other people's pain. I can't just go around saying, "Kill whitey." What does that mean? It may satisfy something, but there's no information there. I can't think through that. And I have to use language that's better than that. What I think the political correctness debate is really about is the power to be able to define. The definers want the power to name. And the defined are now taking that power away from them.

Q: Which authors influenced you when you began writing?
A: James Baldwin. He could say something in a phrase that clarified all sorts of conflicting feelings. Before Baldwin, I got titillated by fiction through

reading the African novelists, men and women—Chinua Achebe, Camara Laye. Also Bessie Head and the Negritude Movement, including Léopold Sédar Senghor and Aimé Césaire. They did not explain their black world. Or clarify it. Or justify it. White writers had always taken white centrality for granted. They inhabited their world in a central position and everything nonwhite was "other." These African writers took their blackness as central and the whites were the "other."

After I published *The Bluest Eye*, I frequently got the question, "Do you write for white readers?" The question stunned me. I remember asking a white woman at Knopf, "What do white people mean when they say, 'I know you did not write that book for me, but I like it'? I never say, 'Oh, Eudora Welty, I know your book was not written for me, but I enjoy it.'" This woman explained that white readers were not accustomed to reading books about black people in which the central issue is not white people. In my work, the white world is marginalized. This kind of ground shifting seems much more common to black women writers. Not so much black men writers. Black men writers are often interested in their relations with white men. White men, by and large, are not powerful figures in black women's literature.

Q: When you began writing, the best-known black literary voices were male—Ralph Ellison, Baldwin, Richard Wright. Did you make a conscious effort to change that?

A: When I began writing I didn't write *against* existing voices. There had been some women writing—Paule Marshall, Zora Neale Hurston, though I hadn't read Hurston yet. When I began, there was just one thing that I wanted to write about, which was the true devastation of racism on the most vulnerable, the most helpless unit in the society—a black female and a child. I wanted to write about what it was like to be the subject of racism. It had a specificity that was damaging. And if there was no support system in the community and in the family, it could cause spiritual death, self-loathing, terrible things.

Once I did that, I wanted to write another book. By the time I wrote the third one, I began to think in terms of what had gone on before—whether my territory was different. I felt what I was doing was so unique that I didn't think a man could possibly understand what the little girl in *The Bluest Eye* was feeling. I did not think a white person could describe it. So I thought I was telling a tale untold.

Q: There's a boom now in black women's literature. Terry McMillan makes best-seller lists. Bebe Moore Campbell's *Brothers and Sisters* is a Book-of-the-Month Club main selection. Is the book world changing?

A: Yes. This means there is now such a thing as popular black women's literature. Popular! In 1992, there were four books by black women on the best-seller lists—at the same time. Terry McMillan's, Alice Walker's, and two of mine. Now that's exhilarating!

When I was a book editor, I had to worry about all the books I was publishing by black authors being lumped together in reviews. Black authors who didn't write anything at all like each other would be reviewed together. Their works were understood first of all to be black, and not, you know history books or novels.

Q: Back to your Nobel. What did you do with the $817,771 that came with it?

A: Put it away for my retirement. And then, of course, the minute I did that, my house burned down. So, suddenly, I needed it and couldn't put my hands on it. [Sighs.] It's probably just as well. Because if I hadn't done that, I would have taken the money and rebuilt my house and it would have been like most of the money I've ever had: as soon as you get it, there's this big hole waiting for it.

Q: Did the fire seem like some kind of mystical leveling for flying too high?

A: No. In the two years around the Nobel, I had a lot of bad luck, a lot of very serious devastations. My mother died, other things. The only thing that happened that was unexpected and truly wonderful was the Nobel Prize. So I regard the fact that my house burned down after I won the Nobel Prize to be better than having my house burn down without having won the Nobel Prize. Most people's houses just burn down. Period.

When I think about the fire, I think I may not ever, ever, ever get over it. And it isn't even about the *things*. It's about photographs, plants I nurtured for twenty years, about the view of the Hudson River, my children's report cards, my manuscripts. There were some months when I wouldn't talk to anybody who had not had a house burn down.

Q: That must have been a limited circle.

A: Oh, I don't know. You'd be surprised how many people had their house burn down. The writer Maxine Hong Kingston and I traded information.

She had her whole house burn down. Right now, I don't want to think about where I live because I'm working hard on a new book. And I am getting deeper and deeper into the book. And I can feel myself getting vaguer and vaguer and vaguer. Pretty soon I will be like someone looking through water—everybody will look to me as if I'm in a tank somewhere.

Q: I read that your two sons didn't particularly like growing up with a writer for a mother.
A: Who does? I wouldn't. Writers are *not there*. They're likely to get vague when you need them. And while the vagueness may be good for the writer, if children need your complete attention, then it's bad for them.

Q: You wrote your early novels while holding a full-time job and raising your sons alone. How did you keep the responsibilities from silencing you as a writer?
A: It wasn't easy. But when I left Washington, I really wanted to see if I could do it alone. In New York, whenever things got difficult, I thought about my mother's mother, a sharecropper, who, with her husband, owed money to their landlord. In 1906, she escaped with her seven children to meet her husband in Birmingham, where he was working as a musician. It was a dangerous trip, but she wanted a better life. Whenever things seemed difficult for me in New York, I thought that what I was doing wasn't anything as hard as what she did.

I remember one day when I was confused about what I had to do next—write a review, pick up groceries, what? I took out a yellow pad and made a list of all the things I had to do. It included large things, like "be a good daughter and a good mother," and small things, like "call the phone company." I made another list of the things I wanted to do. There were only two things without which I couldn't live: mother my children and write books. Then I cut out everything that didn't have to do with those two things.

There was an urgency—that's all I remember. Not having the leisure to whine. Not paying close attention to what others thought my life should be like. Not organizing my exterior and interior self for the approval of men— which I had done a lot of before. It's not a bad thing to please a husband or a lover, but I couldn't do that. It took up time and thought.

Q: There's a lot of sexual violation in your fiction. Why?
A: Because when I began to write, it was an unmentionable. It is so dangerous, it is so awful, so wicked, that I think in connection with vulnerable black

women it was never talked about. I wanted to write books that ran the whole gamut of women's sexual experiences. I didn't like the imposition that had been placed on black women's sexuality in literature. They were either mothers, mammies, or whores. And they were not vulnerable people. They were not people who were supposed to enjoy sex, either. That was forbidden in literature—to enjoy your body, be in your body, defend your body. But at the same time I wanted to say, "You still can be prey." Right now, I've been writing a page or two in my new book, trying to evoke out-of-door safety for women. How it feels. How it is perceived when you feel perfectly safe a long way from home. This new book, "Paradise," has taken over my imagination completely and I'm having the best time ever. I wrote thirteen pages in three days. I've never done that in my life.

Q: When you relax, what do you read?
A: Well, I don't read much fiction when I'm writing, as I am right now. If I read fiction, I want to be in the author's head, and I have to be in mine. I did have some time off recently and I read Marguerite Duras and Leslie Marmon Silko and Jean Genet's biography. When I'm on tour or traveling, I generally read mystery stories—Ruth Rendell, John le Carré, P. D. James and this man called Carl Hiaasen. He has a wonderful ear for dialogue.

Q: Have you been following the O. J. Simpson case?
A: Yes, and I find it very sinister. It's a carnival. Sometimes you think it's about men beating women, sometimes about athletes and their being curried and made into things. Sometimes you think it's about white/black, Hollywood, but it's not. This is just one big national spectacle, and they get to kill him. We get to watch. We get to focus on the detritus, not the victim.

Q: *Beloved* is the story of an escaped slave, Sethe, who kills her daughter rather than see the child live in slavery. Were you frightened while writing it?
A: I had never been so frightened. I could imagine slavery in an intellectual way, but to feel it viscerally was terrifying. I had to go inside. Like an actor does. I had to feel what it might feel like for my own children to be enslaved. At the time, I was no longer working at an office, and that permitted me to go deep.

With *Beloved*, I wanted to say, "Let's get rid of these words like 'the slave woman' and 'the slave child,' and talk about people with names, like you and like me, who were there." Now, what does slavery feel like? What can you do? How can you be? Clearly, it is a situation in which you have practically no power. And if you decide you are not going to be a victim, then it's a major risk. And you end up doing some terrible things. And some not-so-terrible things. But the risk of being your own person, or trying to have something to do with your destiny, is one of the major battles in life.

Q: Do you ever get writer's block?

A: I disavow that term. There are times when you don't know what you're doing or when you don't have access to the language or the event. So if you're sensitive, you can't do it. When I wrote *Beloved*, I thought about it for three years. I started writing the manuscript after thinking about it, and getting to know the people and getting over the fear of entering that arena, and it took me three more years to write it. But those other three years I was still at work, though I hadn't put a word down.

Q: Several of your friends told me you were surprised when you won the Nobel Prize. Why?

A: Because I never thought I had that many supporters. I never thought that the Swedish Academy either knew about my work or took it seriously. The reason it didn't occur to me is not because I didn't think my work eminently worthy. But I was aware of the cautions and the caveats and the misunderstandings that seemed to lie around the criticisms of my work. My books are frequently read as representative of what the black condition is. Actually, the books are about very specific circumstances, and in them are people who do very specific things. But, more importantly, the plot, characters are part of my effort to create a language in which I can posit philosophical questions. I want the reader to ponder those questions not because I put them in an essay, but because they are part of a narrative.

Let me put it another way. I think of jazz music as very complicated, very sophisticated and very difficult. It is also very popular. And it has the characteristic of being sensual and illegal. And its sensuality and its illegality may prevent people from seeing how sophisticated it is. Now, that to me says something about the culture in which I live and about my work. I would like my work to do two things: be as demanding and sophisticated as I want it to be, and at the same time be accessible in a sort of emotional way to lots of people, just like jazz. That's a hard task. But that's what I want to do.

Interview with Toni Morrison

Cecil Brown / 1995

Reprinted by permission of *The Massachusetts Review*, Volume 36, Number 3, Autumn 1995.

Brown: How do you feel about *Beloved*'s being placed, as Stanley Crouch has done, in the tradition of the plantation novel?

Morrison: That's what this is all about. Black writing has to carry that burden of other people's desires, not artistic desires but social desires; it's always perceived as working out somebody's else's agenda. No other literature has that weight.

Q: Gloria Steinem made it clear that Alice Walker's work was a departure from other black male writers. What do you think of that in terms of the prototype black author Richard Wright? Do you think Richard Wright was carrying the burden of that weight to do more for the reader than writing a novel?

TM: He had a very strong program. Powerful as he was—is—as a writer, nobody can surpass him in doing certain kinds of writing. He does action practically better than anybody; also, he is courageous—he was able to look into areas that nobody at that time was willing to look at. But I think he had a legitimate and necessary historical slash political outlook. And that surfaces in his text and that is a legitimate purpose.

The question now as it was then is: how do you make an art form that is both unquestionably beautiful and also political at the same time? But nobody can gainsay that book. Now, I guess he had terrible pictures of men in them, terrible pictures of women in them. If you are asking the characters to function as role models—if that [laughter] is what literature is for, I suppose a lot of people would find him offensive. Black women might find him offensive, vis-a-vis the character's relationship to the woman that he has to rape, mutilate, murder, etc. [deep breath]. We are accustomed as black women, anyway, to that kind of dismissal, even by black men, unless we were the tragic mulatto.

So what is different, I think, is that black women, who seem to be the only people writing who do not regard white men and white women—the white world—as the central stage in the text. White men write about white men, because that's who they are; white women are interested in white men because they are their fathers, lovers, and children, family; black men are interested in white men because that's the area in which they make the confrontation. Those are the people who have denounced them, confronted them, repressed them, and those are the white men who have in large part told them that they are lesser. Black men are serious about this confrontation. Black women don't seem to be interested in this confrontation.

The political situation changed from Wright's time to now. That is the difference now—why black women are not interested in the confrontation. In the 1960s, there were nearly no black women novelists published.

Paule Marshall was published in 1959, and she wasn't interested in the confrontation. Was Zora Neale Hurston? I don't know about this, I'm just wondering if there's a different interest. It is as though black women writers said, "Nobody's gonna tell our story." Nobody but us.

Q: But two things: First, Wright's novel was a depiction of Black life under a brutal system. It was similar to the Hobbesian Leviathan of the short-lived life, the sharecropper's life; the book gave to the whole world a view of black lower-class life. This set the standard in which black writers responded to the political and economic pressure on black life.

Second, since that time, during the sixties, the black writers of my generation responded again. But since that time, the seventies, during the Reagan administration, with the disappearance of radical groups like the Black Panthers, gave a different atmosphere, so that, not just women writers could emerge, but the nation itself turned to a more so that the concern of the woman writer comes to the fore more.
TM: As a kind of trader?

Q: As a buffer between the confrontation of the black male writer and the system?
TM: But that's not true—is it? I mean, has John A. Williams changed what he's writing?

Q: John A. Williams hasn't changed, but his last novel was not published by a big publisher.

TM: There are several ways to write. There're lots of ways to write. There's sabotage, agent-provocateur. There are lots of ways to destabilize racism, and protest novels are only one way. Maybe they're the best way, and maybe they aren't. I'm not interested in that. I'm interested in black readers and me. I think that when you constantly focus on the Nazi, you give him more power than he should have. That's what confrontation in art sometimes does. It's like asking a jazz musician to play his music so white people will like it, and I don't think that's what's going on with black women.

I think that black men have decided that black women writers are the enemy, and therefore we are doing something deceptive by writing less confrontational literature and getting more play out of it. Whereas they are the serious warriors, vis-a-vis literature and they can't get published. And that is just not true. It's not true because they are published. Also, I think it's a mistake—maybe not a mistake—but I just find it interesting that—uh—the play that Moynihan gave of the sinister black woman, which is a white man's idea, is being so beautifully absorbed and digested and surrendered to by a number of black men who are talking about it. The only solution is to do one's work the way you can. But the internecine fighting, I happened to know, is something that any magazine will pay for.

I used to get telephone calls about once a year, another one of those Tell-Us-about-the-Problems-between-the-Black-Man-and-the-Black-Woman calls. Tell how terrible it is. Tell how you all can't get along. And for this you can get infinite amount of space, and you can also have a great talk show. Go on for hours and have a little series. It's inexhaustible. Why is the question about that, and not about what's really going on—black people talking to other black people and enlightening ourselves in an interior way?

Q: How does this question of dissension between black and white men come about? When Gloria Steinem introduced Alice Walker, she made it clear that there was a confrontation between black men's and black women's literature. Here, she said, is an area that black men had not covered. Black men didn't start that?

TM: I can't account for Gloria Steinem. She and Alice Walker are very close friends. She isn't the stamp of approval for me. She may be important to you and a whole lot of people. Gloria Steinem said A, B, C, or D [laughter].

I mean, she and Alice are good friends. They trust one another. Gloria Steinem feels very strong about that. What her agenda is, whether she represents white women in general, I really don't know, and I don't really think she does, as a matter of fact. I don't really know. I'm reluctant to interfere in other people's perception vis-a-vis other people's support systems that black women and white women have forged, for whatever reasons, I can't get into it. I believe I have excluded my work from that area. But I am weary of that kind of endorsement. I think what they wanted at that time—they were very enthusiastic and fearful that Alice Walker's book would not get a lot of attention. They were right. It got bad reviews in the beginning and there was a consistent intention to dismiss the book on the part of publishing. That was real. I know that was real. And it was only through such people [as Gloria Steinem] that it got attention. They used to put flyers on the seats. Now somebody could say that their motives were suspect, you know. I don't know, I'm not willing to comment on that at all.

Because I've seen it the other way around—I've seen white guys thrilled to death with certain books. Claude Brown's book, which was published against the company. They didn't want to publish that book, and then it got this huge response, and there seems to be a large white male identification with that book. Now you could question that, if you want to. Now all these are extra-literary considerations. They have nothing to do with the value of the text, what Claude Brown's book said to me and you. He talked about the way it was received and why it was received that way. And that was the same for *Color Purple*. One of the best books I've ever published in my life was the book by Leon Forrest, and it received wonderful critical acclaim from Saul Bellow and Ralph Ellison. It never sold over two thousand copies. I want to know why black men didn't buy it. I published Henry Dumas to a great deal of reception, and that book never sold over three thousand copies, and now who am I going to blame for that? All the poets came to the parties, but who went to the bookstore, besides me? I mean I bought up all the last copies. Any number of black books by black men have come out and I haven't seen black men in the bookstore buying that book. If I had been able to count on ten, fifteen thousand black men to buy that book then I could take serious this stuff about why somebody gets on top. I can't take it serious, because where are the buyers. I love Henry Dumas, Eugene Redmond loves him, everybody loves him, and I think he is one of the most extraordinary voices in contemporary writing, but I sold not more than two thousand copies . . .

Q: He didn't fit into . . .

TM: It's not about he didn't fit in anything. Black people just didn't buy him. The company published him because I insisted. We printed the books, we put them out, they were not purchased. And we had the publicity, it was in the *Post*, the *New York Times*, stories on him, now who bought him? And this was in the l970s. I published his stories, poems, a novel, in hardback and paper at the same time, so it would be cheaper. So I don't want to hear it. For even when these extraordinary books come out . . .

Q: Do you have many black male readers?

TM: I would imagine so, on the basis of correspondence and the audience and the people who come into the bookstore to ask me to sign them.

Q: Do you have a greater following among white female readers?

TM: I don't know. I can't tell. It seems that, with this book at least, in the academy, I think I have just as many black women who read as white, if not more, but it's proportionate, because there are just more white people in the university. So how can I tell?

Q: I want to turn now to your own novels, the names of your characters. You seem to pun on the names, some of which seem so improbable so that one is sometimes led to believe that the improbability of the names is a kind of pun on slavery itself. That one can never be sure of his own name.

TM: We are very interested in names. There was a whole world of people who call themselves X. I didn't invent that. The whole business of calling yourself X came out of some emotional relationship to a black person's name. There are still people who do it. So somebody is concerned about what a name means to a black person. Is this my name or not? There are spirituals that talk about names: "I ask Jesus if it would be alright if I change my name." Besides, we were named, we just didn't keep our names. In addition, I don't know any musician over fifty who worked with his name. Satchmo didn't, Count didn't, Duke didn't, Leadbelly didn't. It's only after World War II that people begin to use their own name.

Q: Where did they get their names then?

TM: I don't know, Cecil. You know more about it than I do? Where did Leadbelly get his name?

Q: Legend.
TM: What legend?

Q: People.
TM: Well, whatever it is. It's reflected in my book, I'm trying to reflect the milieu. When I was a little girl, all those friends of my father, I never knew their names. Their names were Rocky River, Cool Breeze, Johnnie Dell. I don't know to this day where they got them from, but they used them; they must have had a real name somewhere. But they get or receive names, nick-names. And they generally are names that identify some weakness, as though they are confronting it right away, but it's impossible—if you think about your own childhood you must have been aware of what kind of meanings those names really had. They don't want to call themselves William or some Wasp name. They might want to do it, but you look at records you see all kinds of names. Slaves were called Cato. I don't use that. At least, I use the names that black people are willing to accept for themselves.

Q: How important is the nickname in your fiction? Pauline, in *The Bluest Eye*, has no nickname; she has an infirmity in her foot . . .
TM: She wanted a nickname. A nickname is a personal thing, that intimate people can call you by, and strangers call you by your formal name. But having a nickname, or being the only one who didn't have a nickname, she felt alienated, that's all.

Q: When she worked for this white family, they nicknamed her Polly.
TM: That's right, she was thoroughly enchanted with that. She just gave it up, it was too hard for her. You understand that I don't—people assume so much editorializing in your text that they assume you are recommending things when you are merely describing—I don't want to run around giving people notes on about how to behave and what to do.

Q: Are you describing a particular part of black life by using names in this way?
TM: For the times, sure. Pauline, that's 1923, sure. There are some people in there named Margaret. Cholly's name is just a pronunciation of Charles. Freida and Claudia are nice names. People are talking about the odd names in my fiction but 80 percent of the characters are named Joe. Twenty percent have odd names, which is disproportionate to real life in those days.

Q: Consider Macon Dead [hero of *Song of Solomon*]. The book turns on his name, which is "Dead." It shows . . .

TM: It shows a mistake . . . a clerical error . . . the carelessness of white people . . . and the indifference when they . . . they don't pay much attention to what the records are. My mother doesn't even have a birth certificate. My aunt has a birth certificate and her name is not even on it. It says, Negro Child, that's all.

Q: A critic has said that Macon Dead is supposed to be a pun on "Make Them [Black men] Dead." Is that true?

TM: [Big laughter] Maybe so. I didn't have that in mind, but I'll take it.

Q: Was there an unintentional or intentional parody in *Song of Solomon* of Freud's *Totem and Taboo*?

TM: It was not intentional. I try to stay out of Western mythology. When I use mythology in my text it's usually to show that something has gone wrong, not right. I tend to use everything from African or Afro-American sources. The flying is not about Icarus, it's about the African flying myth. When Milkman walks into that big house, what I have him relating it to is Hansel and Gretel. I have Hagar sometime referring to those beds as little Goldilocks's bed. So it's a signal for me that they are out . . . of their . . . of where they really should be . . . they are thinking of something wrong, they are outside of their history, so to speak. They are pulling from another place that's not going to feed them. The whole Goldilocks thing is an association with the relationship of those three women in that house, and it's supposed to jar. But the people who are connected to the Afro-American tradition or the African tradition are generally the ones who are the wholesome track. So I use Western tradition in order to signal something being askew.

Q: You have a lot of myth-making names, like Milkman, which comes through a kind of legend?

TM: That's the way nicknames are received. [Black people] don't just hand them to you, they wait until you do something that they think represents something. Grownups give them to children, children give them to each other. Milkman got his based on somebody watching that which was going on [his mother suckling him while he was ten years old]. Interesting. In a sense it fingerprinted him. Until he matured, he was dependent on it. The women did everything for him, until he finally grew up.

Q: Is this in the tradition of Black American writing?

TM: I don't—I hope it is—I don't write that way. I don't look back and see what A, B, C, and D did, and decide that I'll do it. I don't work that way. I know the tradition; it's some way that I cannot articulate.

Q: And you were not influenced by Zora Neale Hurston?

TM: I didn't read Zora Neale Hurston until after I'd written *Song of Solomon*.

Q: Really?

TM: Really. I read one short story.

Q: There is such a similarity in both of your works.

TM: In what way?

Q: The style, nicknaming, for example, as a theme . . .

TM: I'm glad because I have since read her and admire her.

Q: There seems to have been with the emergence of your style a return to a former style of writing, bypassing Richard Wright's style. Do you agree?

TM: There are a couple ways of doing it. I remember hearing people screaming, back in the sixties, that we need our own myths, we have to make our own myths, that was Baraka's cry. Well, I think indeed some of us have done that, but I didn't make any, I just tried to see what was already there, and to use that as a kind of well-spring for my own work. Instead of inventing myths, which is a certain body of work which black writers are in fact engaged in, I just didn't do that, I was just interested in finding what myths already existed. There already was a Margaret Garner, there already was a myth about flying Africans. If you go to the Georgia Sea Islands, you hear it all the time. It's all in the narratives of the slaves. The tar baby story is a black story that they invented, I didn't, I used it as a springboard out of which to say something which I thought had contemporary implications, but I didn't invent those stories and I have too much respect for black people's imagination to suppose I can invent something for them. We have always done it. It's just the way in which I can employ them. You know, it's not unusual. Joyce uses the Ulysses myth and people use other things. I just use the ones that already exist, and I appropriate them for texts and characters. When I was

writing *Tar Baby*, I used the characters from the story, the Rabbit, the white
farmer. The reason the white man is in there is because of the white farmer in
the original tar baby story. If he wasn't in the story, he wouldn't be in the
novel. The same thing with *Song of Solomon*. I'd always heard that black people could fly before they came to this country, and the spirituals and gospels
are full of flying, and I decided not to treat them as some Western form of
escape, and something more positive than escape. Suppose they were about
the whole business of how to handle one's self in a more dangerous element
called air, learning how to trust, to risk, and knowing that much about one's
self to be able to take off and to surrender one's self to the air, to surrender
and control, both of those things. That's what that myth meant to me. So
I never go outside of my sources never, never.

And I think that kind of writing is what I'm interested in. It's not to say
that there are not other kinds of writing that are important or more important, but I can only do what I do. That's what fascinates me.

We have already invented so much art. It's just lying there to be picked up
and used and shined and cleaned and there is so much of it that above the tip
of the iceberg has been plundered by black writers, women or men, and there
is so much territory to cover that it seems a pity that critics are describing
what other writers ought to do. That is really painful to be told as a writer
what to do by another black person.

The reason it's so painful is that I thought that the reason those children
had their brains shot out in the street was that people could say what they
wanted to say. And if it wasn't any good it would fall by the wayside. It would
just deconstruct.

Q: Do you find this in the writing of Baldwin, Ellison, Wright?
TM: Ellison does it a bit, not in a large sense, but in terms of families.
Invisible Man opens with the grandfather giving him life-lines, so to speak, a
quotation that would guide him through his life. So he is relating to this
more local myth. Baldwin just looks at the Western myths and deconstructs
them. He looks at Chartres [in *Nobody Knows My Name*] and it's not
Chartres any more. It's somebody else.

Q: Is this a new mode in writing?
TM: It's only mine. I don't think anybody else is much interested in it.

Q: In *Sula* there is kind of fairy tale fantasy and the structure of the book is like a fairy tale with a moral and all. Justice?

TM: Recognition? Yes, my books usually end on a note of epiphany in which somebody learns something about his or her situation as a result of having had the book, which is what novels do.

Q: Any relationship to the fairy structure?

TM: I hate to say that, because that suggests another tradition which I am not interested in—fairy tales—but I am interested in folklore, black folklore, and the end of *Sula* and most of my novels are very much like folktale endings. It's open-ended folkloric tales, sort of open-ended; they don't close and shut the door, which is like the Western tradition, where the moral is—click!—locked up. But in African folktale, the people often say, "You end it," "What do you think?" It's a more communal response.

Q: It invites the reader in?

TM: That's right. And that's what I structure them on, not on fairy tales, which usually have happy endings, optimistic ends, and everything is back replaced properly. I don't do that.

Q: Folk mythology, black folklore—is it conservative? Does it prevent the community from danger? Is it cautionary?

TM: Some of it's cautionary, some of it's prophetic. But the main point is that it's generally discredited. And people think it's simple and simple-minded and not progressive. I think they see it that way because they don't look at it.

In most folklore, there is a lot of hidden gold, a code that may not be easily read; for that reason white people have discredited it. We are a discredited people in their view. And black people discredit it too because they are more interested in what white people think. I have never bought that; it was never discredited to me.

Q: Does this suggest a new, fresh way to look at literary language?

TM: For me it does. Because the strategist I employ is fed by that place, the repetition, a certain structure, the sense of color, the absences, the spaces around the words—all of this is like a call and response thing to me.

Q: Do you think some black male critics have misinterpreted your work because they have a narrow view of our own folklore?

TM: I don't know what that is. There are certain desires in reviews that reflect what the reviewer wants the book to be. I have heard from certain white reviewers that the servant in *Tar Baby* would never do that, that he would never take over that house like that. Now this means they don't want him to. I've read reviews in which Paul D. [in *Beloved*] is regarded as too sweet, too nice. That's because they are used to the slobbering, unloving black man in fiction I guess. So that if you get a person who is strong and tender, they think that character is unreal because they don't know any black men that way, they don't know any strong black men who are not tender, not feminized, but tender, complex in that way.

There are similar desires I recognize in black reviewers, that's their agenda. So when I read reviews, I can tell. It's a risk to write a book because you can reveal all sorts of faults and things, you can be disliked, but also, the same risk is true in the reviewer's text. You can see that he wants it to be about something else. I used to get a lot of criticism because I didn't have any white people in my books. After *Sula*, all the women were mad at me because *Song of Solomon* was about men. And the white people said this book is faulted because there ain't no white people in it. Then my next book, *Tar Baby*, in which I put white people, for my reasons, not for theirs, they said, "Oh, she just put some white people in it!" So that's their agenda! I can't be worried about that! I don't write a novel like a stew, and add ingredients to please other people. It has to have its own integrity. Some work for some people and others don't. When I do five books, you know, some are liked by some people and others by others . . . that's what I do. I read everybody's books, some I like, some I don't. And that's the way they relate to my work and that's how it ought to be. I decided that I wanted to have a career, which means that I want to write books that I want to write, and I have to be permitted to write books that some people don't like. A painter can paint pictures that somebody doesn't like, or a musical can do that. Somebody was telling me that they heard somebody at Suggs [music club in New York] and he was just terrible and the record was awful, and I said, "Are you gonna abandon him?"

Q: Realism doesn't play a part in your conception of the novel?

TM: Realism, yes, but not in that sense. There are a lot of ways to touch realism. It's not documentary, that's not my style, my style is very much in

the line of . . . uh . . . [a long pause]. . . . it's aural [she spells a-u-r-a-l]. It's
visual, it has a sound, that's what I work toward, a place where the reader
can come in, like a congregation, or like an audience at a musical concert,
where they participate in it, and I have to make it open enough so that they
can. You can't be handing out these messages, black people don't buy that
stuff, they buy it for a little while, but not for long. I know when I'm being
hustled and being told this is this and this is that. I don't want to be that
programmatic. I don't know about rich black people, but I know about
poor black people because I'm [laughter] . . . I come from poor black
people. . . . I was a poor black girl, and so we had to get very cunning in all
this, right?

Q: Uh-huh!
TM: And it would require an awful lot of information. So we were not easily
manipulated. So I don't want to patronize black readers. Because I'm one of
them. I want to know as much about what I'm doing as a basketball player.
He doesn't patronize anybody.

Q: Stanley Crouch's review saw your novel as belonging also to the genre of
holocaust novel. To compete with who-suffered-most—blacks or Jews?
Comment?
TM: It's a misunderstanding, but it's more pernicious than that. The game of
who suffered most? I'm not playing that game. That's a media argument. It's
almost about quantity. One dead child is enough for me. One little child in
The Bluest Eye who didn't make it. That's plenty for me. I didn't want to write
about slavery because I didn't think I had the staying power. I didn't believe I
could stay in that world for three or five years, however long it took. But I
think the publications which are interested in that are the ones that
Mr. Crouch works for. They are interested in it.

Q: Skip Gates also measures your success in terms of quantity [*New York
Times Book Review*] when he says Toni Morrison has written five novels—four
more than Richard Wright.
TM: He could have introduced other authors, James Baldwin, for example.
Or, Ralph Ellison, who wrote one magnificent novel. He shouldn't even be
required to write another one, if he doesn't want to. It should be about quality and not quantity. That's what I hate about those arguments about how

many. It's the quality of the book that I want to fail at or triumph at, but I'm not going to withhold writing books for anybody's purposes [laughter].

Q: Are white female readers more conducive to this magic-realism writing than black male readers?
TM: I don't know. I seem to have a lot of black male readers very devoted to my work. Enormous, from what I can tell. People who don't like your work, they don't write you letters. But the people I see, generally, like my work. When somebody doesn't like my work, they just don't want to be bothered with me. I'm that way too. Politically, I'll write a politician a letter in a minute, if I don't like him. But if I don't like a person's book, I don't tell him so; so I just dismiss it. I generally only see people who are curious about my work.

But about the gender conflict among black writers, men and women, as I told you before: I guess I should take it very serious since it seems to come up a lot. But I'm not sure that conflict is not being manipulated from some-where else, outside. We [black men and black women] are subject to manipu-lation, particularly since we are all subject to time and space on the air. And certain kinds of things make good copy. It would make good copy if black women writers began to talk about each other, but we just don't do it at all.

Q: Why don't you?
TM: Because most of us—at least the six or seven I know—are unwilling to participate in a capitalistic search-and-destroy mission that white people fre-quently get black people into. And I refuse to stay on that level. They think in terms of ladders: number one, number two, number three . . . a rank and hierarchy. It looks like a palette to me, and all of them are doing something important. I do this little bit over here, and that person is doing that over there. But I am very different from other black women writers and they are very different from me. It seems to me if you could compare Duke Ellington to Louis Armstrong or Carmen MaCrae to Mahalia Jackson, it's all black in a different style, different solutions.

Q: Why do they do it to black male writers?
TM: They do it themselves. Black men . . . they are males . . . they like to win. They want to know who is on top. They want to be recognized by white men as the best. I can't understand why. They're not talking to each other, they're

not talking to me. So who are they talking to? Those pieces that rank our books are not instructional. They are not going to change the way I write because of somebody's review. It has no relevance in terms of my work. It has some relevance to talking to some white people and some black men and saying "See, what's happening to me and to us." It's like that line I was telling you about the wife getting a letter from a woman that says, "Lady, your husband has been cheating on us!" [Laughter]

I have not seen and cannot think of any black female writer who is interested in being taken up by the white male power structure. I don't know one, not one. And I know them. Because I know the sacrifices they have made and turned down, in order to get their work done. And it has been to their advantage to do it for publicity. I have not done it.

Q: James Baldwin never did it either. Nor has Ralph Ellison.
TM: No, they never did it. And I don't think it's fair to say that black women writers who are getting a lot of publicity are doing it. They are not. That's a cheap shot. Gayl Jones doesn't do it, Gloria Naylor doesn't do it. Paule Marshall doesn't do it.

Q: Michelle Wallace?
TM: Has she written any fiction? She is a journalist and journalism is persuasive. It sets up different criteria. What does Gwendolyn Brooks care about the white male? And I know Alice Walker doesn't do it, as far as white men are concerned, but you are suggesting that she plays to white women? And I cannot answer that, I don't believe it, and the evidence that you have is that Gloria Steinem has been very serious about promoting her. They were colleagues because Alice was her consulting editor on *Ms.* magazine. What magazine was in the position to do that? *Essence* didn't do it.

Q: Do you see this as a media hype?
TM: That's right. It's a media hype. *Ebony* didn't do it. It's sort of sweet that anybody did it.

Q: In *Song of Solomon*, Guitar says, "everybody wants the life of the black man," and in *Tar Baby* this same kind of speech is given by Jadine, that everybody in the world is concerned about the black man. What is your feeling about the position of the black man?

TM: I think [laughs] there's a lot of energy that white people devote to black men. Guitar says, "White women love him. White men love him and so on" because they are always busy doing something about him. They want to kill him or sleep with him, or something. He really is very seriously in the world. Sometimes he wants to be left alone, right? I mean, who needs the Klan, right? But I think imaginatively black men have captured the imagination of the world. The fact that they don't know it themselves is kind of odd, but they have captured the imagination of the world. Everybody is worried about him.

Q: Where does that come from?
TM: Because they are fabulous! They're fabulous! There ain't nothing like them on the earth! Nothing!

Q: But why do we have such a bad time?
TM: Because of that. You don't know how fabulous you are. It's like the adage goes, "If you knew who you are, you would get up off your knees!" [laughter]

Q: When I read *Tar Baby*, I felt proud of being a black man.
TM: Of course.

Q: I couldn't see how anybody could say this was a woman's book and men should not read it. I felt it could have been written by a man.
TM: It wasn't gender oriented. Oh, I like that. It was hard for me to assume that I could write about men. But I felt good about the job of writing about black men that reflected in a way some of what I feel about them, or what I believe about them. And I even think that some of my black male characters—they may not be little models of behavior—but that's not the point. They are just more interesting than anybody else. I've never met one that bored me to death and I can't say that about white men. They are just fascinating people. So I can't write about them and make them little good-goodies, just because it would be nice to have a little man in a suit that is upward mobile. I love Ajax! [*Sula*] And Milkman! [*Song of Solomon*] And Guitar! [*Song of Solomon*] I love that man more than anything. I was sorry about his little number! Son [*Tar Baby*] I thought was heaven, absolute heaven!

Q: How did you create somebody like Son—a black man who comes out of the sea?

TM: I know black men like that! I know people like that. My father was like that! My uncle was like that! Friends who are like that. And I don't have those who are not like that. If they are not like that, I don't have them. But I've known them. I have had really wonderful relationships with men—the best! And once you've been there, you don't want to truck with that other stuff [laughter]. You read my play *Dreaming Emmett*.

I must think their imagination alone is fantastic! Incredible! I don't know why they are always around here drooling. But there is nothing like black men on the globe!

Q: As the possibility for fiction or life?

TM: I mean life! All you have to do is open a door that much [she holds up her fingers] and let them in and they're gone! And you can see why white people are scared of them—they ought to be! I would be if I was a white man, I'd be scared to death!

Suppose those men were saying something important, suppose if we [black men and women writers] got together, wouldn't that be something? I don't want to go to any more Tony Brown things about the black man and the black woman. That's just something for white people to toss around and say, "Uh-huh!" I don't feel any animosity toward black men, but I know it exists because people tell me it exists, so I guess it exists. But I don't feel it. I don't feel it with my own sons. They like me. They have their little man thing but I don't bother them; they can do what they want to do. I don't want my sons to be like those people. The only unfortunate relationship I ever had with a black man was their father. But I can't blame him for not liking me. I don't like it, but what can I tell you [laughter]. But he's not the devil. He wasn't even from this country. There was some other kind of woman he wanted to be bothered with, it wasn't me [laughter]. He didn't want anybody like me running around with a big mouth. He wanted a little quiet girl, who will just shut up and do what he says. That makes sense, that's alright. It was inconvenient and problematic and painful, but I can't say he is a monster.

Q: There is no castrating woman in your prose. I didn't find it.

TM: You won't find it in Toni Cade either. Her male characters are fabulous. Those men are delicious. So I get disturbed when I see black men cut themselves down to size for some coat which some white man has cut for them. That's what I get upset about. That ain't the coat he is supposed to wear, he may not even wear a coat. But when you see them they eat up the whole place.

Q: So this question—this issue—has gotten to be a very trivialized one. You have moved beyond that.
TM: I'm not in that one. NO I'm not going to be in that one.

Q: Do reviewers and interviewers talk to you about this in your work?
TM: No.

Q: Why not?
TM: They always talked to me about easy stuff. They don't ever talk to me about what I really think; most of them come with a preconceived idea. But most of them don't ask me questions like the ones you have put to me that would lead me to say personally what my own version is, about my regard, my fascination artistically, and my awe, as well as love for black people. That stuff is not to be played with. This is serious business. And I'm not going to make choices between my sons and my brothers and some white folk. That's not a choice. I'm not in that gender fight.

Q: When you create a strong black male character, do you think you create a threat in your reader?
TM: Yes, that's right. I create a threat, and then some readers began to ask about what their roles were. They say, "How come all your black males leave home? How come they don't stay home and take care of their children?" Black and white readers ask me this. I say, "Well, what characters?" They say, "Ajax, for example." I say, "Well, he can leave home. Ulysses left home, and you all said he was a hero. But when a black character leaves home you say he is irresponsible. He might be on an adventure." I think that's one of the best things black men ever did was leave home, because they could because they knew somebody was going to take care of business. And that's alright with me. I don't have problems with that. They are always trying to force my black male characters into some kind of nuclear white family with the father, the mother, and the children, something they don't even like. The Africans had nine homes, they kept their land that way, they would have a farm two

hundred miles away with a woman and some children, many wives and another farm over there. And they could take care of thousands of miles of territory. But when you come in there and make them monogamous, they took their land because they didn't have anybody over there guarding it.

Now, I'm not saying that polygamy is the solution. All I'm saying is what the practical consequence of this is. What are they talking about, anyway? They are trying to confine Ajax to his little nuclear house. They won't even pay a mother on welfare unless she ain't got no man in the house. So I'm not befuddled by all that.

Q: What about white writers like John Updike and Norman Mailer and sexism?

TM: They don't even ask them that kind of question. They don't care. They don't say, what about this character, he didn't meet his sociological obligations, you know, if they get divorced and do mean things. Think about violence in the white media. Everybody remembers Jimmy Cagney smashing that grapefruit in that woman's face. Did anybody have a debate on television about white males being violent to their women? No! [laughter]. I've been looking at that all my life. When a black man does it in a little book called *The Color Purple*, the whites say, "Ohh!" She must be saying that all black men. . . . Look at Mickey Spillane. Look at all those white men running around beating up women in their books, or having contempt for them! Look, they talk about Norman Mailer now, but all those years nobody said a word!

Q: So sometimes they use a sociological criterion for the black writer and the literary criterion for the white writer?

TM: Yes, and that's because the black man is still on their mind. Whatever I have to say about you, or whatever you have to say about me—black man and black women—they are going to weight it with some extra-literary criterion. I'm trying to deal with the exhilaration and the complexity of black men—black men are very complex (not that women are not, I find women equally complex), but you have to weight that through. Black men, the least of them, are more complex than any man I've ever met.

And that is what I want to show. That doesn't mean that they are going to always be following some program set out by whatever the movement is at that moment. There is lots to complain about, I suppose, but I'm not so much interested in the man in the white hat as opposed to the man in the black hat. That's why I like Leon Forrest's and Henry Dumas's books so much, for in their works you get that sense of who these male characters are. I want to do my male and female characters that way, because art is like that. I'm not going to make my characters smaller than life because it's desirable and fashionable.

Q: What about your drama *Dreaming Emmett*? Do you use the same technique of subtlety to draw his character?
TM: That kid tore the place up. The whole play was about what was on his mind.

"I Come from People Who Sang All the Time": A Conversation with Toni Morrison

Sheldon Hackney / 1996

From *Humanities* (March/April 1996, vol. 17, no. 1). Reprinted by permission of the National Endowment for the Humanities.

Sheldon Hackney: I'd like to talk a bit about your view of life in the late twentieth century, basically as it comes out in your literature, which really fascinates me.

Let me ask you first, though—in *Jazz*, I take it the title comes from the structure of the narrative itself, from the way you tell the story.

Toni Morrison: I was very deliberately trying to rest on what could be called generally agreed-upon characteristics of jazz. There are so many arguments going on about jazz: What it is, when it began, who are the authority figures and who is the best, who has debased *it*. There is however agreement about some things that have been true all along. One is that jazz is improvisational; that is to say, unanticipated things can happen while the performance is going on, and the musicians have to be alert constantly. One of the reasons being that it isn't written and rehearsed for permanence on the page, and the other that there's a kind of egalitarianism in it, or meritocracy. One person doesn't dominate the whole performance—or if he or she does, he or she will have to take close, close notice of what another voice or instrument is doing or saying, and listening to the other voice may, and frequently does, affect or alter what the other voices might do or say.

Hackney: So you have various voices telling the story from different points of view.

Morrison: Exactly. No one voice is the correct one, the dominant one, the one that has all of the truth, including the narrator, or especially the narrator. I wanted to get rid of that notion of the omniscient narrative voice.

Hackney: Is that why the narrator isn't even very definite at times about what happens or what a character feels or thinks?

Morrison: I didn't want gender or age or even race or anything to be identified. I wrote it as though it were literally a book speaking, so that the verbs that I used in connection with the "I" voice would be only those things one could associate with the book. The book says things about its imagination, about its dreaming, about its yearnings and its assertion of knowledge, and then its admission at points that it was wrong. I wanted it very, very dissimilar to *Beloved*, which had a kind of classical, spiritual gospel feel, a largeness to it, which I think I could easily associate and did associate with the music during the late nineteenth century. But for the beginning of the twentieth century, I wanted that feeling of dislocation and inventiveness and startling change that was representative of those enormous migrations that were taking place among African Americans, and certainly is characteristic of the music.

Hackney: But I also notice that, as in jazz, there is a melody and there is a narrative here, a story.

Morrison: When I listen, or as anyone does, to a jazz performance whatever they're playing, you hear the melody and then it goes away or seems to, or they play against it or around it or take it off to another zone. Then sometimes it comes back and you can recognize it. I wanted that narrative line or melody to be established immediately in the first pages, and when the question becomes whether the narrator was right in his earlier expectations of exactly what the story was, that is the "melody" being taken to another zone.

Hackney: But there are surprises all the way through.

Morrison: All the way through.

Hackney: In *Jazz,* Joe and Violet do find some sort of happiness or satisfaction. I guess what the reader is called upon to do is to figure out how or why. Life is hard, as it is in all your books. Did Joe and Violet come to terms with life's imperfections?

Morrison: I think so. I think so. It's not quite as tentative as some of the relationships that I've written about. These are older people who had powerful and grief-stricken losses as young people, and in their somewhat helpless adult life in the city, which is less about the city than it is about that sort of intensity where all of the unresolved problems of their personal histories are mangled in the city. They do terrible things because they haven't sorted it out yet. But they do sort it out. There is some redemption, in a way, for them. They are not guiltless. Who is? I was surprised myself a little bit that they could look forward to that shared experience, a real conversation, and holding on. That was a little surprising, although I sort of thought maybe . . .

Hackney: Did that surprise you when it came out that way?
Morrison: Yes. I was not sure what their relationship would be. I had invented these people based on some anecdote I heard about a girl killed in 1926 at a party, who insisted on letting her ex-lover, the one who shot her, get away, and just wouldn't tell anybody who had done it, and bled to death. That seemed to me, when I heard it, since she was only eighteen years old, so romantic and so silly, but young, so young. It is that quality of romance, misguided but certainly intense, that seems to feed into the music of that period. I was convinced that that reckless romantic emotion was part and parcel of an opportunity snatched to erase the past in which one really didn't have all those choices, certainly not choices of love.

In *Beloved,* for example, or any books in that period that I make reference to, the people marry the people next door or the people on the farm or the people down the street, because they don't travel. But with the migration from the South or even to the West, one of the things that must have been an absolute thrill for the people in that period was to get somewhere where they could choose this illegal thing, which was falling in love. It meant so much because it was rare. The lyrics are all about that, the willingness to give up everything. Like the blues, too, although there are all sorts of themes and extremes in the blues.

What was interesting to me was the willingness to abandon everything for this chosen beloved. I wanted this young girl to have heard all that music, all the speakeasy music, and to be young and in the city and alive and daring and rebellious and, naturally, to get in trouble. The adults, however, have to come to terms with their own lives bereft of love.

Hackney: In that sense, Violet and Joe's being enmeshed in their own history and the problems of life stand in contrast to much of contemporary literature. In fact, they don't get away from their past, do they?
Morrison: No, not at all.

Hackney: Do any of your characters get away from their past?
Morrison: I hope not. No. I don't want anybody to get off scot-free.

I think what I want is not to reinvent the past as idyllic or to have the past as just a terrible palm or fist that pounds everybody to death, but to have happiness or growth represented in the way in which people deal with their past, which means they have to come to terms, confront it, sort it out, and then they can do that third thing. But denying it, avoiding it, and evading it is a sure way to have a truncated life, a life that has no possibilities in it, generally speaking.

Hackney: So even if it's problematic, your past is enriching.
Morrison: Indeed. I think an individual or even a country needs that. I mean, a certain kind of amnesia is just intolerable. In personal life, you have to know what happened and why and figure it out, and then you can go on to another level freer, stronger, tempered in some way. Constantly burying it, distorting it, and pretending, I think, is unhealthy.

Hackney: In that sense, your characters really are existential in that their choices make a difference in their lives and they are made to seem responsible for themselves and for their lives. Is that a conscious thing?
Morrison: Oh, yes. I sometimes think—I'm not quite sure—but I sometimes think that the experience, in large part, of African Americans in this country was classically existential. Coming here in that manner, being mixed up in that way—the deliberate putting together of people from different tribes and regions, the forbidding of marriage—all of that which was economically sound for slavocracy would dash certain traditional related cultures of their past. They're all just being thrown somewhere and having to make it up. And also, trying to hold on to those pieces that you do pass on, because there were large blocks, sections, of knowledge that were passed on, maintained, kept, and might disintegrate and then resurface. By and large, the desperate way in which that hanging on took shape meant that there was a lot of fragmentation. So here you are with certain kinds of choices, constantly fighting for more, and having to do it rather quickly.

Hackney: One of the other things that one notices in reading your work is that your characters do live with their past always. They live in history, but not in a self-conscious way, as Faulkner's characters frequently are quite self-conscious about history with a capital *H*. You know, Quentin Compson thinking about Pickett's charge.
Morrison: Yes. They do historicize themselves.

Hackney: Yours don't, but clearly they're in the flow.
Morrison: They play a very interesting power game, you know, Faulknerian characters, brilliantly intricate American forays into the past or the failed maintenance of the past.

The past for my characters, I believe, is—I was going to say more intimate, but I don't mean intimate. Why don't we put it this way: I understand that in many African languages there is an infinite past, and very few, if any, verbs for the future, and a major string of verbs for the continuous present. So that notion of its always being now, even though it is past, is what I wanted to incorporate into the text, because the past is never something you have to record, or go back to. Children can actually represent ancestors or grand-mothers or grandfathers. It's a very living-in-the-moment, living now with the past, so that it's never—calculated; it's effortless. Sometimes that causes a great deal of trouble to some of the characters.

Hackney: Part of the problematic in your stories is coming to terms with that.
Morrison: Oh, exactly.

Hackney: Would you go so far as to say that that sense of the presence of the past is taken from black English's use of the present tense, frequently, for events in the past?
Morrison: I've been told that, and I've read books on so-called black English in which children, for example, who come to the first grade are confused by standard English because it has only two present tenses. Whereas black English, I am told, has five or six present tenses, some of which involve space and time, some recent time, some longer time, and so on. It's a very interest-ing way in which the verbs are understood to be constructed. I am unwilling to commit on that because I don't trust people who talk about black English who don't know African languages.

Hackney: I share that.
Morrison: It's a fascinating subject, but black English has along with it some devotees who I think are misguided because they want to teach it or make it a secondary language. I think all the people who speak it know it and don't need to be taught, and its formalization seems to me to have some other agenda.

What is certainly true is that the language we speak in this country and, I know, the language spoken where there are a large number of black people all over the world alters in some very fascinating, interesting ways. It was my intense desire to capture the vernacular, the lyric, the sermonic—all these layers of English that play about in the way African Americans speak.

Many people have tried to grasp that in literature, and usually they do it in a way that I find very offensive. They just make it ungrammatical, or earlier they used sight spelling, just changed the spelling to something nobody could possibly read at all. Remember George Bernard Shaw was trying to represent cockney for about two pages, and then he gave it up in *Pygmalion*—it was sort of like that, but I think writers understood there was something going on in the speech of black Americans. I know there's something going on, but I try to represent it in choice of metaphors, rhythm of the sentence, the kind of image that would surface in order to say something theatrically. For certain people with a certain kind of education, obviously the language would be nonstandard, but I try to blend colloquial vernacular and standard. Then, as in my family, when something terribly important was to be said, it was highly sermonic, highly formalized, biblical in a sense, and easily so. They could move easily into the language of the King James Bible and then back to standard English, and then segue into language that we would call street. It was seamless, and this was extremely attractive to me to hear. Just listening to my great-grandmother, whom I knew, and my grandparents and my uncles and my mother and father and all their friends, it was fascinating, and it was quite different from street language.

I became sensitive to languages very early, not just in school, but because I grew up in a steel town where there were so many immigrants, East European and Irish, European, Italian, all sorts. It was very much a mixed bag because it was in the thirties and because there was a steel mill there. It attracted all sorts of people. It's strange, but I take it for granted people now don't believe such places exist much.

I was in Barcelona two years ago and I met a man from Lorain, Ohio, who was in the diplomatic corps. We were at a party, and we were talking about the way things were back then. Nobody at the embassy—Americans or the people from Barcelona—understood what we were trying to say. I don't know if the experience is unusual or the representation is all that unusual, but the racial and ethnic mix was so tight and so unhostile, and there were no black neighborhoods. I mean there were wealthy neighborhoods but all of the poor people, which we were—the workers—lived next door to each other. Of course, they went to different churches, and so on, as adults. Even now I think of the names of the people who live next door to my mother's house. It's quite different from the media stereotype. It's the way I thought New York City was, and it isn't.

Hackney: It is not. Right.
Morrison: It is not.

Hackney: In Lorain, though, despite the great heterogeneity in the backgrounds, there was something that everyone shared, apparently.
Morrison: There was. We all shared the small space, one high school, three junior high schools, these totally dedicated teachers, poverty, and that kind of life.

Hackney: Was the language part of that sharing? Language is very important to you.
Morrison: I have to think about that a little bit, because there was a certain exchange of language also.

I remember being a reader in the sixth grade for what they called then "partially sighted," I guess, people who were blind. I used to read for one or two of those students after class, and I got very excited about the kinds of questions they asked.

Also, I used to be put next to children who couldn't speak English. I remember in the second grade, there were some children from Italy, and, of course, children pick up language very quickly. I would be selected frequently to read and talk to them. So when you say language sharing, that immediately came to my mind because of those exceptional circumstances in the classroom. At the same time, there was a lingua franca of the town.

However, groups did retreat socially, in terms of their family lives, into certain enclaves. But the public space of the schools, of the PTA, of the workplace, of the shopping place, of the neighborhood, of the streets, belonged to all of us.

Hackney: I'm going to leap a little bit now, because that strikes a familiar chord. One of the projects that I'm most interested in now is something we call the National Conversation on American Pluralism and Identity, which is a project that's seeking to bring together millions of Americans to talk and to listen to each other about what they share amidst their heterogeneity. Are there any common commitments? One of the things that comes up in these discussions frequently in the small heterogeneous groups that get together and talk about this, is the notion of public and private—basically, that there is a public sphere, not just a governmental sphere, but a public sphere in which Americans seem to want to be able to come and be just American, in some sense, where everyone comes as an undifferentiated individual. But they also want this other sphere where they can honor their particular heritage, their particular identity, and they want both at the same time.
Morrison: They should have both.

Hackney: I believe that also.

Morrison: I think that's very important. You said not necessarily government space, but what shot up in my mind was that monument down there, the Vietnam veterans' wall.

Hackney: Yes, yes. Terribly moving.

Morrison: But there's a serious problem about public space that seems recent to me. It's as though our public space is being privatized so quickly. Here we have—here meaning New York City—there are fights about the parks, there are fights about the streets, there are fights about all sorts of public spaces. These are class problems.

Hackney: Right.

Morrison: Severe class problems. And because there are so many dispossessed homeless and itinerant people, it fosters grave, truly grave problems.

I find architects to be particularly annoying these days, well, I don't mean annoying. In trying to develop public space, they think of it as an enclave for a certain kind of public person. I say—I have a son who's an architect—I say, "You know, if you were given all the time and all the money, could you design a city that could accommodate the poor people?"

Hackney: That's a wonderful challenge.

Morrison: They can't even think of what it would look like, except as in Paris—where all the Algerians and poor people live outside the city in tenements hidden behind the trees. It leaves a city without any sense of being urbane, because you don't confront anybody. You don't see anybody. You don't mix in that sense. Now, it's true, the crowd's flow in New York is like that, but it's so unusual to share public space without hostility. Bryant Park, next to the New York Public Library, is a sensation because it was redesigned to do precisely that: offer beautiful unhostile space to all sectors of the public.

Hackney: I saw you quoted somewhere saying that as long as the children of poor people are thought of as "them," we would have a problem in this society.
Morrison: Very much.

Hackney: I believe that also. One of the tasks is getting to "us" somehow. That comes back to your sense of community, which is there in the novels. Is that consciously a big part of your view of life?
Morrison: Oh, yes. Being one of "them" for the first twenty years of my life, I'm very, very conscious of all—not upward mobility, but gestures of separation in

terms of class. Community, for me, is extremely important, not in the sense of there is a community that has to be maintained at all costs the way it is or was, but that communities offer some very positive things and they offer negative things. The tension is between the community and the individual always. It seems to me that one builds a community, also.

When I first moved to New York, my family was alarmed because they said I had no family here, meaning there was no one who felt responsible for me here. They were very upset with my coming here.

Hackney: Is that your definition of community, people who feel responsible?
Morrison: Exactly. When I walked down the streets of Lorain, any adult could stop me or tell me, "Take that lipstick off"—and I would have to respond.

Hackney: Yes, yes, right.
Morrison: So even though I was in my thirties, my mother was alarmed. I said, "Let me have this one year, and if I can't do it, I'll come home." But she did find somebody, a very, very ancient man who was like a tenth cousin. He could hardly walk. She felt relieved that he was here. I was so tickled with that.

But here, I found what she said was true: I needed people who felt responsible. So what I had to do, along with some other people, was make a community. Now, that meant not the people on my street necessarily or on my block, but the people nationally, if not globally, the people that you could count on. If a friend's child was in trouble, I could say, "Send her to me." Or if my children needed respite from me, somebody would say, "Send them to me for a week," or a summer, or what have you. Or they would just appear under times of stress and clean house and go to the market. I relied heavily, of course, on my family. I went home a lot, and my children spent the summers there. It always amuses me a little bit when people say, "You reared your children alone," meaning you were separated or divorced, because I don't know many women who really do that if they have a family.

Hackney: No one rears a child alone.
Morrison: No. It's just not possible. Even two parents isn't enough.

Hackney: You need a village, as the saying goes.
Morrison: That's right.

Hackney: Going back to your statement just a second ago about the tension always between the community and the individual—it must be true. What the community gives the individual is an identity, a place, a certainty. What it sometimes demands is a loss of choice, though.

Morrison: Oh, yes. Their demands are sometimes repressive.

I remember, as a teenager, walking down the street in Lorain, and somebody came up to me and said, "Are you a Willis?" which is my mother's maiden name. And I said, "Yes." And he said, "I thought so. You walk like one."

Now, when I moved to New York . . .

Hackney: Nobody said that.

Morrison: People said, "What do you do? What job do you have?" But the place where somebody has some notion of what a Willis female walks like is entirely different. That kind of comfort of being recognized for those things that are—you know, I didn't even know what a Willis walk was—but it's a kind of comfort that I wish everybody had.

At the same time, I was very, very interested in getting out of there.

Hackney: Opportunity was elsewhere.

Morrison: Was someplace else, right. Also, how could I know what that community was and how valuable it was if I had not left it?

Hackney: So, as modern men and women, as we make the trade-off between a community in which you're known for who you are, and in a modern community where you're known for what you do, is our fantasy replacing that sense of community where you are, who you are, rather than what you do?

Morrison: I think we have settled and resigned ourselves, in large part, to the latter so that people want to be known for what they do, and that becomes their only identity. That is who they are. You are your job, you are your position, or you are your clothes. If it's not possible in very poor communities for this to exist, then they feel that isolation or that absence so profoundly that people do unbelievable things. When you hear about young people stealing icons—I call them icons, you know, jackets or shoes.

Hackney: Right. Nike shoes.

Morrison: Yes. What on earth is that about? It really is a symbolical acquisition of "I am this" in a country that, on the one hand, offers wide, inconceivable freedoms, but at the same time seems to be training consumers rather than citizens, so that we are asked to value ourselves, certainly in the media, by what one can accumulate or what one can show. In order to do that, one's interior life must be hollow, truly frail.

Hackney: These attempts to buy an identity are acts against being made anonymous—aren't they?—being just shoved into the mass. Maybe that's also American individualism demanding that we be individual somehow.

Morrison: Both things, actually. The public persona . . . Having a public self first before you have a private self is what is alarming, although it is true that the people who came voluntarily to this country were trying to forge a new identity, erase all the terrible things of the so-called corrupt, classbound life of the Europeans. This was a clean slate, as it were. The only thing that mattered was one's back and one's inventiveness and opportunity seized. That is part of the national characteristic. Now it's exacerbated, I think, by a reluctance to believe that anything is real if it's not publicly stamped. Therefore, the easy purchase of an identity has wended its way through all strata of the population.

Hackney: That's true.

I saw also somewhere in one of your interviews that you made an interesting distinction between creativity and entertainment; it sounds like it's connected here.

Morrison: It seems very obvious to me which is which, but it's hard to articulate it. I think something that is created, that is either intentionally or consequentially created, is something you can find new things in the second, third, or fourth time around.

With entertainment, you can repeat that performance or repeat one's access to it, but it closes at a certain point. It closes and leaves no echoes. It moves along in that context I was talking about, dance and music among African Americans. The singing and the dancing that I remembered was not limited to entertainment; it was a kind of meditation. I know that it's true in my own family because I come from people who sang all the time. It was a kind of talking to oneself musically.

Hackney: Sustenance for the mind and spirit.

Morrison: Yes. I could even hear the different ways that my mother would sing a song, whether it was classical or spirituals or whatever, depending upon what was on her mind. It wasn't just to make herself feel better. It was also a kind of probing into something and then working it out in addition to whatever release it provided. It had a great deal to do, actually, with my feeling that writing for me is an enormous act of discovery. I have all these problems that are perhaps a little weary and general and well-worked-over that I want to domesticate and conquer. Then I can sort of figure out what I think about all this or get a little further along.

Hackney: You don't know what you think until you've written it.
Morrison: Right. You know, when you bring the dramatis personae into it, all sorts of debates and arguments and positions and stages of growth come into play. I sometimes am surprised. It's a way of sustained problematizing for me, writing novels.

Hackney: Well, have you discovered the meaning of life? What is the meaning of life?
Morrison: I think only one thing about life; it is certainly original. That's about all I know about it.

Hackney: The life of your characters is always full of problems.
Morrison: Oh, yes.

Hackney: So, life is tough, but redemption is to love and nurture. I'm inferring from your characters.
Morrison: I regard the problems as part of the excitement of living that original life, which is not to discredit grief. But the mind is designed for that alone—problem solving, the acquisition of knowledge. That's all it does. And if we don't acquire healthy knowledge, we acquire some other kind. But the brain is never not doing something. Our instinct should be and is to find out about the unproblematic life, which I suppose is in some ways desirable when you think of what the nature of certain problems can be but it is not food for a novelist, not worth talking about.

The man who goes back and forth across the lake every day without consequence is lucky. But it's when he sinks that the novelist steps in.

Hackney: Ah, yes. Fortunately, reality is on the novelist's side here. There are very few lives that are unproblematic at some level.
Morrison: At some level. That's true.

Hackney: But yours are problematic in history, which is why they're so gripping.
Morrison: I'm glad to hear you say that—gripping—because I want the narrative to be compelling. People who don't like what I write are frequently depressed by all these hard-going situations in them and complain bitterly about the tests to which my characters are put. I keep saying over and over

again, "No, I'm not saying my work is representative of one's typical life, but it is about something that is serious." I hope there is some humor.

I am interested in who survives, what form redemption takes, and I'm very open in the endings because I don't like the closure that means I, as a writer, know all the answers, even though I certainly do. But I like the reader to participate in this debate, in this dialogue.

Hackney: Yes. Fill in the blanks.

Morrison: Yes. Fill them in. What do you think? What would you like? Of course, if it's worth reading again, you might want something else later.

Hackney: That's right. But even the reader then is, when filling in the blank at the end, constrained by what you've already written.

Morrison: By what I've written and what I've left out. Also, the reader's baggage, what we bring to a book.

I love reading some books over and over and over again at different times. I change, they change. Nothing remains constant in those extraordinary books that you know you would never like to be without. I wanted that to be a bit more deliberate.

Again, what you mentioned earlier is very much to the forefront in *Jazz*; that is, in forcing the reader to like the music, the music of jazz itself. If you're listening to it, it forces you to appreciate its artifice and to linger on its invention and to recognize how well practiced the performer is. It doesn't wholly satisfy; it kind of leaves you a little bit on edge at the end, a little hungry.

Hackney: It certainly does.

Morrison: That sort of absence of tying every final knot—I mean, I'd like to tie all the narrative knots, but there's a quality of mystery in the books that I recognize and underscore.

Hackney: And you leave the possibilities there.

Morrison: Very much so.

Hackney: Well, thank you very much for such a fascinating glimpse of the artist in search of redemption amidst the realities of life.

Toni Morrison

Zia Jaffrey / 1998

From *Salon.com* (February 2, 1998). Reprinted by permission of Zia Jaffrey.

I met Toni Morrison at her apartment in SoHo. She hung up my coat and offered me a drink, and we settled in for a conversation. I was immediately aware of the gentleness in that room—her listening presence. Morrison's seventh novel, *Paradise*, had just been published by Knopf, and throughout our talk her phone rang continually with news—from her son, her sister, a friend—of the reviews the book was getting. An unhurried and thoughtful speaker, she took it all in stride. *Paradise*—which opens with the startling sentence "They shoot the white girl first"—involves the murder of several women in the 1970s by a group of black men, intent on preserving the honor of their small Oklahoma town; they see the women as bad, a wayward influence on their moral lives. It's an intense, deeply felt book that easily ranks with her best work.

Toni Morrison was born in Lorain, Ohio, in 1931. She attended Howard University, then received a master's degree in English at Cornell University, where she wrote a thesis on William Faulkner. Her first novel, *The Bluest Eye*, was published in 1969, followed by *Sula* in 1973. Then came *Song of Solomon* (1977), which won the National Book Critics Circle Award for fiction, *Tar Baby* (1981), the play *Dreaming Emmett* (1985), and *Beloved* (1987), which received the Pulitzer in 1988. Her novel *Jazz* appeared in 1992, and in 1993 Morrison was awarded the Nobel Prize for literature. Last year she was the co-editor, along with Claudia Brodsky Lacour, of a volume called *Birth of a Nation'hood: Gaze, Script, and Spectacle in the O. J. Simpson Case.* An editor at Random House for many years, Morrison now teaches fiction writing at Princeton University.

ZJ: Do you read your reviews?
TM: Oh, yes.

ZJ: What did you think of Michiko Kakutani's strongly negative review of *Paradise* in the *New York Times*?

TM: Well, I would imagine there would be some difference of opinion on what the book is like or what it meant. Some people are maybe more invested in reading it from a certain point of view. The daily review in the *New York Times* was extremely unflattering about this book. And I thought, more to the point, it was not well written. The unflattering reviews are painful for short periods of time; the badly written ones are deeply, deeply insulting. That reviewer took no time to really read the book.

ZJ: You don't feel you need to protect yourself from listening to critics?

TM: You can't.

ZJ: You need to know what's being said?

TM: I know there are authors who find it healthier for them, in their creative process, to just not look at any reviews, or bad reviews, or they have them filtered, because sometimes they are toxic for them. I don't agree with that kind of isolation. I'm very much interested in how African-American literature is perceived in this country, and written about, and viewed. It's been a long, hard struggle, and there's a lot of work yet to be done. I'm especially interested in how women's fiction is reviewed and understood. And the best way to do that is to read my own reviews, for reasons that are not about how I write. I mean, it doesn't have anything to do with the work. I'm not entangled at all in shaping my work according to other people's views of how I should have done it, how I succeeded at doing it. So it doesn't have that kind of effect on me at all. But I'm very interested in the responses in general. And there have been some very curious and interesting things in the reviews so far.

ZJ: *Paradise* has been called a "feminist" novel. Would you agree with that?

TM: Not at all. I would never write any "ist." I don't write "ist" novels.

ZJ: Why distance oneself from feminism?

TM: In order to be as free as I possibly can, in my own imagination, I can't take positions that are closed. Everything I've ever done, in the writing world, has been to expand articulation, rather than to close it, to open doors, sometimes, not even closing the book—leaving the endings open for reinterpretation, revisitation, a little ambiguity. I detest and loathe [those categories]. I think it's off-putting to some readers, who may feel that I'm involved in writing some kind of feminist tract. I don't subscribe to patriarchy, and I don't think it should be substituted with matriarchy. I think it's a question of equitable access, and opening doors to all sorts of things.

ZJ: Because the book has so many women characters, it's easy to label.
TM: Yes. That doesn't happen with white male writers. No one says Solzhenitsyn is writing only about those Russians, I mean, what is the matter with him? Why doesn't he write about Vermont? If you have a book full of men, and minor female characters—

ZJ: No one even notices. No one blinks that Hemingway has this massive problem with women.
TM: No one blinks at all.

ZJ: Many of the male characters in *Paradise* have severe problems. I was wondering if you yourself identified with any of them as morally strong characters?
TM: I suppose the one that is closest to my own sensibility about moral problems would be the young minister, Rev. Maisner. He's struggling mightily with the tenets of his religion, the pressures of the civil rights, the dissolution of the civil rights.

ZJ: And he's worried about the young.
TM: And the young. He's very concerned that they're being cut off, at a time when, in fact, he probably was right, there was some high expectations laid out for them, and suddenly there was a silence, and they were cut off.

ZJ: He's like Lev in *Anna Karenina*.
TM: Right.

ZJ: Struggling with the moral—
TM: He's not positive about all of it, but he wants to open up the discussion. He wants to do this terrible thing, which is listen to the children. Twice it's been mentioned or suggested that *Paradise* will not be well studied, because it's about this unimportant intellectual topic, which is religion.

ZJ: *Paradise* has also been called a "difficult" book.

TM: That always strikes me—it makes me breathless—to be told that this is "difficult" writing. That nobody in the schools is going to want to talk about all of these issues that are not going on now.

ZJ: Do they say that about Don DeLillo's *Mao II*, because it involves cults?

TM: No, there's a different kind of slant, I think. Different expectations. Different yearnings, I think, for black literature.

ZJ: You mean, they want you to step into what they've already heard?

TM: And say, once again, "It's going to be all right, nobody was to blame." And I'm not casting blame. I'm just trying to look at something without blinking, to see what it was like, or it could have been like, and how that had something to do with the way we live now. Novels are always inquiries for me.

ZJ: Did you have any relationship to the word "feminism" when you were growing up, or did you have a sense of yourself first as black and then as female?

TM: I think I merged those two words, black and feminist, growing up, because I was surrounded by black women who were very tough and very aggressive and who always assumed they had to work and rear children and manage homes. They had enormously high expectations of their daughters, and cut no quarter with us; it never occurred to me that that was feminist activity. You know, my mother would walk down to a theater in that little town that had just opened, to make sure that they were not segregating the population—black on this side, white on that. And as soon as it opened up, she would go in there first, and see where the usher put her, and look around and complain to someone. That was just daily activity for her, and the men as well. So it never occurred to me that she should withdraw from that kind of confrontation with the world at large. And the fact that she was a woman wouldn't deter her. She was interested in what was going to happen to the children who went to the movies—the black children—and her daughters, as well as her sons. So I was surrounded by people who took both of those roles seriously. Later, it was called "feminist" behavior. I had a lot of trouble with those definitions, early on. And I wrote some articles about that, and I wrote *Sula*, really, based on this theoretically brand new idea, which was: Women should be friends with one another. And in the community in which I grew up, there were women who would choose the company of a female friend over a man, anytime. They were really "sisters," in that sense.

ZJ: Do you keep the company of female writers? Do you find a need for that?
TM: I really have very few friends who are writers. I have some close friends who are writers, but that's because they're such extraordinary people. The writing is almost incidental to the friendship, I think. It was interesting to me that when books by black women first began to be popular, there was a nonarticulated, undiscussed, umbrella rule that seemed to operate, which was: Never go into print damning one another. We were obviously free to loathe each other's work. But no one played into the "who is best." There was this marvelous absence of competition among us. And every now and then I'd see a review—a black woman reviewer take another black woman writer, a critic usually, on—but usually it's in that field of cultural criticism. Because it was always understood that this was a plateau that had a lot of space on it.

ZJ: Have you noticed a change in the intelligence of the criticism of your books over the years?
TM: I have. Over time, they've become much more intelligent, they've become much more sensitive, they've given up some of the laziness they had before. There was a time when my books, as well as everybody else's books, were viewed as sociological revelations. Is this the best view of the black family, or not? I remember once, in the *New Yorker*, being reviewed, I think it was *Beloved*, and the reviewer began the review and spent a lot of time talking about Bill Cosby's television show—the kind of black family to be compared with the family in *Beloved*. It was so revolting. And that notion—once I was reviewed in the *New York Review of Books*, with two other black writers. The three of us, who don't write anything alike, were lumped together by color, and then the reviewer ended by deciding which of the three books was the best. And she chose one, which could have been [the best], but the reason it was the best was because it was more like "real" black people. That's really discouraging. So if you have that kind of reduction to the absurd, you just have to keep on trying.

ZJ: Do you see a place for gay literature, Indian literature, black literature, black women's literature—in a positive way?

TM: Oh, absolutely. It's changing everything. They may take longer; the marketing shapes how we understand these books. Some Native American writers enjoy being called Native American writers. I had a student who was Native American and I told him, "You're going to have trouble getting this book accepted, because there are no moccasins, there are no tomahawks." And he did. He had enormous trouble. I mean, submissions, I don't even want to repeat the number, but he finally did have this book published, and you know, it's a first novel—it got excellent reviews—but the point was that the rejections, I know, were based on the inability to think of Native Americans, in this particular case, as Americans.

ZJ: You teach writing at Princeton. Can writing can be taught?
TM: I think some aspects of writing can be taught. Obviously, you can't expect to teach vision or talent. But you can help with comfort.

ZJ: Or confidence?
TM: Well, that I can't do much about. I'm very brutal about that. I just tell them: You have to do this, I don't want to hear whining about how it's so difficult. Oh, I don't tolerate any of that because most of the people who've ever written are under enormous duress, myself being one them. So whining about how they can't get it is ridiculous. What I can do very well is what I used to do, which is edit. I can follow their train of thought, see where their language is going, suggest other avenues. I can do that, and I can do that very well. I like to get in the manuscript.

ZJ: How did you juggle being an editor, being a writer, and being a mother?
TM: When I look back at those years, when I was going into an office every day, when my children were small, I don't really understand how all that came about. Why was I doing all these things at once? Partly, it was because I felt I was the breadwinner, so I had to do everything that would put me in a position of independence to take care of my family. But the writing was mine, so that I *stole*. I stole away from the world.

ZJ: So when did you write?
TM: Very, very early in the morning, before they got up. I'm not very good at night. I don't generate much. But I'm a very early riser, so I did that, and I did it on weekends. In the summers, the kids would go to my parents in Ohio,

where my sister lives—my whole family lives out there—so the whole summer was devoted to writing. And that's how I got it done. It seems a little frenetic now, but when I think about the lives normal women live—of doing several things—it's the same. They do anything that they can. They organize it. And you learn how to use time. You don't have to learn how to wash the dishes every time you do that. You already know how to do that. So, while you're doing that, you're thinking. You know, it doesn't take up your whole mind. Or just on the subway. I would solve a lot of literary problems just thinking about a character in that packed train, where you can't do anything anyway. Well, you can read the paper, but you're sort of in there. And then I would think about, well, would she do this? And then sometimes I'd really get something good. By the time I'd arrived at work, I would jot it down so I wouldn't forget. It was a very strong interior life that I developed for the characters, and for myself, because something was always churning. There was no blank time. I don't have to do that anymore. But still, I'm involved in a lot of things, I mean, I don't go out very much.

ZJ: Who is Lois? Your book is dedicated to Lois.
TM: My sister. The one who just called [laughter].

ZJ: Who's your editor at Knopf?
TM: I have two editors.

ZJ: Erroll McDonald and Sonny Mehta?
TM: Yes. You know, I had an editor, Bob Gottlieb, for all my books through *Beloved*. Then he went to the *New Yorker*. I had to find an editor. And everybody said, "You don't need one, do you?" And I said, "Yes, because I used to be one. I know the value of a good editor." I mean, somebody just to talk to. Bob was very good at that. I learned a lot, just in the conversations. He's funny, he's literate and really able to tell you things—it's not so much writing in the margins of the manuscript, but . . .

ZJ: Macro-thinking?
TM: That's right. And so Sonny followed him at Knopf—whom I like a lot, who is terrifically smart about books and publishing. But he was the president of Knopf. Bob Gottlieb was also the president, but he was the only president that also edited manuscripts, who line-edited. Sonny doesn't do

that. I mean, he shouldn't do it. Most presidents don't do it. But I wanted
someone who . . .

ZJ: Would have that capacity . . .
TM: That's right. So they said, "What combination do you want?" Even
though Erroll McDonald works at Pantheon.

ZJ: So Erroll is your actual editor?
TM: He's my . . . yes. My lines. I have no hesitancy about his abilities at all;
he's extremely good, oh man, and he's read everything, he can make connections. And he monitors the book in-house, you know, to see what people are
doing—you know, the covers—the fabric and paper and all of that really
important stuff. *Jazz* was pretty much complete when I engaged this dual edi-
torship, so he had less to do with that. With *Paradise*, I was able to send him
the manuscript, say, when I had a hundred pages, and get some feedback on
it. So the levels of intensity have been different because I've submitted the
manuscript under different circumstances.

ZJ: So did he actually line-edit the full manuscript, or is it hands off on the
fiction?
TM: What he does is write me long, interesting letters. And the letters
contain information about what's strong, what's successful, what troubles
him, what stands out as being really awful, that kind of thing. Which is what
you want.

ZJ: You have stated, I think it was in the *Times*, that there was still work to be
done, you realized, on *Paradise*.
TM: I regard them all that way, all those books I've written. Years later, I read
them, or read them in public, and say . . .

ZJ: "Should have done that . . ."
TM: Or "Should not have done this," or maybe, you know, this line. And it
goes on forever.

ZJ: In terms of *Paradise*, what is your personal assessment of—
TM: Of what I could have done? I wanted another kind of confrontation
with Patricia, the one who kept the genealogies together.

ZJ: Yes, which she burns at the end.

TM: And some of those young women. You know, like Anna. She has a confrontation with Rev. Meisner—but you know about her, what they think about her, but she has a very subjective view. She's the daughter of someone whom she felt they despised, so she has an ax to grind. So she's reevaluating everything, and has come to learn some terrible things, she thinks, about this town.

ZJ: A friend said to me, "Why don't you ask Toni Morrison what makes her really angry?"

TM: You know, I've lost it [the anger]. It's a very, very strange thing. I was telling someone this summer that I felt some [turning point], and I didn't know what it was, you know. It's because I've lost the anger now—and I'm feeling really sad. And that seemed so sad to me. Really sad to me. Now, I did get angry recently, about this daughter [in the book]. And I hadn't felt that furious about someone who isn't in my personal life. Because I get angry about things, then go on and work. And today I was a little angry about Justina.

ZJ: Justina?

TM: Justina was that little girl whose mother helped the lover kill her.

ZJ: Oh God. In the *New York Post*, yes.

TM: And the part that reduced me to just smoldering anger was when she says she held her hands, as she was drowning.

ZJ: That was just the most horrible detail.

TM: And I dwelt on it, and dwelt on it, until I was in a state. Yes, I really wanted to write about her, the child. So I get enraged about something like that, but generally speaking, I guess it comes with being over sixty-four, you just get sort of melancholy.

ZJ: Melancholy—meaning you're resigned, or passive, in your responses?

TM: It's overload. You sort of struggle to do four good things when you're my age, and then not deal. I even tell my students that: four things. Make a difference about something other than yourselves.

ZJ: What are those four things?

TM: That I do?

ZJ: Let's say, in the last year?

TM: Well, I think the book is one, [my teaching] is another, and the other two, I don't want to talk about.

ZJ: Can we talk about O. J. for a second? [Morrison laughs.] What about this notion of "black irrationality"?

TM: The story of the case is a marketable story. And that story is made up of black irrationality, and black cunning, and black stupidity, and the black predator. That's what the story is about. So if you take black irrationality out of it, you don't have a story. Black men in particular, and black people in general, are supposed to be able to do opposite-ends-of-the-scale things, and we don't have to make sense. We've always been considered to be irrational, emotional, lunatic people. So if you have someone that was accepted in the mainstream world as exactly the opposite of that, the threat that one may fall back into chaos is always there. That's not just in this case. It was just played out theatrically, although it's true in almost everything—narratives, stories, about black men in particular. So what concerned me was not even what my little hunches were . . .

ZJ: But your hunches, you have written, were that he was innocent.

TM: Absolutely. I have never been more convinced of anything than that, precisely because of "motive" and "opportunity." Forty minutes.

ZJ: Forty minutes. You mean, how could it be done in that short a time?

TM: Well, I'm sure that, scientifically, it could be done, but it is truly irrational. Truly almost impossible.

ZJ: Physically impossible?

TM: It's not impossible.

ZJ: You mean there had to have been two people, or something like that? What is your theory?

TM: I have no theories.

ZJ: He had these dream-team lawyers, and they never even bothered to—

TM: No. They decided to just get him off, and not produce an alternate—a television show would have found the guilty party. But that's not the way the legal system works. But the rest of it is, you know—there was a lot of money involved in that case. People got jobs, whole industries started up. Every issue surfaced in it. I think sometime we'll know a lot about it.

ZJ: The kids—I don't understand how they heard nothing.
TM: They heard their mother crying.

ZJ: But then they heard nothing afterwards, with this violent thing, and the dog barking . . .
TM: No, it's a very intricate, strange case. He's not very helpful himself either, in clarifying much. But my feeling about it was sort of like . . . you know, like when prostitutes can't be raped in court, because, well, they're prostitutes. It's that kind of thing. If you're going to be specific, and try to find out if someone did this thing, that's what you ought to do. Part of the reason that the truth never emerged was not just the success of the defense team, but the media's layering on. All these other issues were layered into this.

ZJ: Here's a different question: Whose work, among contemporary authors, do you rush out and read?
TM: Hmm. I follow Márquez. I read anything by Márquez. Peter Carey is someone I've read off and on, but now I've become devoted to. I read Pynchon. I buy those books, list price. And who else? Jamaica Kincaid has a new book out that I haven't read. I love her work. I relish her work. It is incisive and beautiful at the same time.

ZJ: Do you want to get remarried? I mean, did your marriage change your thinking about the notion of marriage?
TM: No, I like marriage. The idea. I think it's better to have both parents totally there, and delivering something for the children. Where it's not preferable is if that's all there is, if it's just a mother and a father. That's an isolated horror. I would much rather have a large—a connection—with all of the members of the family, rather than . . . Because, usually, marriage, you think, that little atomic family, which I deplore. But I learned a lot in marriage, in divorce. I think women do. They don't know that they do. I remember sitting around with some friends, all of them who had either been divorced, or separated, or on second or third marriages, had had that in their lives—some collapsed affair. And I said, "You know, I suspect that we all talk about that as a failure. But I want you to tell me, what did you learn? Wasn't there something

really valuable in the collapse of that relationship?" And they began to think, and I did too; and they said extraordinary things. One woman said, "I learned how to talk. For the first time, I learned to talk." And another woman said, "I learned high organizational skills. See, I was a mess, as a young woman, you know, keeping house," and her husband was worse. So, to stay in the house together, she had to really get it together. The skills that she now uses all the time. So I said, you know, we should stop thinking about these encounters—however long they are, because they do not last—as failures. When they're just other things. You take something from it.

ZJ: What, for you, was a lesson?

TM: I learned an enormous amount of self-esteem. Even though the collapse of the relationship suggested the opposite. For me, I just had to stand up. When I wanted a raise, in my employment world, they would give me a little woman's raise, and I would say, "No. This is really low." And they would say, "But . . ." And I would say, "No, you don't understand. You're the head of the household. You know what you want. That's what I want. I want that." I am on serious business now. This is not girl playing. This is not wife playing. This is serious business. I am the head of a household, and I must work to pay for my children.

You can't always explain [divorce] to the children. My children were, you know, accusatory. They were teenagers. Now, of course, they're delightful people, whom I would love even if they weren't my children. But when they were young, five and six, they didn't understand what this was about. And I never, never, ever spoke ill of their father, ever, because that was their relationship. And I wouldn't do that. You know, maybe I was wrong. I didn't want to put that burden on them. I didn't want them to choose.

ZJ: When raising your sons, did you try to protect them or guide them through the racial issues that they would encounter?

TM: No, I failed at that. Miserably, in fact. One of my kids was born in 1968. I thought they were not going to ever have the experiences that I had. I mean, there were going to be political difficulties, obviously, the haves and the have-nots, and so on. But they were never going to have that level of hatred and contempt that my brothers and my sister and myself were exposed to. Or, worse, my mother. Or worse, her mother. That it was all getting better. Not perfect, and not even good, but that at some level they wouldn't have that. I was dead wrong.

ZJ: Because the 1980s came along . . .

TM: And black boys became criminalized. So I was in constant dread for their lives, because they were targets everywhere. They still are. I mean, if you can find police still saying they thought a candy bar was a gun, or they thought whatever they thought—things that would never be coherent if they had shot a white kid in the back. Could they tell those parents, "It looked like a gun to me, but it was a Mars bar"? It's just surreal. So that is what they are prey to. And I just couldn't fathom it, for years and years and years. That it was *that* bad. I knew it was really bad, but I didn't know it was that bad.

ZJ: Did either of your sons go to Howard, where you went?

TM: One did go to Howard. In architecture. Didn't like it. Thought it was not the best place for that. It was a personal decision about the school of architecture. But they were not averse to going to places like that . . . Unlike me, they were focused on where's the best school for what they wanted to do, rather than on the sociological myths, and so on. I appreciated that. But a very close friend of mine, Angela Davis, has known them since they were children. The kinds of women that I had as very close friends were very independent women, very progressive, so they grew up amongst those kinds of women. So they have a different feeling; they're very sensitive about social change, and so on. But what I didn't know was just how, on a day-to-day basis—step into an elevator, and everyone gets out . . . I just couldn't have imagined. If I had raised them earlier or later, I would have said, "Now look, this is what you do." And I would say things like the things my father would always tell me, "You don't live in that neighborhood."

ZJ: You don't live in that neighborhood?

TM: No, you don't live in that imagination of theirs. That's not your home. What they think about you . . .

ZJ: The reality that they think you are, you are not.

TM: That's right. You are not.

ZJ: He told you that? That's amazing.

TM: He was wonderful. He was very insightful. Go to work, get your money, and come home.

ZJ: He was a welder, right?

TM: Yes. So . . . That helped me, because I always looked upon the acts of racist exclusion, or insult, as pitiable, from the other person. I never absorbed that. I always thought that there was something deficient—intellectual, emotional—about such people. I still think so, but I didn't communicate it to my children enough. I think they have suffered. And being male, too. They' re competitive, they feel it in a different way. Maybe as a woman you get so used to being abused and dissed, that . . .

ZJ: You just think, "I'll shut this out."

TM: Right. I'm not even going to deal with that one. But they don't do that.

ZJ: They deal with it.

TM: They try. And it causes them, I think, more pain than it did me.

ZJ: My stepfather, who is black, recently said he would advise young black men to go into therapy. It's helped him come to terms with prejudice. I thought it was interesting.

TM: That is interesting. Because I used to complain bitterly that psychiatry never considered race. I remember saying that, you know, in the moment when you first realize you're a boy or a girl or your toilet training is this or whatever—all these little things that happen in your childhood—no one ever talks about the moment you found that you were white. Or the moment you found out you were black. That's a profound revelation. The minute you find that out, something happens. You have to renegotiate everything. And it's a profound psychological moment. And it's never talked about, except as paranoia, or some moment of enlightenment. It's just as devastating on white children, I read in those novels all the time. Those moments when you found out you were white. In Lillian Hellman—any of those Southern writers—the moment when black and white children play together, and then there's a moment when that's all over, because they can't socialize together. And then the white child, sometimes it happens with their nurses.

ZJ: It's like: I love this person, and then, boom, she's gone.

TM: And now this person is gone. Then you don't trust your instincts. You mean, I loved something unlovable? I loved something that's not really among us? I mean, the trauma of that is interesting to me. And I mentioned it in a lecture once, and some psychiatrists asked me to lecture further on the subject. And I said, "No, you ought to be thinking about it."

ZJ: I read recently that you once suffered a terrible house fire. Did you lose manuscripts? What happened?

TM: Oh, *I remember that*. It was my house up in Rockland County. It was just a routine, stupid Christmas fire, in the fireplace, with the coals and the pines smoldering. The wreaths, you know—the detritus, the dried needles were around on the floor and not swept up. And the fire leaped to one of those and leaped to the couch, where it smoldered, and no one knew. I wasn't there. One of my kids was there. And by the time he got downstairs, it was shooting through the roof. So he called the fire department, but it was a terrible winter, and the water was frozen in the pipes. And I lost . . . I write by hand . . . I was able to save some books, but I had all my manuscripts, notes from old books, in my bed-room on the second floor, in a little trundle underneath the bed, where there was some storage space. It went up first. I said to somebody later, "Why did I think that having those things near me was safer than having them in the basement?"

My manuscripts, I didn't care, I mean, I'm never going to look at that stuff again, so that wasn't the hurtful part to me. They had a value, I think, to my children. As an inheritance. But I know I would never look at that stuff again. I would never look at *The Bluest Eye*—seven versions, in hand, of it—again. So I was not that upset about that. Other people might be interested in that. For me, it was the pictures of my children and of myself. Family. And I have nothing. Everything's gone. So, I'm sorry about my children's report cards, I'm sorry about my jade plants, certain clothes.

I also had first editions of Emily Dickinson, first editions of Faulkner—I mean, all the stuff that you just hang on to. Only about thirty or forty books, but they were all marked up. I had a Frederick Douglass—not the first edi-tion, but a second edition, done in England. And letters, over the years. Whatever there was is gone. It's just the wrong place to store stuff. No excuses. The house burned. I lost a lot of stuff.

ZJ: Have you ever been to Africa?
TM: No.

ZJ: Do you have an urge?
TM: A big urge, yes.

ZJ: Do you think it's an important journey for black Americans, in general, to make?

TM: I don't know. We romanticize it so much. But maybe so, for that reason. Because we're so easily drawn, you know, into the myth of—whatever—a history—a useful little test story. And I want to go to Senegal, because I've been invited there by Ousmane Sembène, and I'm desperate to go. And now, South Africa, I've gotten a number of invitations there.

ZJ: Right at this moment, it's like watching 1776, but with black people deciding.

TM: That's something I'm determined to do, because now, I'm hoping I can really make the trips, you know, that are not research trips or whatever else I've been doing all my life. But you just go, sit there and watch, and look, and talk.

ZJ: I was there writing a piece on the Truth and Reconciliation Commission. I was there for the Winnie Mandela hearing. Do you think it's finally shifted so that people can acknowledge that, look, things went horribly wrong with Winnie Mandela, and maybe we ought not to embrace her?

TM: A South African woman, who was very close to Mandela, asked me, "Why do black Americans feel close to her?" And I was quite taken aback by her question, because she was very enabling and ennobling to black women in this country when she came, and she has endured things that are unspeakable. And it was only after that that I began to wonder whether there was some clouding over the eyes—deliberate and willful. It's very difficult among many women here, professionally, to say anything derogatory about Winnie Mandela. Anything. I don't know what I think about her. I have enormous—frankly, enormous—admiration for Winnie Mandela, but it's based on her legendary past. And when she came here and I saw her, she's terrific, she's just magnetic. And then when I hear other kinds of things from Africans, or South Africans in particular, I have to fold that into my equation. So now I am curious, very curious, about what is the truth. I mean, what is the real person?

Of course, Nelson Mandela is, for me, the single statesman in the world. The single statesman, in that literal sense, who is not solving all his problems with guns. It's truly unbelievable. Truly.

Conversation: Toni Morrison

Elizabeth Farnsworth / 1998

From *The NewsHour with Jim Lehrer* (March 9, 1998). Reprinted by permission of MacNeil/Lehrer Productions.

Elizabeth Farnsworth: Novelist Toni Morrison, who has received the Nobel and Pulitzer Prizes, is on the bestseller list again this month with her new novel *Paradise*. It's set in an all-black Oklahoma town called Ruby, population 360. It's a place with a complicated history, going back to slavery and haunted by incidents of prejudice among ex-slaves, themselves. It's also the story of a former convent just outside Ruby, where a group of women gather to heal their broken lives and in the process seem to threaten Ruby's very existence. Toni Morrison's first novel, *The Bluest Eye,* was published in 1970. She's also the author of *Sula, Song of Solomon,* and *Beloved,* among other works. She teaches literature at Princeton University. Thank you for being with us. Is Ruby a place that's based in history? There were all-black towns in Oklahoma formed by ex-slaves, weren't there?

Toni Morrison: Absolutely. It's my invention of the all-black town that might have lasted until now, until at least the '80s. It's based on towns that did exist and some that are still there.

Farnsworth: And did you come to the idea through reading the history of those towns and reading about the migration of slaves from Louisiana or Mississippi to Oklahoma?

Morrison: Part of my idea came precisely from that research and thinking about that whole period when ex-slaves, freed men, left plantations, sometimes under duress because Southerners frequently wanted them to stay, but managed to take advantage of the land that was offered in places like Oklahoma and to build whole towns, churches, stores, banks, many houses. And some of them are still there to see.

Farnsworth: Explain the idea of separation. It's almost a utopia that's built in Ruby. It's very separate, and in some ways I felt that the book was a meditation on this idea of separateness. This is a place, after all, where nobody dies until the end of the book. Tell me about that, about the separateness.

Morrison: The isolation, the separateness, is always a part of any utopia. And it was my meditation, if you will, and interrogation of the whole idea of paradise, the safe place, the place full of bounty, where no one can harm you. But, in addition to that, it's based on the notion of exclusivity. All paradises, all utopias are designed by who is not there, by the people who are not allowed in.

Farnsworth: And am I wrong to consider it a meditation on the dangers of exclusivity? This was a place that was very beautiful in some ways but very dangerous in others.

Morrison: Well, isolation, you know, carries the seeds of its own destruction because as times change, other things seep in, as it did with Ruby. The '50s, that was one thing; the '70s, that was another, and they refused to deal with the changing times, and simply threw up their gates, like any gated community, to keep everything away. And, in fact, that was the necessary requirement for the destruction of their paradise.

Farnsworth: Ms. Morrison, is there something in African-American history that makes you especially interested in this separate place?

Morrison: Yes, because only American—only African-Americans were not immigrants in this rush to find a heaven. They had left a home. So they're seeking for another home, while other people are doing the same thing, except the other people were leaving a home that they didn't want to be in any longer, or couldn't be in any longer. Native Americans were being moved around in their home. African-Americans were looking for a second one and hopefully one that would be simply up to them, their own people, their own habits, their own culture, and to contain themselves in that. So it makes the motive for paradise a little bit different.

Farnsworth: Then there's the convent outside of Ruby, which is another sort of paradise, at least that's the way it seemed to me.

Morrison: Yes.

Farnsworth: Women—Ruby's ruled by men, the convent is all women, and there's this dichotomy: The convent that is ruled by women who have been hurt and the town that's ruled by men. Tell us, how did you think about that dichotomy and come to that idea?

Morrison: Well, Ruby has the characteristics, the features of the Old Testament. It's patriarchal. The men are very protective of their women, very concerned about their role as leaders. The convent, as it evolves, becomes a kind of crash pad for some women who are running away from all sorts of trauma, and they don't seek the company of men. They have been hurt profoundly by men, so that even though they quarrel and fight most of the time, they're in what they consider a free place, a place where they don't have to fear that they are the people to be preyed upon, but the values are different. You have a very profound Protestant religion in Ruby, and you have something that verges on magic that is non-institutional religion in the convent. The values are entirely different. The women are examples of the '70s. And the conservative black community is affronted and horrified by that.

Farnsworth: Would you read the first couple of paragraphs from the book for us from the book.

Morrison: I'd be happy to. "They shoot the white girl first, but the rest they can take their time. No need to hurry out here. They are seventeen miles from a town which has ninety miles between it and any other. Hiding places will be plentiful in the convent, but there is time, and the day has just begun. They are nine. Over twice the number of the women, they are obliged to stampede or kill, and they have the paraphernalia for either requirement— rope, a palm leaf cross, handcuffs, mace, and sunglasses, along with clean, handsome guns."

Farnsworth: I was struck by this for many reasons, but that first line, "They shoot the white girl first," I have read the whole book, and I don't know who that was. And I imagine you did this on purpose. It doesn't matter what color the girls in the convent are. Was that your point?

Morrison: Well, my point was to flag raise and then to erase it, and to have the reader believe—finally—after you know everything about these women, their interior lives, their past, their behavior, that the one piece of information you don't know, which is the race, may not, in fact, matter. And when you do know it, what do you know?

Farnsworth: How do you work? What are the rituals for getting started? To me, this book is almost in a different consciousness. It's like at a high level of kind of poetic prose. How do you get yourself there?

Morrison: Well, I try to write when I'm not teaching, which means fall and most of the summer. I do get up very early, embarrassingly early, before there is light, and I write with pencil, yellow pads, words, scratchings out, but, you know, long before that, I've spent a couple of years, probably eighteen months, just thinking about these people, the circumstances, the whole architecture of the book, and I sort of feel so intimately connected with the place and the people and the events that when language does arrive, I'm pretty much ready, I don't have to discard so much.

Farnsworth: What is next for you now? Your books have plumbed the history of African-Americans in this country. Do you plan to stay—to keep writing about that?

Morrison: I don't know. I have no ideas now. I am about to fall into a very dark melancholy if something doesn't happen soon.

Farnsworth: You kind of wait until the ideas come to you.

Morrison: Yes.

Farnsworth: Well, thank you so much for being with us.

Morrison: You're welcome.

Loose Magic: A. J. Verdelle Interviews Toni Morrison

A. J. Verdelle / 1998

From *Doubletake* (Summer 1998). Reprinted by permission of A. J. Verdelle.

My hands-down flat-out literary hero has always been James Baldwin. I have adored him since before I understood the word "adore." His boldness and directness and wide-eyed pursuit first offered me the gift that language is mine. But the sad truth of history is that heroes get snatched. And so where my living hero once wrote and thought and spoke aloud, now there's only a memory, and a thundering shelf of books.

Second to Jimmy, I have loved Toni Morrison. Not knowing her personally, I really loved her work. As a young reader, I swallowed library books whole: I knew the fiction shelves and the E185 section as if those books belonged to me. Among them, I read Baldwin's *Beale Street* and his *Another Country*, and then not long after, Toni Morrison's *The Bluest Eye*. Morrison's first book ricocheted into the crass race debate in the early seventies. Much as it has diminished now, blue-eye envy lived fresh as fish then. Writing was scarcely a thought in my mind.

Toni Morrison changed my life twice. The first time was when, graduating from Baldwin, I cut my teeth on *The Bluest Eye*. A character named Cholly lives in this first book. Cholly, in literature, mirrored the experience of one child in America, a she who happened to be me. This dialect spelling acknowledges a certain ear; reveals a loving proximity, care, concern, true wit. C-h-o-l-l-y. This considered, determinative spelling finally privileged a maligned kind of speech. "Charlie"—a name I had forever read—had associations both plain and pernicious. "Cholly"—a name I had forever heard—I had never before then seen. This little studied Cholly placed me in the narrative's geography. By its own fictive omniscience, the book elevated my

Cholly, my neighbor down the street. Through this one little care, among a million novelistic cares, Morrison zoomed in on my personal landscape, swept up my neighbors, their names, their concerns.

The second time Morrison changed my life, I was a big grown woman, like now. I had already published my own first book when Morrison stepped into my life in person, a great mind's authority in a veteran's high boots. Morrison pronounced my first novel a book she "really loved." *The Good Negress* took off then, at Morrison's lofty urging. The book I had so carefully scripted would now be read for sure. It was rare like magic, this book endorsement, this great good fortune.

I admit that once or twice I harbored reckless fantasies that my literary hero, the one living one, might see my book sometime and like it—find in it reach, effort, mettle, grit. But I never believed it would really happen. Morrison found my little book, for certain, though what she found in it, I haven't had the grit to ask. Before I had the chance to meet her, Toni Morrison saved me from the sinkhole of literary obscurity, from the blinding white void of the many books written, but neither bought nor read.

The first time I saw Toni Morrison up close, she was flush with the heat of stage lights, New York City, summer 1995, Lincoln Center for the Performing Arts. Toni Morrison, Max Roach, and Bill T. Jones collaborated on a performance piece called *Degga*—a Wolof word, a West African ancestor of the expression "Dig it?" which means something like, "Do you understand?"

Morrison entered the stage seated at her own lectern, equipped with a pedestal and a decorative spiral stair. The dancer, Bill T. Jones, had crossed the stage on his knees, wheeling her out. Morrison sat reading upon the pedestal, not one jolt in her husky voice. Her entrance was very dramatic. Max Roach and his drums sat high up on scaffolding. Bill T. Jones danced between them, fashioning an illusion of a little staged family: young Bill, father Max, mother Morrison. Father Max, in a rare moment, contributed a vocal number. But the rarest moment of all was when Bill T. partner-danced with Morrison. She took to the wide stage in her bare feet. Three geniuses, one stage, daring, dauntless details: the drummer's singing, the dancer's parents, the writer's naked feet.

No magic or foretelling forewarned me that when *Paradise* was published I'd be watching in the wings. I knew her book was being finished, her publishing plans being laid. Last July on one of my visits to see her, we talked about the coming August, the four unfinished chapters at the end of the book: an unusual turn in the writing process for her, by her own acknowledgment. Now on the plus side of a million hardcover copies sold, has *Paradise* renewed the public life of literature? Is the complex book revived?

Paradise coils around questions of good and reward, evil and comeuppance, theocracy and kingdom. Big questions, to which the Morrison imagination responds: *the prisoner wine; rose madder and umber; blossom and death; shriveled tomato plants; land flat as a hoof, open as a baby's mouth; language made especially for talking to heaven: ora pro nobis, gratia plena; adding a half-starved baby to their own quarter-starved one; the mutiny of the mares; the young thinking of elsewhere, the old full of regret.*

We think that questions twin with answers. To think otherwise is to be transgressive, revolutionary, or at the very minimum avant-garde. To say *the question has no answer* is heresy, hard to get away with, an idea for the mature. In *Paradise, the text will not answer the question.* You should know that going in.

Maybe for the first time in all her books, the magic in Morrison's latest novel is "explained." Ideas, events, and visitations that seem like pure fancy, like nonsense or like leaping invention, are in fact fundamental to how paradise is defined. When I asked about the difference between the new and the old, Morrison reported that her earlier books had "loose magic." She is right: the magic in *Paradise* is tight. Morrison writes about Candomblé, about the Catholic Church, about people having sightings that they themselves call up. Men do the unthinkable, women whisper or are silent or run away.

In *Paradise*, Morrison fashions an oven where the whole town cooks. A testament to places built and left and reestablished. The crisis of *Paradise* happens in a coven. Inside an old convent on the outskirts of town, women hide and sequester themselves, trying to live, to survive. The men in *Paradise* cannot understand them, so they fell the women, failing themselves, hell-bent on making prey. In *Paradise*, Morrison makes two brothers identical. After a whole lifetime, one looks at the other and finds he doesn't like himself. This transformation happens in an instant. A panoramic story with a wandering eye, *Paradise* rides the wave of an undulating climax in this little death, this instant shift of self-regard.

In *Paradise*, race goes in one sentence from its usual state of ultraprivilege to nothing, silence, annihilation. Much of the talk about *Paradise* has to do with its one mention of race, a subject which never rises again. To nullifying the race signifier, I only say, *Olé*. Unlace race from the fictional fabric. Strike the nasty words. Build a new kind of story, a short-order heaven. Scratch the words that mean evil that also mean black.

There are greater states of grace than race.

Once I visited Morrison at her office at Princeton, in a gray stone corner of the quad decorated with gargoyles and fleurs-de-lis. I brought the British edition of my book, which is not called *The Good Negress* as it is here, but is titled more poetically, *This Rain Coming*. (The British behave more delicately, they believe, about race; and so, this title difference, poetry in a race signifier's place.)

The little brown girl on the cover of *This Rain Coming* looks so much like all of us here, between these shores. She shocked me then and still gives me pause; this little girl recalls the diaspora, the historic separation, which resemblance discredits in its own aggressive way. I inscribed this book to Morrison: "This little girl lives in England, and she wanted to come and be by you." Morrison looked at the book, read my little note, and said in reply: "I'm going to England next week; I could meet her."

The tiny secret hopes we harbor hardly make a difference in this huge, unwieldy, postmodern world. Every blue Monday, when I'm feeling daft, I get the trepidations about trying to be a writer in Morrison's time. In the wake of her sprawling mysticism, her well-turned history, her elaborate language, her flat-footed faith, my words seem thin as consommé. But when I come to my senses, the daft day's done. I accept my "youngish" forays. I stop time and consider what a hero I have.

A. J. Verdelle: You've said on a number of occasions that you write your novels from a question. Was there a question that informed your writing of *Paradise*?

Toni Morrison: The question was two-pronged, and the two parts didn't seem to relate to one another at the beginning. The first part was, how do fierce revolutionary moral people lose it and become exactly what they were running from, that is, destructive, static, preformed? I was thinking about certain African Americans in the public scene who had abandoned and changed their political beliefs over the course of thirty or forty years.

Everyone says that happens as one ages, that such passions are only the passions of youth. And that as one grows older, one gets more conservative, even repressive. That's always been the shibboleth for everyone.

AJV: It's always been the—what's the word?
TM: Shibboleth. A kind of saying, an inaccurate or generalized observation about the passage of time.

On the other hand, youth is for fervor, romance, positions of high morality, and complaint about social injustice. As you grow older, you are perhaps dissatisfied with the social order, but you begin to appreciate the stability of the past. You don't like change; the young are threatening. I wondered what that process was. It wasn't true for so many people who—even if they're not as active as they once were—have nonetheless stayed the distance and remained as fierce in their moral positions, in their passions for justice, in their understanding of who the enemy really was. They never wavered from that. So, I was interested in exploring the difference between the young and the old. That was the question.

The associative question became how the fight for social justice or for the good life when one is young is a struggle for a kind of paradise where everything will be the way it ought to be. Is paradise the manifestation of the vision that you had when you were young? If you're an African American, what does paradise mean and what are the threats? The book became for me an interrogation of paradise, of the idea of paradise.

AJV: Is it possible that the political and moral shifts that people experience as they age also have to do with feeling certain about what they know? You know, how older people sort of feel like, I've been through history, I've learned from history, even though the lessons of history might not fit the present time.
TM: Yes. And when that certainty of knowing is not accompanied by constant learning, you reach a plateau at a certain age—it can be at forty, or it can be at eighty. And for some people that may seem enough. It's true in every discipline that after thirty years of education most people really don't want to learn anything new, because you've spent years solidifying, clarifying, analyzing, coming to terms with all of the knowledge that comes from experiences you had. So, to constantly learn and change is frightening to some people. You may remember that there was a complaint in *Paradise* that these

people have wonderful stories to tell about their fathers and their grand-fathers, and nothing to say about themselves.

AJV: Right.

TM: They have nothing themselves to pass on. And that is when you freeze history, and you simply just pass it off as preformed, already made, already understood, already furnished. And that kind of history is valuable, but it's not porous. If it's not porous, if it doesn't translate, then it is a museum piece.

AJV: You've said that history can be toxic if you don't understand it.

TM: Yes.

AJV: What do you mean by that?

TM: You can romanticize it to such an extent that you cannot join the modern world. You can find it so overwhelming and so frightening and so wicked that you can't separate yourself from its wickedness—say slavery, for example—so that you feel sullied and stained and incompetent and hurt all of your life. So there's kind of a negotiation that has to take place between one's self and one's national past, one's cultural past, one's personal past, and one's racial past.

AJV: These questions that you've talked about give rise to a number of themes that I found while reading the book. I made a tiny list of them.

TM: Oh, good, it got very complicated for me!

AJV: Well, I don't know if I got them all right. But let me just run quickly through them and you tell me if I covered the most important things. One being the search for home. How we make home. How we have families or choose our families. That's one.

TM: Certainly.

AJV: Then there's another, related theme about how we incorporate theology and spirituality into our lives. A third one would be the way communities often dread and suspect newcomers. There's the newcomer group of people who migrate west in *Paradise* and then there's the newcomer group of the young people.

TM: All of them were newcomers.

AJV: Right.

TM: Their history was the history of the newcomer, over ten generations. And then when they finally reach this place, it's the newcomer that they fear—the very thing that they were and are.

AJV: The fourth theme we were just talking about, the conflict that arises between older people and younger people. And then, five, I have the passage of time. What gets retired. What gets introduced.

TM: Yes.

AJV: So, did I miss anything?

TM: A big one.

AJV: What is it?

TM: Race.

AJV: And what about race is thematic in this book?

TM: Or maybe I'm wrong. Maybe it's not thematic. But what the book invites the reader to do is to examine, recognize, hold onto, or dismiss, the racial baggage, which is frequently cultural baggage, that a reader brings to a character. I say and flag "race" in the first sentence of *Paradise* and never mention it again as far as the newcomers go. The reader only knows that of those four women, one of them is not black. One of them is white. But the language of the book refuses to identify which one she is. The text will not answer the question.

So I'm interested to know whether it matters to the reader. I'm interested to know if it ever matters, or when does it stop mattering? And I was mightily interested in the language you have to create in order to not signal race. You think automatically if a person's race is not mentioned that they're white. All the others are flagged, either by skin color or some cultural code. To refuse to do that was in some ways daunting for me, and also I felt crippled—the language was crippled—because I couldn't take those shortcuts anymore. I had to say something else about a character or nothing or probe into some other places. I had a reader of the book very disturbed about that. He felt cut off in some way, blinded somehow. He felt as though he didn't have some critical information.

AJV: Because you didn't mention race again?

TM: Because he didn't know which of the girls in the convent is black or is white. Is it Seneca? Mavis? Gigi? Or Pallas?

AJV: Why is the question of race worth resisting, or why is it worth pursuing?
TM: It's a question of freedom, writing anything you want any way you want
in order to say several different things. I want to be able to write highly
marked, black language with black characters steeped in black culture. I want
to be able to write about the wild differences among black people, and very
much in this last book, *Paradise*, I was concerned about the variety among us.
We're so generally understood as *the* black woman, or *the* black man, or what
have you, and it's just, you know, burdensome. So one of the ways for me to
get specifically at the differences was to have a population, a part of the book,
that is wholly unraced. I mean, the reader knows that the majority of those
women are black, they just don't know which ones. *I* know. But not signaling
race frees me up to talk about the characters in all sorts of ways—to not have
race be the only way in which they are understood.

AJV: Out of this roll call of characters in the town about ten or twelve turn
out to be major. And by chapter 3, you feel like you know who those people
are. They remind you of your family and neighbors like your cousin Cynthia,
your uncle William, your grandfather Joe, your grandmother Louise. Was this
a way of developing this notion of the everyman?
TM: [Laughter] I'm not going for that. Now, there are recognizable people
here but to me they are very specific in the distinctive ways that they look
and act and in their speech. It's the vague characters who cannot be associated with one's aunt, one's cousin, and so on. I could have made the dramatis
personae very lean, but then I would have lost what I really wanted and what
was paramount for me, which was the community, the town, and their connections. I don't know where one finds that in literature among African
Americans, although it is easily the most obvious thing about us—which is
the connectedness, the history of family and personal relations, people's atti-
tudes toward one another based on anecdotes and legends about them that
you may not have even known. And how all of that pulls into and mixes and
becomes a community. All their secrets. All their confrontations. All their
reconciliations. The hierarchy within. There is a part in the book where
someone is speculating on how Zechariah would have felt when the community was broken up. The horror for him was in having that consortium of
families scatter, because how would he then be able to know or see himself in
the grandchild? How could he recognize a family by somebody's eyes or jaw?
When I was a little girl, people would recognize me instantly—I would go

down the street and somebody would say, "Are you a Willis?" And I would say, "Yes, my mother's maiden name." And then, this particular man would say, "I thought so. You can tell by the way you walk."

When I left my hometown, that never happened again, obviously. People say, "What do you do?" Or, "What work do you do?" And so on. But nobody says, "Are you a Wofford?" Or "Are you a Willis?" as they used to. "Are you Buddy Wofford's daughter—you must be." And they know something about us, just by looking. There's a kind of comfort and thrill in that. It's also a little claustrophobic if you want to get out of it.

That security within a community is hard to describe. It has to be part of the activity, part of what they think, what they know, what they're holding against other people. So, we have to bring the readers in and let them feel as, say, Pat feels: "This town will never like me because they didn't like my mother."

AJV: There's a place in *Paradise* where somebody refers to the young people as the "young disobedients." I'm wondering how this relates to this concept you were describing as frozen history. Do we romanticize history so that the people who are dead and gone were obedient and wonderful and that's how they got things done?

TM: Yes. They were wonderful and powerful, and they got things done. Everybody did what they said. But that's the cohesion of the family. I am appalled by what contemporary young people think and do in their parents' company. It appalls me, which is not to say they should or should not be obedient. But the liberties that they are allowed to take are stunning to me. Which is to say that the quality of respect that you give to old people—not because they are right but because they are old—has dissipated. And no one probably even knows or even remembers what that time was like. Here, when a young boy doesn't even say "sir" it's like . . .

AJV: Right. It's a big deal.

TM: Yes. The novel says, "You say 'sir' when you speak to men." You do what the parent says—that's an important thing. And it holds communities and families together. In my life, there was no one who couldn't stop me, no adult who couldn't stop me and tell me what to do. And my parents relied on that. Now, you have to buy that—in baby-sitters or in housekeepers or you test your friendships with that. People today are very busy *not* getting involved in other people's affairs—certainly not their children's—and the children miss it. They want lines and boundaries. They want to know, "How far can I go, and will you catch me if I fall? And who's going to pull me aside and tell me?" Today you have to create that sense of responsibility with the big movement. The big movement, where two million appear and say, "This is what we're going to do." It was unthinkable to even have to say that in those days. All these various millions. Million women. Million men. And there'll be another million.

But that's interesting. It's all spectacle. Because the only way, I guess, to translate the idea, one at a time, is to stage a spectacle and say, "See how many of us there are." You have to have a spectacle in order to remind people that these are good things to do: take care of your family; take care of your children; be responsible for your life; love one another. These are all very basic Sunday school lessons.

AJV: So you think we're making efforts to reclaim it? Is that what I'm hearing? Even though we have to do it in a much more systematized way somehow?
TM: Oh, sure.

AJV: Do I hear you correctly in saying that the children are evidencing this lack of attention?
TM: They're yearning for it. They don't know how to say it, but that's what they want. When they act out, they're saying, "Stop me."

AJV: Values, theology, and belief are huge aspects of *Paradise*, relatively speaking. And I wonder, do you think that the theology as presented in *Paradise* is as necessary as the book makes it seem?
TM: Do I think it's necessary in life?

AJV: Yes.
TM: No, it's not necessary. It's just interesting. Totally compelling and interesting. You know, thinking about good is one of the most compelling intellectual ideas there is. It has no peer. Being a moral person is not, to me, just doing good deeds. It's how to live morally in a world that may itself not be interested. Being immoral or being weak or being lazy or being evil—it's not interesting to me, intellectually. It's intellectually lazy. It's simplex. It only is

about more of itself. And it's, you know, greed. A very simple infantile relationship with other people, which means they don't exist, it's only me. That's not interesting to me. What's interesting and compelling to me is how people do give up something in order to make it better for somebody else. How does that happen? What makes that possible? I understand there's some ego in that also, but I'm talking about the concept of living in a good space and wanting goodness for its own sake, not for its glamour, not for its feel-good qualities, not for its notoriety, but in and of itself. The other always needs headlines, as I said. Corruption always needs a loud voice.

AJV: From the outside, one might argue that you have attained a kind of paradise of your own. You're the first African American woman to do a lot of different things, including the biggest, which is to win the Nobel prize. You've got an endowed chair at Princeton University, which is where we're conducting this interview. Do you think that you have achieved a kind of paradise for yourself?
TM: Absolutely not.

AJV: Have all the accolades and laurels affected your day-to-day life?
TM: Well, I don't know how to put this without sounding churlish. I love prizes and accolades and so on. But my responsibilities are to do the best work I can do and to be the best human being I can be. Now the Nobel prize doesn't help that. It doesn't make it easier to write the book that I had to write. None of it helps that. What it does do, I think, which is one of my assumed responsibilities, is make it thinkable, possible, doable for others— other African Americans and other women. If one, then why not two? If two, why not twenty? So in a representational sense, it's extremely important to me. It would have been extremely important no matter who had won it. I happened to be the one that did. So, *that* is extremely important to me. And I feel, representationally speaking, responsible for what I do. But the other person I am is somebody who's just not available to the public, which involves my life as a parent, as a teacher, as a writer, and as a friend. And that doesn't get any easier. That stays tough. And it should. And if I'm able to keep learning, putting myself in a position where I can learn something else and putting myself in positions where I can make it possible for somebody else to learn something, those are the major successes, you see.

But I would hate to tell you how pedestrian my daily life is. If you are interested in a writer's paradise, I cannot tell you. I get up early in the morning, and I go to work. And minor ecstasies have to do with gardening and friends on the phone. Very ordinary and very delightful. I don't have the big picture. I don't ski or climb mountains. The most spectacular thing in the world is my mind. To me, anyway. That's where everything's happening.

AJV: Well, Leontyne Price said, "I like nothing better than the sound of my own voice."
TM: I agree with her there. [Laughter]

AJV: In *Playing in the Dark*, you said your job as a writer was to figure out how free you could be—"how free I can be in this genderized, sexualized, wholly racialized world." What about this notion of freedom, or this question of freedom, or this quest for freedom? How does that affect what you do or what you aim for?
TM: It is *the* problem of the writing, to let my imagination have full rein, and for me to be the only one to rein it in. It's the situation I was describing to you before. As an African American writer writing about African Americans, can I talk about evil in a certain way without demonizing people who have been traditionally associated in the minds of bigots and racists with evil? I have to claim that, as we all do. Do I have to use skin privileges when I describe people? What can I do about the color coding? Can I change the language so that it's harder for me to do it? Can I give up the inherent power of signaling race? It *has* a power.

AJV: So, the question of freedom is the problem of writing and not so much a problem of life?
TM: No. I mean, I'm not free. I'm not free. But then freedom is choosing responsibility. So, maybe I am close to it. But the real freedom is in the work.

"Things We Find in Language": A Conversation with Toni Morrison

Michael Silverblatt / 1998

From *Bookworm* on KCRW Radio (October 22, 1998). Reprinted by permission of Michael Silverblatt.

Silverblatt: My guest today is Toni Morrison. She is, of course, the author of *Beloved* and the author more recently of *Jazz* and *Paradise*. She began publishing with *The Bluest Eye* followed by *Sula, Song of Solomon, Tar Baby*. And she really is one of my most admired American writers. I wrote her a letter two weeks ago, knowing that the movie of *Beloved* would be coming out and wanting, not even having seen the film, to talk about the book because it's my sense that after a movie hits the public, a book is altered by it and that there are things that we find in language, in the shaping and writing of literature, that a movie cannot touch. Not because it doesn't want to or because it's inadequate, but because they're different art forms, because it can't. Now it seems to me that at the center of *Beloved* is not the thing that people always talk about. They always talk about a story that happened in the days of slavery in which an actual woman killed her children rather than seeing them brought back and living the life that she had led on the plantation. But it seems to me that while this is the background of the book, what the writer has done is bring to it the question, which becomes the question in your following two books, *Jazz* and *Paradise*, what kind of love is too much and when does love of another eclipse the love of the self?

Morrison: The question is, how are we able to love under duress, and when we can, what distorts it for us and how can we negotiate the various kinds of claims on love that we choose in order to make it include ourselves, the love of the self that is not narcissistic, not simply selfish. And also how do we love something bigger than ourselves in a way that is not martyrdom, not setting oneself aside completely. How do we negotiate between those two extremes to get to some place where the love is generous.

171

Silverblatt: Yes, now it seems to me that in the same way that one finds oneself afterward on a path without knowing when one's embarked, that the books, all of them, lead up to this. The first book, *The Bluest Eye*, is about the consequences of self-loathing. And the books that follow take the impaired self into the world where attempts at love are made. And in a sense, it's not until *Beloved* that the question of a transfiguring love, one that might destroy the self in the process of being enacted, becomes the central subject of the book. So in a way, all of the books have been a sequential path from the frightened self to the self that begins to risk in the world, and then the self that is taking grand and possibly disastrous strides.

Morrison: True. Yes, because the frailty of the first book—of that child who is fairly doomed by things outside of her control and collapsing really emotionally—moves all the way to another kind of child I suppose in *Beloved*, whose hunger for disrupted love, whose lack of love, abandoned love, matches the ferocity of mother love. And mother love is on the one hand laudatory and on the other something that can actually condemn everybody, not just her child but the mother herself and her living child and make love impossible for her with a man. This all-consuming love, which is an exaggeration of course of parental love, involved loving in a fierce, unhealthy, distorted way under circumstances that made such a love logical. I mean Sethe's not merely psychotic; she didn't just erupt into the world that way. But I was trying very hard as a writer to put into language the theatricality and the meaning of these kinds of distortions in order to reveal not only their consequences but what one should be warned against, what we should look out for, what we should be wary of. And I thought *Beloved*'s circumstances, the book's circumstances, were not limited in any way to 1873 or 1855. I think for those of us who live in 1998, male or female, the problems of trying to love oneself and another human being at the same time is a serious late-twentieth-century problem, a very serious problem. And I thought, in particular, mother love is a very serious problem in late twentieth century because of the choices that women can make now. You don't really have to have children. Some women feel that not having children is the freedom they seek. And some women feel that having children is the fulfillment they seek. But in both cases, you know, things can go completely and terribly wrong. And what happens if you don't understand, and no one does instantly, what that means. So I thought that it was interesting to me to write, in 1984 I guess I started, about how one woman felt, that she was only free and complete when she asserted herself as a mother as opposed to those feminist notions of not having to be forced into motherhood as a way of completing, fulfilling the self and expressing one's freedom. So it's not so much that they're contrary, it's just the same area, the same park in which I wanted to work and work out the problems of *that* kind of love as opposed to say the notions of *romantic love* in the so called "jazz age" as compared to our notions of romantic love these days. I think I'm trying to stress the point that . . . I think I'm echoing something you said earlier which is, whatever the historical background, my hope, my earnest hope was that the relevance of these people, whatever race, whatever region, whatever their historical circumstances were, they would resonate powerfully with contemporary difficulties.

Silverblatt: Years ago, you mentioned you brought the manuscript of *Beloved* to your editor, Robert Gottlieb, feeling that it was not complete, that it was one part of a trilogy of novels and you didn't even know if it could be published on its own. In each of these books though, a triangle, or a configuration, emerges, and it's as if the brilliance of the book is to rotate that configuration, which I see as a triangle, from every conceivable angle. In *Jazz*, because the metaphor is jazz, the characters at the vertices of these figures, they do their solos, they speak, they have arias. In *Beloved*, too, one senses that the whole novel has been directing itself toward a moment that in my mind a film can't possibly realize, a moment of locked gaze and psychic transfer that seems at the heart of the narration of all these books, that there be a moment when there is an exchange of eye and feeling of mind and touch that allows people to know each other's stories without speaking them.
Morrison: Well, you have a major void in a movie which is you don't have a reader, you have a viewer, and that is such a different experience. As subtle as a movie can be, as careful and artful as it can be, in the final analysis it's blatant because you see it. And you can translate certain things, make certain interpretations and wonder, and certainly there could be mystery. But the encounter with language is such a private exploration. The imagination works differently. The things that I can create and hint at via the structure, via the choice of words, via the silences are not the kinds of things that would be successful in any movie, and when it becomes pointed and successful that way it loses something. So for me what you call the exchange of mind and self and touch, none of that they would even attempt because that's not what movies do or do well. And I had to realize, although I was not very interested

in selling any book to the movies ever, and when I was persuaded to complete the sale of this one I thought I would let them do what they do, and I would go home and do what I do. And I had no further contact with it until, indeed, they were filming. And I went there to say certain things that I thought might be helpful and might be used but probably would never be, but I felt it important to simply say these things. And my judgments were powerfully structural—where to linger, where not to. And they were really unusable. They were literally unusable, by anybody, because they were not cinematic.

Silverblatt: I want to explain the context here. I think the trust and the agreement between a writer and a reader is very important to her. And so when I wrote a letter to her several weeks ago, it was not only that we would talk, but we would talk from her home because that was a decision not to be going out on the road again to be making pronouncements or flaking for the movie. The movie is a separate thing and so we're talking from Toni Morrison's home. It was out of respect for the writer that led to this particular circumstance. It seems to me that your fiction does bring the reader to a space that cannot be defined. That must be called, for lack of better terms, the sacred or indeterminate space of the imaginative experience. That words are the inadequate clothing of that experience when you're reaching the heart. Up until that point, the writer's choices word by word are immensely important. When you reach the heart, no word can be correct. You're talking about an experience that is close to a mystical experience.

Morrison: I wanted precisely that point to be rendered in a couple of occasions in *Beloved*. But particularly when the women are in front of Sethe's house, having been persuaded that enough is enough. And when they go there they come with what they've got, whatever faith they've got, whatever superstition they've got, whatever religious iconography they have using all the symbolic world. And then they pray, and they do things, and then there's a moment when none of that, not the symbol they hold in their hands, not the cross they may have around their necks, not the desire to have their will done. The only thing that works is to go very, very far back before language, when there was only the sound. The sound is a kind of choral singing in this case which works, I think in terms of the folklore, in terms of who those people were. But it's another way of saying, of their saying and my saying, I can't *say* what this is. There are no words to tell you how to get there from here.

Silverblatt: Now opposed to that that can't be voiced, there's another kind of silencing that runs through the work that is not helpful to a writer, that a writer fights with every straining instinct against. That is the silence that fills the master's wife's throat. She can no longer speak. It is the silencer on the gun that kills Dorcas. She is silenced in *Jazz*. And I wondered if you could talk about the ways these books combat silence.

Morrison: Well that's an interesting way to put it. I think the signal instrument of silence for me in *Beloved* was the bit, which was a kind of familiar and frequently used homemade instrument that you put into a person's mouth, which you could adjust. And there are quite a variety of them. And whatever other feature they had, they were not to keep you from working because you worked with them, but they were to shut you up so that you could not say, you could not talk back, you could not articulate a contrary position, or do any violence with your tongue or your word. And that was a complete erasure of all language that the victim or the oppressed had. So for me it was operating this way. I would try to say what they were prevented from saying.

Silverblatt: It seems to me that the writer's role in work of this kind is to save the characters from the silencing of society and bring them to that point that can only be quasi-articulate of the witnessing of the holy or the miraculous.

Morrison: Precisely. Indeed it is. It's bearing witness on the one hand, in a way you mentioned it yourself; it's not quite secular, let's put it that way. It's not quite secular work.

Silverblatt: Yes, now in that scene of the bit, there is what I consider to be one of the signatures and triumphs of your way of looking and writing. In the scene in which this brutal silencing occurs, several tortures and punishments are going on at once, several witnesses without voices. What we see instead is that rooster, and I wondered if you would tell me about him.

Morrison: (Laughs) Yeah, imagining it myself, the sort of "what must it feel like, what must it look like," this man under those circumstances being treated like a beast. So you're trying to not just reemphasize that, but to have him look at something that is edible, something that he brought into the world, but nevertheless roosters have a kind of royal way of behaving sometimes in the yard. And you have him compare himself to a creature so beneath him but who, visually—if you visualize a rooster you see the crown, you see the beak, you see the eye, you see something close to an eagle so you see something painterly—you recognize as having at least a certain kind of authority, the rooster crows, etcetera. But you know really that it's just three or four pounds of a little nothing. And to have him feel less than that, and to, more importantly, know that rooster. He has a name. He remembers when it was born. He remembers naming. And they named it "Mister" because it was so tough. So here we have a man who will never be called Mister, walking out of that yard, looking at a rooster that is already called Mister.

Silverblatt: And also participating in flashback in a ritual of male birth. That he has in some way mothered this rooster. It's so amazing. Now this, of course, is what a movie cannot do because it can only show you a rooster. It can't tell you where the rooster came from. It can't make the red of its comb pulsate the way yours does, it cannot enter the mind of the man who named it "Mister," whose mouth is filled by a bit. These are those things that in a book last beyond the book, they're intersections that the author has structured that editing in movies can only rarely . . . one needs an Eisenstein to think of a structure that would allow for so much association, so much fullness to go on in the midst of such devastation.

Morrison: They're so different. It's the most obvious thing to say, but I had no idea how very different the whole experience is, what you're being driven to. And it's not even a reduction, it's just a powerful difference. First of all, it was important to me at least on the paperback jacket, not to see Beloved's face—that she must be someone that the reader invents. Well, already, when you're in a movie situation, you have a face. It fixes it. So it moves from there to other kinds of scenes, gestures, voices . . . some of which enhance, I have to tell you, what the dialogue might be. You hear other things with very good actors, and they're very good in this movie. On the other hand they're just whole areas that not only are not there; they're not gestured toward, but the mechanics of cinema doesn't work toward that anyway. The part that you work so hard for is of no use whatsoever. They cannot use it and should not. I remember a scene in *Paradise* in which I worked a long time with a couple of scenes to make sure that the pallette was right, that the same colors that were in the scene were also in another scene. And I don't expect a reader to necessarily know all that. But I do believe that because I painted the scenes the same colors, there's this sort of undertow or urtext where it may not look comparable in terms of the two scenes, but the reader may not even know

that they're getting the nature of the comparison because I have painted
them that way.

Silverblatt: Well, it's very deeply embedded in the work and what I find
myself saying about that, it's kind of wonderful. It came to me in *Beloved*
with Baby Suggs's quilt in which there are two patches of orange and Baby
Suggs is working on pink that what's going on in this book is that we are
thinking about color in new ways.

Morrison: In a fresh way. I wanted it to be absolutely raw and in the rest of
the book, nobody mentions color. And then when Sethe meets Paul D again,
and she thinks about maybe this could work, she thinks about color, maybe
she'll look at turnips. It's a pleasure; it's a deep, sensual, gratifying pleasure.

Silverblatt: And not only that, it's a way of making new what a Black writer is
supposed to do. He or she is supposed to think about color and here it is
you've got it—I'm doing it right now (Laughs).

Morrison: (Laughs) You got it!

Silverblatt: I've been speaking to Toni Morrison, the author of *Beloved*. It is a
conversation occurring on the occasion of the film but not about the film. It's
the attempt to celebrate the depths of a book that a film can't touch. Thank
you very much for joining me Toni.

Morrison: This has been a pleasure.

Blacks, Modernism, and the American South: An Interview with Toni Morrison

Carolyn C. Denard / 1998

From *Studies in the Literary Imagination* (no. 31–2, Fall 1998). Reprinted by permission of Carolyn C. Denard.

Denard: You are not a Southerner. You were born and grew up in Lorain, Ohio. So your sense of the South and what African Americans value and/or hate about the South comes largely from your parents' memories of the South—the stories told to you when you were growing up. What was the perception, the sense of the South that you gained from your parents?

Morrison: They had diametrically opposed positions. My father was born in Georgia. My mother was born in Alabama. Both were from very small towns in those states. My father thought that the most racist state in the Union was Georgia and that it would never change. My mother had much fonder memories. She was very nostalgic about the South. But she never visited it—ever. While my father went back every year. Quarreling and fussing all the way, he went back to see his family—aunts, uncles—there. So I grew up with a complicated notion of the South, neither sentimental nor wholly frightening. On the one hand, with no encouragement, my mother was nostalgic about the Alabama farm, yet she would talk in a language of fear about her family's escape from the South. On the other hand, my father recounted vividly the violence that he had seen first-hand from White southerners, but he regularly returned.

Denard: What about your own impressions of the South when you toured with the Howard Players, or when you taught at Texas Southern University, or when you've visited since then?

Morrison: What impressed me when I first went to the South for a sustained period of time (with a theater group from Howard) was the sight of so many people like me, like my relatives. I think Ralph Ellison said something elegant but similar when he was trying to answer Irving Howe. Howe had asked why would he have any good feelings about the South, and Ellison said that the South was full of Black people. Well that's suddenly what I realized. When you go there, while it was true that I was going into a white domain, what I was aware of primarily are the Black people there, and they were like people in Lorain, Ohio. And I didn't have to change my language or my manners. The accents were different but the language was not. I recognized and participated in the culture. I mean the food, the music, the way in which you behaved in other people's houses, what you don't do with strangers, what you do—they were no different whatsoever from the way I had been reared in Lorain, Ohio. Also, I had a sense of—I hate to use these over-taxed words—a sense of belonging and community that was lifesaving. I used to tell my children about how I felt when my sister and I as young girls were in the company of so-called vaguely criminal men in Lorain. Men who gambled, sold illegal liquor, or what have you. But when we saw them on the street they were safety zones for us. If we needed to get home, they took us. If we were someplace where we shouldn't be, they told us. If we needed protection, they gave it. So I always felt surrounded by these Black men who were safe. I knew I was safe with them; the people I ran from were not them. I felt the same thing traveling through the South on trains. The porters—even when I was a grown woman traveling with my children the porters were the praetorian guard. They were the ones who gave me extra orange juice and didn't charge me for it because I had a little boy with me; they were the ones who gave me the pillow anyway whether I purchased one or not. It was a kind of chivalry that I had come to expect from Black men. You see a Black man, you know you're safe. And that was precisely the feeling I had in the South, of protection and care and solicitous, unflirtatious behavior. This very recent notion of Black men as threats stuns me.

Denard: Were there other people in Lorain, other family members or friends or people you met at Howard, who had lived in the South and who expressed the similar views of the South that your parents did?
Morrison: Many.

Denard: Tell me about those people.
Morrison: Many of my father's people lived in Chicago and most of my mother's people lived in areas around Ohio, Michigan, and California, but all of

them had come from the South originally. My mother came north very young. She was six. And she went to school in Ohio as did her sisters and brothers. And her parents, along with many of the aunts and uncles in Cleveland and Lorain, made up a culture that I didn't identify by region but only as Black. I learned later how pronounced the variations of culture—from state to state or region to region—are. I've never felt that sense of familiarity within variety anywhere else except in Brazil where you see evidence of intrinsic, even dominant, Black cultures—each one of which is strikingly different in cuisine and dress and music from the others, and they all speak different kinds of Portuguese. But somehow, however, they relate to each other. When you are in that company, you feel as though you are in exalted company.

There is another aspect of the South that I remember which exemplifies that notion of community that we talked about earlier. When I first went South with the theater group from Howard, we couldn't count on living quarters. I mean they made adequate reservations in advance, but we were traveling in several cars, and sometimes we arrived too late and the rooms were taken. As faculty members, they were all dedicated to making sure that we were all safe. So they looked in the yellow pages of the telephone book and called up churches. And invariably, the minister or his wife would answer, and the faculty would tell them who we were and where we were from and that we were on our way to do a performance at some school or whatever and then ask where we might find lodging. Invariably, the minister said "call me back" or "come." He would find three or four parishioners who were pleased to house us.

Denard: This sounds very familiar. This kind of house-lodging continued right up through my high school years in the late '60s. We would go to conferences at other schools, and we stayed at people's homes. That's the way it happened; they never tried to get hotels. Instead, they had a registration table with a list of people's homes and addresses. So they didn't choose not to have the conference because they didn't have lodging. They just facilitated it with the help of the members of the church or others who were willing to offer their homes for the church.

Morrison: Well when we went there, I thought that was fascinating, not because I wasn't accustomed to that kind of hospitality within the community, but because these were emergency circumstances, it was like an underground railroad. This included places to eat. I remember when we were in Virginia and there was no restaurant in this tiny little town where we could eat at all.

But one of the faculty members knew or had heard of a man who had been a chef in New York who was retired now. He didn't have a restaurant, but he cooked for guests in his house. And that was easily one of the best meals I've ever had.

Denard: I'm sure. When we travel now, we often look for these small mom and pop kind of places in Black communities rather than the large restaurants so we can we can have what we still consider the "better" food.
Morrison: And it was. The preserves they had canned, the biscuits were homemade. It was like eating at my grandmother's table.

Denard: In the novels, the ambivalence that the migrant characters feel about the South rings so true. It rings true to the experiences that your parents had and that I had with my family. The ambivalence echoes the feelings that migrants expressed in letters to the *Chicago Defender* and ones collected by Emmet Scott, where repeatedly they said things like "I miss the folks down home, please send me vegetables and preserves," but they also said "there's no Jim Crow car; I can sit anywhere I want," or "here I can be a man or a woman with a decent paying job."
Morrison: You give up a lot, you know, to take advantage or benefits of urban or working life elsewhere: The problem is trying to balance those two environments. Sidney doesn't want to live in Baltimore. And Pauline could not go back either. Some of the fault of the urban areas, it seems to me, was it took a longer time to become part of that community. Urban Blacks were very much on the defensive. We used to joke about calling up relatives or friends in New York and they'd greet you by saying "where are you staying?"

Denard: (Laughter) They were trying hard NOT to be southern. I wonder whether part of the tension of living in the North really was mediating between the way you remember yourself versus the new way you wanted to be. In every novel there is this tension, of course the saddest being Sethe's re-memory of Sweet Home in *Beloved*. There's Pauline in *The Bluest Eye* and then there's Violet in *Jazz* who says it all—"I knew who I was before I came up here and got my mind all messed up." These instances point clearly to the tensions. No one has articulated that tension in literature in the kind of sustained way that you do in your fiction.
Morrison: Maybe because they are mostly women who feel that tension in my books. When men come to the city, perhaps they feel more urgency to

conquer and make their way out in the street, so to speak. For women, because they are domestic, they remember domestic support—friends, exchange of food, and so on—and they have difficulty trying to reproduce it in the urban North. In a very large city you have to pick your clan very carefully. In a small town like Lorain, it would just be easier to be near a city like Cleveland, but not in it.

Denard: John Leonard said in his review of *Jazz*, that if you read a Morrison novel, "you know sooner or later she's going to go South." It may be, he says, "all the way back to antebellum or sometimes it's the trials and tribulations and the horrors," but it is also for what he calls "those ghostly waters and that bag of ancestral bones." When you start to write, in terms of character development, and in trying to say something about the characters' past and the impact of African-American history, of African-American identity and psychology, how important is the presence of the South in that development? Is it just drawing an authentic character and that's how they flesh out, or were you thinking first of placing the South self-consciously in the development of the character?
Morrison: It starts with characters. When I think about the context in which to put a character, I think about the characters' preceding generation. I didn't want to create an "atom"—a family just sort of sitting there in a vacuum—which seemed to me to be at one time not just current in literature but demanded. In the '50s and '60s in certain literature certain authors preferred to create characters in isolation. Hemingway never writes about his character's families; Fitzgerald writes about family in terms of what a character is running away from. But it's all very much now—the woman they're falling in love with; the work they're doing at the moment. When they describe a region—Michigan or Paris—that's enough to give the narrative its context. For me, in doing novels about African Americans, I was trying very hard to move away from the unstated but overwhelming and dominant context that was white history and to move into another one. So in thinking about place and where these people come from, I did the inevitable thing because what I knew most about were the people I lived among and where they had come from and my own sense of what the place was like. I was trying to do a very modern novel and comment on what I thought were contemporary issues between Black men and women. Nevertheless, even in dealing with an orphan like Jadine—and although she despised being an orphan—at the same time she relished the freedom of not having any familial or cultural weights. But the people who did feel responsible

for her—her aunt and her uncle—were themselves very much a product of the South even though they lived in splendor in a sense—as servants they lived a comfortable life.

Denard: In *Sula*, there is less of a sense of an affective South. In most of the novels, both sides are shown—Cholly Breedlove remembering his humiliation with Darlene and his father on the one hand and Pauline remembering blackberry vines and lemonade on the other. Or Sidney priding himself in being a Philadelphia Negro while dreaming refreshing dreams of Baltimore. There are always both sides of the memory. *Sula*, however, seems to be the only novel where there is no affective memory of the South—except perhaps Nel who realizes some sense of herself as separate when she returns from the South when she says "I'm me, I'm me," but it's not an affective memory of being in the South.

Morrison: In that book—it was the second book I wrote—that culture was intact for me. It was like a moveable feast—you could take it anywhere, and you didn't have to identify geographically with anything because it was all there.

Denard: So it works thematically not to bring in this other history.

Morrison: It's almost as though it didn't matter where Black people were in the '20s and '30s. They were still operating under the aegis, or umbrella, of a culture that had probably been reconfigured in the new world in the South. Most of the major themes and threats I think had originated there.

Denard: I often wonder whether this lack of an affective connection to the land or the community is some of the difficulty with Sula—with her trying to create an existential self and not really being able to do that. I think sometimes because she does not have that tie to the land or to something larger than her household, she flounders. There is the hint that she goes South to Nashville—although she doesn't seem to find anything there.

Morrison: The enterprise of being a complete individual, which is what she wanted to be, is associated with—not necessarily bound to—the goals of solitariness. I am complete by myself or maybe with my friend. When I lose comfort in my solitude, I have nothing. She had few normal responses to col-lective things—at all—not to her neighbors, her hometown, her friend, not to her mother, not to anyone. I find her eccentric, but it was only by using a very eccentric character—for her time—that I could talk about the relationship between the two of them and give each of them something the other wanted a little bit of.

Denard: *Sula* was the first novel that I read and surprisingly Medallion—a (northern) Ohio town—had great resonance for me. It was a lot like Black community life in the small southern town I grew up in. I have always been curious about that resonance, and I have wondered whether or not this is just Black resonance or southern resonance, or small community resonance. What do you think accounts for what I am calling the Black southern resonance that Medallion has?

Morrison: The problem even now is the question of what's southern and what's Black, and as a writer I can't always figure it out. I just place things once I know where they ought to be. Even when I took Black people out of the United States altogether in *Tar Baby*, the dynamic still operated. Here you had Son who is a southern boy—who hadn't been there in a long time, but that's where he's from. All of his noble instincts about what women ought to be and what people ought to be come from that milieu. He didn't learn that in the Navy or at sea.

Denard: In addition to the sustaining aspects of southern community life, there are also obviously aspects of the South that you think are repressive, or are obstacles for a full self-awareness. I am thinking specifically here of the women like Geraldine and Helene Wright in *The Bluest Eye*—those domestic women from southern towns like Mobile, Baton Rouge, and Meridian, who you say are so prudish that they will not allow "the funk to erupt." Tell me about those women or those aspects of the South.

Morrison: Well at that time I was thinking of the repression in the South for nefarious purposes, for pleasing White people—not for the health of the community. I meant those women who won't dance—not for religious reasons, but because they are afraid to express joy or sensual pleasure, because both are associated, in White culture, with lack of discipline. Maybe they've all died now. I remember a lot of them. They were very busy. The eye that looked at them was not another Black person's eye. It was a distant White eye that looked at them that they were aspiring to emulate or correct. That was what I thought was sad—not the Southern regions from which they came, but how they absorbed the dominant culture. They could have come from Detroit.

Denard: Most of the manifestations of the South in your work are of memory—an historical consciousness of the South that exists in their minds. Are there other places where or ways in which you are trying to bring in the South in your work? I remember, for example, the passage in *Jazz* when Joe Trace comes in to Felice's apartment when the other women are there, and there is that "pitch" in his voice that reminds them of people down South who sat on the porch and wore their hats—a southern, rural metaphor.
Morrison: There may be a different sense of the South for men and women. I found Joe's incorporation of the South in the city different from Violet's. Even though they met there, they fell in love there, they got married and they left. Her memories are not good. He had terrible things happen to him as well in the South, but he does not feel devastated by the South.

Denard: What about the language? Many reviewers talked about the Harlem community in *Jazz* as a place where women "quit" their husbands, as if "quit" were a word they had not heard before. It seemed very southern to me. Is "quit" one of those language hold overs from the South, or is it Black, or just old fashioned?
Morrison: That's all I ever heard.

Denard: It's all I ever heard.
Morrison: "Did she quit him?" "Did he quit her?" "Yeah, they quit." That's just memory of the way we spoke. The only way you can hear it now is in song.

Denard: As in "Please Don't Quit Me Baby"
Morrison: Or "Hit Me, But Don't Quit Me." (Laughter) Can you imagine?

Denard: Exploring the specificity of the words like that, that have been forgotten or gone out of use, is a good space for the criticism of your work.
Morrison: I work at that, you know. To get the language that is particular, very particular. And I know I use words that contemporary authors or critics may not know, but I can't help that. It's hard to hear different varieties of English now because everybody talks like people on television. Even when you go to interview people, they sound like some version of themselves—the language becomes mass produced—their choice of words, all the clichés, and so on.

Denard: What about what we might call "southern ethics," manners, expectations? You deal with this with some of your women characters—in *Sula*, although not in a southern setting, but more specifically in *Tar Baby*, where you have Jadine violate these ethics in a southern community.

Morrison: Well there are some very interesting things happening with Black women and they are risky and experimental and were not all of four or five stereotypes. I've always thought that if Black women don't know it, it's not known really in the collective because they've had to know. They've experimented in existential ways, in collective ways, in urban sophisticated ways, in Pilate-Dead ways—they're always out there trying to figure out how to get it done—how to walk on water. And sometimes they're successful, sometimes they're not—more often not because that's the nature of being out front—that somebody's going to knock you down—and I don't want to say or even imply that these ventures of theirs necessarily have heavy consequences. But any explorer—spiritual explorer, geographic explorer, or somebody trying something different—is going to put oneself in danger. Sula is in danger, Jadine is in danger. It's a different kind of danger from, say, the one that Eva is in, but they're all in danger. They are the people with the least power in the body politic and at the same time with the most influence, and they are always searching for small escapes. There's a certain type of Black female adventurer that has nothing to do with going to war—or the big male type adventures. In order to function at the front lines you have to break rules, cross boundaries. Being a working, single parent without the protection of an extended family would require a shift in ethics. So would being a career woman on one's own in a foreign country.

Denard: In the case of Jadine where she rejects those expectations of her, what could we say? In order to do the adventurous thing you have to give up something else, which you talk about with Sula—the Bessie Smiths, the blues-singing kind of woman who has to leave the community. How do you mediate those expectations of other generations or your small community as you go out on your adventure? Are there some adventures that are so necessary that we should no longer be held accountable to the expectations of the communities from which we come?

Morrison: We are all accountable. Jadine is definitely accountable. What I'm trying to suggest is that she can be judged the way Ondine judges her. She tells her, "You have to learn how to be this person, and I failed you if you don't know it." While at the same time, an ideal person would have put those two expectations together, but I don't know who those people are. I don't know people who can be a success in the fashion world in Paris and come back and be comfortable in their small community. I'm sure they exist. But the point of the book is to show how painful and difficult that is. You separate these entities so that you can look at them, then the reader has to figure out how he or she would mediate. It's not for me to solve that problem.

Denard: But there is the implication that they need to be mediated.

Morrison: Oh yes. You know I get a lot of flack about Jadine—why I seem to sympathize with Son, or how I did her a disservice. The point of writing the novel is to do everybody justice. But, she's apolitical, and she's very much in love with him; still she doesn't want to be like Ondine. She doesn't want to be a servant. She doesn't want to be dependent on a man.

Denard: And even with the validity of that independence, she still has to negotiate.

Morrison: Of course. She knows that.

Denard: And she's already tried to negotiate the two worlds and the different expectations by going back to visit her aunt and uncle.

Morrison: You're on the side of the women of Eloe. Some readers are furious with those Eloe women. That's what I meant when I said these readers think I have done her a disservice. They think that she should get out of there as fast as she can, and "what kind of man is he hanging her out the window; she should leave him alone." Because they are clip-clopping in New York, they don't want to be bothered with the rules of the women of Eloe. They really don't. They're into Louis Vuitton, and business, and security. You know, and I can't judge them, I can't condemn those women—well I can, but that's not my work.

Denard: You do get the sense that Jadine is at least wrestling with this issue—that she is not callous.

Morrison: Neither one of them is. They know what to do when it comes to love; they don't know what to do when it comes to cultural compromise. She's going back to zero, she says, when she goes back to Paris. "Let me start all over again." And he is trying to make a choice. I don't know where he's going—off to the mystic past or back to that house with Sidney. The nature of the metaphorical language suggests that he allows himself to stay in history—embalmed in history. But they can't make a life together until they straighten out these problems.

Denard: As they work them out, however, neither of them is in Eloe.
Morrison: No, no one is in Eloe.

Denard: I want to go back to a point we talked about earlier—and that is the difference in writing *in* the South versus *about* the South—or an experiential South versus a reflective South. One of the interesting things about your work, and to some degree the works of other northern Black writers whose characters have moved North—John Wideman in *Damballah*, Rita Dove in *Thomas and Beulah*—are their reflective quality. How important do you think distance and memory are for being able to articulate—particularly an affective memory of the South?
Morrison: I think distance is important even if you're in it. You need the distance in order to see. Whether you're not there or living in it, you establish a certain kind of distance anyway. I guess there are some people who have to be in it and write about it. But for me, I always find it necessary to have a kind of third eye about things so that you aren't overwhelmed by the details, so that you can control them. And also, it really is about vision. I do see places better when I'm not there. I don't always know what I'm seeing if I'm in a place. You're doing things and thinking things, but not selecting things. But when I leave it, it's clearer to me. Because what surfaces are some things I did not know that I was noticing at the time.

Denard: That is the value, to me, of your novels, as a writer whose characters are from the South but not in the South. In a sustained way, in nearly every novel, there is some character who is remembering the South. So one gets this articulation through memory that one would not get otherwise. Do you think that Blacks who are still in the South, who never left, are as self-conscious about the South as a cultural homeplace as Blacks who left and went North and had to invoke their memories of it? Migrants often have a way of embellishing things and making us see our surroundings in ways that I don't think we would have without their reflective, outsider's vision. It seems to be the peculiar vision of those who left, and I wonder if that generation prior to integration—who did not leave and who were not part of the post-integration generation—ever focused reflectively in this way?

Morrison: They probably didn't. They knew city ways versus country ways. The city was understood in those days as being always wicked; the city is always considered wicked no matter where you are, but also very modern. Now it is understood as very retrograde, because we have accepted a contemporary media version of what's in an inner city. It can be wholly false, however.

Denard: I also wonder whether there are some Blacks in the North, some transplanted southerners, unlike your characters and unlike many of the migrants who wrote letters to their relatives in the South, who both seem to have understood the tension or at least were able to articulate it, who are still wrestling with the tension of being a southern small-town person living in the urban north. They don't know the source of their tension, or perhaps they just can't name it?

Morrison: Yes, but maybe less now. Some people pay lip service to it. And age makes a difference, too. But it's very scary for a lot of Black people—women in particular who want a career, marriage, children, who want everything we've always wanted, and sometimes they feel great pressure to leave home to get these things. There are more Sulas out there—but they may not be as mean as she is.

Denard: What do you think that suggests for the future—where women are not so conscious of the past and not as reflective?

Morrison: I don't know; I'm not sure. I have mixed feelings about it. I just like for women to do interesting stuff. I think the trajectory of Black women has been very different from the freed White women—in interesting ways. But more important than those differences, are the similarities and I like it although I know the risks; I know they're going to be very lonely. I know they're going to die like Sula, maybe not that young, but that's what happens.

Denard: I know that there are many older couples who move back to the South when they retire. It's as though they've just being trying to live long enough to retire and go back.

Morrison: Oh sure. Oh I would. If I were from the South, I'd go back.

Denard: Why?
Morrison: Oh it's nicer; it's cheaper than most places.

Denard: Tell me about the new novel. This time you have people leaving the South traveling to the West. How does the South manifest itself in *Paradise*?
Morrison: Well I'm not yet sure. They're moving from Louisiana to Oklahoma. Oklahoma is different; so much sky and the land is flat. I read a lot of newspapers about the people who went to Oklahoma. About soliciting people to settle Black towns all over Kansas and Oklahoma, particularly Oklahoma. And I got interested in one little sentence, which was in a column in one of the Black newspapers, encouraging people to move, work your own land, etc.; and it had an ad that said, "Come prepared or not at all." It encouraged people to come with a year or two or three of supplies or money, so that if things didn't go right they would be able to take care of themselves. And the newspaper articles indicated how many people came with fifteen thousand dollars and so on, but there was a little paragraph about two caravans of Black people who got to Boley or Langston, or one of those towns, and were turned away because they did not come prepared; they didn't have anything. So I thought about what it must feel like to make that trek, and be turned away by some Black people—maybe for good reasons but nevertheless turned away by Black people—because they were too ragged and too poor to come into their town and homestead. So I've taken that route—these people just go somewhere else. They're determined to make it, and they do. But it makes them very isolationist. They don't hurt anybody except themselves. It's a closed town. The novel is somewhat about that "run" into Oklahoma, but it's very "inter." It's about conflicts within the race. Outside is whatever is out there. But this is a big story—I mean it's got a lot of people in it—but it's a very interior terrain. What that one town becomes after very revolutionary and hardworking activity to build it with no help. They're very separatist people.

Denard: It sounds as though there are two moments that seem "unlike" the culture—first Blacks being turned away by Blacks, then that turning away, breeding more independence—more turning away.
Morrison: That's right. But we have some of those communities here. Separatist movements of people who wanted a whole state for themselves or wanted to return to Africa. Oklahoma was one of those states. But these people

don't cultivate any romance about Africa. I also wanted to explore unpopular ideas about the difference between liberation and conservation. The liberation movement, the movement to free oneself to be completely independent—as a community not as an individual—is marvelous. But how one moves from liberation to conservation is what I explore. How you can make a liberationary gesture and how it can make you end up as the world's most static conservative. These are also very religious people. They do not want to hear anything from the outside. The outside is hell, is Babylon to them. They don't want anything stirring up, they don't want any civil rights, they don't want any of that.

Denard: Would you say that this is a '90s book—a book we need for now? *Beloved*, for example, was about slavery but written in 1987, and it spoke to some really present issues. Many readers realized in reading *Beloved* that some ghosts of the past had not been put to rest, had not been faced, and in many ways the book was redemptive for the present generation. What will we mediate on in *Paradise*, or are you ready to say yet?
Morrison: Well, a number of things. It stops in 1975. There is conflict between the sort of the '60s and '70s mentality, and an older mentality. These days we say everybody loved Martin Luther King, but they didn't. Right now, other things have happened; he has survived as a man with a powerful message and a powerful mind. While he was around, however, there were a lot of people who thought he was a demagogue. The students from SNCC took issue with him. I'm not trying to destroy what has survived, but it's no good to paper over these kind of Du Bois versus Washington splits. They just reconfigure themselves in other ways, and they're much more complicated now. And I just want to talk about the inevitability of—well I want to suggest something about negotiation that is applicable for the '90s. There are a lot of neo-cons, a lot of activists, a lot of pacifists, people for integration, people against integration, who are still out there. These are still current issues, and people change their minds on them a lot. And part of that is seeded in, or many of these ideas are seeded in, *Paradise*.

Denard: How does religion function in *Paradise*?
Morrison: There are lots of conflicts in the book, and religion is one. Not religious believers versus non-believers so much as what turns out to be conflict between politics and faith. What does a young minister go through who

is very political with other ministers who are not? The point is faith without politics or politics without faith. They oppose one another—sometimes arguing—sometimes they're just wary of the person who is introducing new ideas. Thurgood Marshall went to Norman, Oklahoma, to do this case for the NAACP in 1947. They were building separate rooms for the law students, for the Black graduate students who could not go to the University of Oklahoma. The law said separate but equal, and they were going to build a whole new section of the law school for Blacks. You know people have forgotten. I don't think this generation knows at all what was going on in 1947 as far as Civil Rights are concerned. They think it all began in the '60s. It's interesting to me to re-examine that period—'50s, '60s, and '70s era. Black people made a lot of money in this period right after the war. Yet, that was the moment of Emmett Till in 1955. When Blacks do well, Whites get very nervous.

Denard: We don't hear of the successes as much. We hear mostly the anger. So we can't appropriate anything but the anger.
Morrison: So it's hard going really. There's a lot of research involved. And I haven't done it all. I've done some of the research enough to move through a draft of the narrative, and I've been to Oklahoma, but the part I'm moving toward in the novel is very different. You can see the sky from here, over to there, so Oklahomans have a very fecund imagination.

Denard: That's going to be very different for you. You've had sycamore trees, champion daisy trees, hills, robins—all very lush settings in the earlier novels.
Morrison: Yes, very different. I've found a lot of subtle variety, but there is that unremitting sky. It's a great place for religion, too. There are churches everywhere. You know you have liquor stores in Washington and banks in New York—a bank on every corner in New York. Well in Oklahoma there are churches—two or three in a block, or just a large parking lot in the middle of nowhere and a nice church that people will go long distances to attend. In the little town of the novel there are three churches: a Methodist, a Baptist, and a Pentecostal.

Denard: Is it based on Boley?
Morrison: No, it's not Boley. It's a new town. The old town they remember was a 1908–1950 town. But that one has collapsed. And these are just some veterans who have gone off to do it again.

Denard: Well, I have just two more questions and one of them has to do with the place of the South in our understanding of the African diaspora. When you reviewed Albert Murray's *South to a Very Old Place* in 1972, you first complimented him that he had found new avenues for exploring the Black sense of belonging to the South—talking to Blacks and southern White liberals like C. Vann Woodward, Robert Penn Warren, Hodding Carter—but you also criticized the book because Murray stopped the connection to the South in the "American South"—in his case, in Mobile, Alabama. You suggested in the end of that review that Blacks will never understand their history if they think that it begins and ends in Mobile, Alabama—that there is a place older and "souther" in Black American history than Mobile. Given that the South does operate in some way in your novels as home, although it is in fact not the first or the oldest home for African Americans as your review points out, how would you describe the place of the South in the African Diaspora? What does it mean, should it mean, to us as African Americans?

Morrison: Well for us it's home, I guess, in the sense that it was the first stop when we left the ancient home—and sure there was the Santa Domingo and Caribbean thing—but it was. . . . You see my struggle with the South is to keep it from being just the old place, and what I was trying to say, even in that review, is that what Black people did in this country was brand new. Even if they did it a long time ago. These people were very inventive, very creative, and that was a very modern situation. It was, philosophically, probably the earliest nineteenth-century modernist existence. And out of thrown things they invented every-thing: a music that is the world's music, a style, a manner of speaking, a relationship with each other, and more importantly, psychological ways to deal with it. And no one gives us credit for the intelligence it takes to be forced into another culture, be oppressed, and make a third thing. Other cultures who get moved like that die or integrate; or because they're White, they don't even inte-grate, they disappear into the dominant culture. That never happened to us; I think we would have wanted it because it was better than being isolated and so on. But in view of that, in spite of that, they made something else. For me, jazz was the moment when Blacks took the country over in terms of its tone—not its money, not its business—but it was all in its blood by then, it was all there. So what happened to African Americans is not what happened to Africans in Africa—more like what happened to Africans in South Africa, but not even that because that was their home. But this is a whole new experience—and it is a modern experience. So that there is some modernity and some grasp on the future that the South holds more than any other place. Although I understand the nostalgia about it being everybody's past, and the good old days, and ma and pa and grandpa and so on. But for me the actual thing that was going on was this wholly modern thing.

Denard: So it was a starting point, the site of modernity for the Africans who came as slaves. I don't think many people have thought about it in quite that way. That has been an essential question for me. What is the larger more philosophical, metaphorical way even—to think about the South and its meaning to African Americans than just as "down home?"
Morrison: Yes, there is some way to make it down home but to also make it this jet—it was a rocket too. You have to get rid of the look, the look of it—I don't mean the Atlanta look. I mean the look of the South in the eyes and minds of certain folks is mansions and little houses, a slower pace, and all of that, and I think that's true in parts of Africa, as well as in the art.

Denard: Do you think the South is where we claim our Americanness? Is the South the native ground beginning for us in the same sense of where we began the modern experiment?
Morrison: It's where the modern experiment begins, oh yes, there's no question about that. But I don't think people understand that though. I think when Black people think about the South, they think of it as down home.

Denard: Where what is modern is not happening.
Morrison: (Laughter) Yes, we started there, but we left to go where it is happening.

Denard: But starting there is very important, given what we were dealing with when we arrived.
Morrison: Yes. My mother always said something, and I'm sure it's not true, but I haven't figured it out yet. She said, "No Black leader would ever appear who wasn't from the South." And I said, "I beg your pardon." And she said, "Who?" I couldn't think of any people. No northern Black had produced one Black leader—that activism and modernity begins in the South. Whatever happens to it ultimately originates there.

Denard: One of the things that has been so fruitful for me as a Black southerner in this exploration has been the possibility that finally we can claim the South on our own terms. Historically, it has been filled with the metaphors of the Confederacy, and the signs of the White South. Whites have always been in the subject position when it comes to the South.

Morrison: Well, Whites have been thinking about it exclusively as their history. There was no history for Whites in the South other than the South. Although some promoted and romanticized their connection to Scotland or whatever. For Black people it was their past but not their history. Their history was some-place else. What they did with their past is to create something brand new. I think the South is now, finally, getting close to the edge of the modern world because Black people are there. Once White people gave up the legal claim to the things they were doing—killing Blacks, bullying them, and pushing White supremacy, ideologically and personally—they stopped to see what was in their best interest. Then and only then, did it become a modern part of the world.

Denard: What difference do you think it would make if we knew the cultural and philosophical meaning of the South collectively? Do you think we'd all move back to the South or would we all claim Americanness and stop gestures of separatism?

Morrison: We wouldn't have to think about it in those tired old ways—as your greens are better than any other greens—or like my mother and father. My father wouldn't have to go back there every year in order to refresh his soul. My mother wouldn't have to stay away because something was scaring her even though she was talking about it as though it were paradise.

Denard: And that's what happens in *Beloved* and *Jazz*. The characters don't go back; Milkman goes back, but Violet and Joe Trace finally are able to negotiate it right there in Harlem. And Sethe and Paul D say in *Beloved* that we have more past than anybody, we need some kind of tomorrow.

Morrison: And their daughter is going to Oberlin College. Denver, the last person you'd think would ever leave the house.

Denard: The clearest indication that the next generation will be alright.

Morrison: I hope that's right.

Interview with Toni Morrison: "The Art of Teaching"

Ann Hostetler / 2002

Previously unpublished interview that took place at Princeton University, on April 17, 2002. Published by permission of Ann Hostetler.

I met with Toni Morrison in her office at Princeton University's Council for Humanities to learn more about her teaching philosophy and practice. I had sent her a number of questions beforehand. When I arrived I saw the questions on her desk, handwritten responses penned in her elegant cursive in the spaces between them. Although it was our first meeting in person, she greeted me warmly as a member of the Toni Morrison Society, and I suggested she begin by answering the questions that seemed most interesting to her. —AH

TM: There was something that interested me in the paper you are writing about one of my books for the upcoming conference.

AH: I am working on a paper entitled "Consolata's Classroom" in which I compare Pat Best and Consolata Sosa as teachers in communities and investigate both the perils and opportunities inherent in their teaching. Would you care to comment on this?

TM: Teachers have to figure out whether to be safe or to take risks. Some avoid taking risks and some take risks. Likewise, they encourage their students to either avoid or take risks. Pat Best was a scholar. Her research was based on data, minus intuition. Consolata, on the other hand, is all intuition and no scholarship. Each method, taken by itself, is deficient. For good teaching you need to use both.

Connie's teaching is based almost entirely on her own experience. She's not trained as a teacher, but she has that background learning from those nuns that the church has forgotten all about, doing what they think is best to train the Arapaho girls that have also been forgotten. And she has the experience of her own despair and recovery to draw on.

For the town of Ruby, on the other hand, Pat's intervention, her data—research into genealogy and family history—is vital. But she lacks the intuition that would reveal its significance to her.

Good teachers need both research and experience, both analysis and intuition. Teaching is also, of course, about the creative mind as it works through whatever problems present themselves to it.

AH: But there also seems to be something dangerous about Consolata's pedagogy. It heals the women, but it also puts them at risk. It jeopardizes their lives and they end up dead.
TM: They wouldn't have been attacked like that if the men hadn't perceived them as strong. Just as it is today, when women are strong, they are subject to attack.

AH: So in a way the attack was a "compliment"—that's not quite the right word—a "tribute" to their strength?
TM: The men of Ruby took those women on as though they were men. If the men of Ruby had come after the convent women a year earlier, for instance, things wouldn't have unfolded the same way. The women would have run, they wouldn't have resisted and fought back. It's too bad they lost. But *did* they lose?

To say that the women lost is to forget all that they learned. They claimed their own voices and found a ground from which to speak. They were able to acknowledge their desires and to use their dreams and their art to realize their own identity. And at the end of the book their lives take on other dimensions. They appear as whole, healed women to those who loved them, however imperfectly—Mavis to her daughter Sally, Pallas and Seneca to their mothers.

That's why I chose to use the New Testament motif of resurrection. After his resurrection, Jesus appears to those who want to see him. Vision is a kind of life. The women of the convent in *Paradise* are not deified, but after death they appear to those who want to see them, just as the risen Christ appeared to his disciples. It's bigger than nostalgia. The person who has the vision, converses with it, becomes larger than themselves. The language of these passages in the novel is not just lyrical, but transitional, as between two realities.

Thus the spiritual elements in the book offer alternate explanations for what becomes of the women at the end.

Love of God is what the book is about. It's about spiritual love—how it gets played out and how it gets corrupted. For instance, the old nuns at the convent are literally abandoned by the church to which they have given their lives. Ruby is founded by the vigor of black Protestants who survived and prospered. But what saved them in the past could not be transferred along the generations.

The idea of Paradise is based on boundaries, on exclusion, which is not love. The vision Piedade has at the end of the novel—of a ship—hints at a vessel on which there is no hierarchy, no exclusion. That's why the "paradise" at the end of the novel is supposed to have a lowercase "p." In the first edition it had an uppercase "P." (We check the paperback I have with me—it's been changed to a lowercase "p.") True paradise is what we enact here. Salvation occurs in context and history. The community of Ruby has not developed a language to accommodate the new, the non-hierarchical notions of community emerging at the convent, so they fear it.

As a novelist, my job is to take ordinary assumptions and to push them to their logical conclusions. Just as I took a friendship between women—in 1969, when no one was writing about friendship between women—and tested that friendship in Sula.

Love is in all of the world's religions, but it keeps getting covered up. The basis of all of them is love, but it gets mangled. The nuns at the convent loved the Arapaho girls, but they didn't know how to respect their culture, and shaped them as they themselves had been taught.

What Consolata does with the women at the convent is what an artist does. Within the death outlines they draw of each other, she encourages them to use paints and chalk to recreate themselves. They lie in a spot of their own making. She encourages them to tell the truth to each other. Only after this can they get beyond the petty fighting that has plagued their relationships with each other. When Consolata says, in the garden, to the green-eyed male, "Oh, you're back," who is he? Is it a male version of herself she has reconnected with? A trickster figure? Jesus? Death?

What I had to do here was to take away the labels of "psycho-babble" and to show the healing. This is difficult, but the hardest thing to do in this novel was to make visions ordinary and not exotic for the characters who have this thing called "faith."

AH: I remember when the full spiritual dimension of *Paradise* first hit home to me. I was sitting in a presentation at the Second Biennial Toni Morrison Society Conference in Lorain, Ohio, when Eleanor Traylor from Howard University broke into song. "He comes to me in the garden, while the dew is still on the roses . . ." and the audience joined in at her urging:

TM: "And he walks with me and he talks with me." My mother is one of those deeply spiritual people who had a personal relationship with Jesus. She would have long talks with him regularly. When I made the money from my first book—$3,000.00—I decided to surprise my parents and my sons with a vacation to Aruba. I chose Aruba because it was beautiful, but also affordable. The only problem was that we had to fly to get there and my mother had a great fear of airplanes. When I told her about the vacation, she said, "I don't fly."

"Then you can't come," I replied. She didn't say anything further, but as we began the process of getting ready, she packed her suitcase, I bought the tickets, and she got on the plane when it was time to go. After we arrived and settled in, I asked her what had made it possible for her to change her mind and fly.

"I had a talk with my maker," she said. "And I told him, that if he was going to let me get up there in the airplane with my daughter and her family, and then was going to let it crash, I didn't want anything to do with his religion."

The mind does what it does when it needs what it needs with whatever canvas religion provides.

AH: What informs your pedagogy in the classroom?

TM: The two most important things in teaching are analysis and passion, and they often fit inside of each other. That is why, for the classroom, neither Pat Best or Consolata, by themselves, has a strategy that is sufficient. They each have something that the other one needs. I was a teacher before I was a writer.

AH: And you were a reader before you were a teacher. Do you think of the reader when you write? And does that awareness of the audience inform your work as a teacher?

TM: Yes. I think of a reader when I write. I am a reader when I write. So the reader I am writing for is at least partly myself. I prize my ability to read in depth. And I try to foster this ability in my students. I think that readers knows more than they think they do. And I try to get my students to see that they, too, know more than they think they do.

AH: I remember hearing Oprah tell the story of how she called you up after reading *Beloved*. She asked you whether it was "normal" to feel compelled, as she did after reading this novel, to go back and reread parts of a story in order to understand the meaning. She says you responded, "Yes, my dear. That is called r-r-r-reading!" I like to tell that story to my students.

TM: She makes me sound so pompous! But that is what reading used to be. A book is a place you can inhabit and return to. When did we get afraid to go back, to reread? Maybe it was that woman back in the 1960s who taught us all to speed-read . . . Evelyn Wood. I'd like my books to be read more than once.

Teaching a book is about asking your students about how they occupy the space of the world the writer has created. I regard the reader as a companion in my books. It's a very intimate relationship that reading provides. I like books that insist on a certain kind of meditation, books that put the reader in a position where they might think about something a little bit differently, that capture the warp and woof of a particular time and place.

AH: What have you found to be your best teaching strategy?

TM: One on one! The classes I teach at Princeton are small—five or six students. I meet individually several times with each student during the writing of each paper and discuss the student's work in detail. I enjoy the editing and the close working with a text line by line. It's a very intimate relationship that reading provides. It's like life—you don't know what's going to happen or what's important. That's *alive!*

AH: And in the classroom?

TM: Placing students in a world closely related to—but different from—what they inhabit. A good book asks students to go to a new place for which they don't need visas—a place that is as deep and rich as your mind is. In teaching, I ask my students to consider how they, as reader, occupy the space in the world that a particular work of literature creates.

I like to think of a class as ending with really interesting questions. Just as when I'm writing, I don't like my books to end, but rather leave the reader with questions that will prompt them to circle back into the text.

A good book may prompt you to go out and learn more about something that hasn't interested you before.

AH: And when you are teaching creative writing?
TM: I do more editing than anything else. When my students begin writing their stories, they often don't know what is important or what they are about. They don't know where to stop on one hand, or where to develop the writing, on the other. I try to open up space in students' writing so that they can glimpse new possibilities. I show them how to pause and look. How to go back and find places like gold mines—places that say something—moments in the story that form connections with the urtext underneath. That give it life.

AH: How do you teach students to listen to each other's work in the classroom setting?
TM: I try to help them to develop a language—a critical, conversational language—so they can tell the truth without hurting others' feelings. We focus on the work, not personality. For each assignment I have four conferences with each student in which we work through an idea they have. In the first conference we discuss their subject, they bring an outline and a first draft to the second conference, in the third we go over the second draft, and in the fourth we go over a third draft.

AH: When did you come to Princeton?
TM: I came to Princeton to work for the Council on Humanities in 1989. Here I developed a course entitled "Studies in American Africanism," which I taught for six years. It is out of this course that the essays in *Playing in the Dark* came. I also teach two courses in creative writing each year.

AH: What have been some of your most difficult moments in the classroom? What did you learn from them?
TM: The greatest difficulty is talking about race without getting students mad at each other. In my course on "American Africanism" I gave lectures to hundreds of students. Then we broke down into small groups for discussion.

The strategy in this situation is to use the language of good literature. The language of real cogitation, rather than name-calling. We live in a culture of name-calling. "Terrorist," for instance. But a true discussion is not a war.

Art is a route into developing a language in order to talk about all sorts of things that are unspeakable. Take for example, Gertrude Stein's *Melanctha*. There is a reason that she's writing about Black women. Through them she creates a world in which she can escape the limits of her own racially constructed reality. One of my students in this course wrote a fine paper about the lithographs from the original edition of *Huckleberry Finn* and examined them in light of their relationship to the text—who was infantilized, etc.

America is a nation of immigrants, and one of the greatest needs of immigrants is to feel at home. How do you do that? One way is to hate Blacks. That makes you White. American. It's a scene you see enacted over and over again in literature, in film, in life. There's a wonderful film called *America, America*, about a Greek coming to America.

At the very end, in a scene not directly related to the plot, a Black man walks through and the Greek immigrant tells him to get out.

In political life, the president of the United States needs to signal something about race. Even Bill Clinton, whom I adore by the way, had to fulfill the demands of this spectacle by pronouncing, "Sistah Souljah is a racist."

AH: Your book of essays, *Playing in the Dark*, grew out of this course?
TM: There were twelve lectures in the course, "American Africanism," but only three of them are in *Playing in the Dark*. When I gave these lectures at Harvard in the early 1990s, the English department was just appalled that I would "race" such writers as Hemingway, Cather, and Stein. The African American Studies department was appalled, too. They wondered why I was focusing on these traditional white writers. "I'm expanding the field of African American studies," I told them. If it hadn't been for Cornel [West], no one there would have taken me seriously.

In giving these lectures, I was simply claiming the space that writers used to have as cultural critics. I thought that this course, these lectures, would be an incisive but narrow intervention in the discussion about race. But it turned out to be something much larger than that.

AH: Will you ever do something more, in terms of writing, with the other nine lectures for this course?

TM: I'm working right now on an essay called "Scarlet and Her Sisters" that comes from a lecture for this course on Hawthorne's *The Scarlet Letter*. Originally I developed this lecture for the College de France when I spent three months in Paris several years ago. However, I lost it on my computer and have had to totally rewrite it, since the college couldn't locate the tape they made of the lecture. I will be delivering the new version—I think it's probably much better because of the rewriting—at an upcoming lecture at the University of Toronto.

AH: *Playing in the Dark* introduced readers to a whole new way of talking about literature and addressing issues that lurk beneath the surface. I used it in a course I taught on your novels in connection with Faulkner's and Virginia Woolf's, and it opened up all sorts of new connections and conversations.

TM: Learning how to read race is very important. For instance, in *Paradise* I begin with the line, "They shoot the white girl first." And then I never mention the race of the women in the book again. Readers must then learn about how they read race. And they will discover that race gives us very little information about a person. In fact, the race of a person is the least important thing you can know about them.

AH: I found this to be true for me as I read this novel, that in wondering about the race of the characters, I confronted stereotypes I didn't know I possessed.

TM: Where I grew up in Lorain, Ohio, I lived among a mixture of peoples—Italian, African American, Irish—all brought together by jobs in nearby industries. I had good friends there—not black or white friends—but friends. Certainly there was some name-calling, a child's language is one of name-calling, but the personal experience we had denied the labels. I didn't realize how different my community was until I went to Howard and, for the first time, encountered people who had grown up in predominantly black neighborhoods.

AH: It must have been a culture shock.

TM: It was! I remember, for instance, telling one of my friends at Howard that a good friend of mine was studying at the Goodman Theater. "I didn't know that there were any Black students at the Goodman Theater," she replied. What she didn't realize is that my friend wasn't Black. It didn't occur to her as a possibility. And then in the 1950s and '60s, we suddenly had to prove that we were Black. Just as today's rap artists have a style that claims a certain set of ghetto attributes for "Blackness," even though most of them never grew up poor.

AH: Although we know that readers resist "what has a palpable design upon us," as Keats would say, do you see yourself as a teacher through your fiction?
TM: Each one of the novels has a pedagogical impulse. That is what the creative enterprise is about—helping people see the world.

The novels place readers in worlds that show them "this is what race feels like," or "this is what friendship is like."

Sula talks about friendship between women at a time—I was writing it in 1969—when women and women's friendships weren't considered worthy subjects for fiction.

In *Song of Solomon* the reader asks, "How did these men get educated?" "How do they learn about the heroic possibilities for men?" and "How does this relate to women?"

Tar Baby asks, "How do people from entirely different cultures know love?" and "How do they not come together because of cultural difference?"

Beloved takes, of course, the story of Margaret Garner, a story no one wanted to remember, the buried past, and resurrects it. But it is as much about the obsessive love of mothers and children in the context of slavery as it is about history.

Jazz was my attempt to reclaim the era from F. Scott Fitzgerald, but it also uses the techniques of jazz—improvisation, listening—to ask questions that I want to ask of myself.

Paradise is about going out into the wilderness and attempting to create utopia, then asking, "Why does it collapse?"

AH: Why did you choose to leave editing for teaching? What has kept you going as a teacher over the years?
TM: Publishing and editing are very hard work and, as the industry changed during the 1970s, it became less interesting to me. What I enjoyed most was line editing, working with the actual text. Editing became more about acquiring works from superstars and less about discovering writers and working with their manuscripts. Copyeditors took over more and more of the actual

work with the manuscript and book editors did less and less. Nurturing writers that publishers don't want to publish is also not very rewarding.

AH: There are many teaching opportunities outside of the classroom. In your work at Random House you brought a number of new writers to the public and created resources such as *The Black Book*. Do you see yourself as a teacher in your work as an editor and a writer of nonfiction?
TM: I learned many useful strategies from my work as an editor. For instance, when I put together the collection of essays on Clarence Thomas and Anita Hill, I knew quite a few people who were able to write essays for that book. "The last word on this subject will be Ted Koppel if I don't do something about it," I thought.

AH: Some creative writers view classroom teaching as a necessary chore that can detract from their writing. You have been both a teacher and a highly successful novelist for many years. How do you view the relationship between these activities in your life?
TM: Teaching is a way of thinking for me, as is writing. But I can give up the teaching, whereas I can't give up the writing. And, quiet as it's kept, they pay me.

AH: I suppose at this point in your career, with small classes and a select group of students, that teaching taking away from your writing time is not so much of an issue.
TM: Oh, no. There is no doubt that it does take away time from the writing. [Ms. Morrison breathed a sigh familiar to every teacher-writer I know.]

Our interview came to a close as another visitor arrived. I left Ms. Morrison's office feeling that I had had the privilege of being one of her students for several hours.

Star Power

Adam Langer / 2003

From *Book* (November/December 2003). Reprinted by permission of Adam Langer.

Toni Morrison looks weary. The seventy-two-year-old Nobel laureate has just returned from a doctor's appointment and she's complaining of eye trouble. Lately, she says, she's been having difficulty doing the crossword puzzle. She says she is putting off eye surgery because of an upcoming book tour, and her doctor has scolded her for focusing more on her career than her health. "Priorities, Ms. Morrison," the doctor said. "Priorities."

Appearing before a large group or on television, Morrison is an expansive and charismatic figure, not merely a writer but *the* writer, the high priestess of American literature. In person and out of the spotlight, though, she can seem worn down, and often when she speaks, her voice does not rise above a whisper. Occasionally, when she tells a wicked story about, say, the ineptitude of would-be shoe bomber Richard Reid, or, at a photo shoot when her makeup artist regales her with tales of celebrity romances, suddenly you can see that glint in her eyes, hear her roar with laughter. But then, just as suddenly, she'll stop and stare into space, her eyes gazing out in the indeterminate distance. One wonders what she might be looking for.

Though she has seemed ubiquitous over the last decade, thanks in large part to Oprah Winfrey, who named four of Morrison's books to her book club, since receiving the Nobel Prize in literature in 1993, Morrison has only published one novel, 1998's *Paradise*. That book, an ambitious but unrelentingly grim exploration of guilt and revenge, received some rave reviews but also some of the worst of Morrison's career. The 1998 film version of Morrison's 1987 *Beloved*, directed by Jonathan Demme, was coolly received by critics and was a disappointment at the box office. A writer for *Variety* called it a "neutron bomb," suggesting that, though it did not destroy the studio that produced it, it effectively killed the careers of many humans

206

involved. Morrison's most recent published work has been the first book in her series of Who's Got Game children's stories, co-authored with her son Slade. The books, written in a faux hip-hop style and illustrated by Pascal LeMaitre, attempt modestly to subvert Aesop's Fables, just as Morrison undermines traditional literary genres in her adult fiction.

Now Morrison's first novel in nearly five years arrives with great expectations and a remarkably economical page count—only some very spacious typesetting allows *Love* to reach two hundred pages. At first glance, the length would seem to suggest that Morrison may be slowing down. The only problem with this theory, though, is the novel itself, which, despite its slimness, is a powerhouse. Taut and uncompromising, *Love* is a compact meditation on the aftermath of the civil rights movement, a chilling ghost story about a friendship destroyed by the whims of a wealthy and respected patriarch, an epic saga about the generation gap, a concise reflection on the African-American experience in the twentieth century. Dreamy, nonlinear, vigorous, and vital, it explores enough Big Issues to keep Morrison scholars busy for decades to come while keeping Morrison readers second-guessing their own presumptions. Earlier this year, Morrison told the audience at a booksellers convention that the new book is "perfect," and when we meet, she says it again. She says it with her tongue partly in her cheek, but she also adds that she has only felt this way about one previous novel: 1992's *Jazz*. Her writing, she says, is better than ever.

"Only in other ways," she observes ruefully, "am I slowing down."

Toni Morrison is sitting on an ottoman in the apartment she owns in a jaw-droppingly opulent down-town Manhattan building. She divides her time among her New York apartment; New Jersey, where she is on the faculty at Princeton and runs the Atelier program, a collaborative arts program that she founded approximately ten years ago; and a converted boathouse in Rockland County, New York. That house burned down on Christmas Day 1993, shortly after she won the Nobel Prize, but it has since been rebuilt.

Morrison has been working on last-minute edits for *Love*. Though she has not worked as a full-time editor for nearly twenty years, she still behaves like one on her own projects. She is savvy about the publishing process. Earlier this year, when Simon and Schuster was publishing *Who's Got Game: The Ant or the Grasshopper?*, she would not talk about *Love*; now that Knopf is publishing *Love*, she prefers to keep discussion of the kids' books to a minimum. For *Love*, she has kept a close watch over all aspects of the process—from the evolution of the title (first, the novel was called *A Sporting Woman*; next, simply *L.*; and now *Love*) to the cover ("It's hard to get that color that's not purple, that doesn't suggest Danielle Steel," she says. "We had to take it down, bring it up, move it over") to punctuation. Lately, she says, she's been fighting with her editor about commas. "I don't like the comma that comes before 'and,'" she says. "I hate it. You've got the 'and.' What do you need the comma for?"

Morrison's editor, Robert Gottlieb, chuckles about Morrison's remarks, saying the editing process on *Love* has been smooth. "This particular book didn't require any large editing. It didn't need rethinking," says Gottlieb, the New York publishing legend who has edited such authors as Robert Caro, John le Carré, and Joseph Heller and was, from 1987 to 1992, the editor of the *New Yorker*. Gottlieb, who has known Morrison since both were editors at Random House, had edited all of Morrison's books from 1974's *Sula* to 1987's *Beloved*, but did not work on *Jazz* or *Paradise*. "Toni appears to be such a formidable person, and *is* such a formidable person, that people assume that working with her could be difficult," he says. "It's exactly the opposite. Because she has been an editor and because she's smart as well as talented, she gets it right away and she knows whether it makes sense to her or not."

Gottlieb places the new novel very high in the canon of Morrison's work. "It knows the story it wants to tell," he says. "It's found the language in which to tell it. Nothing is there that shouldn't be there, and everything that should be there is there." Gottlieb may be biased, but in this case he is also right.

Love is set on the site of a long-shuttered resort, the sort of black-owned vacation spot that flourished in the first half of the twentieth century. It is a resort much like Amelia Island, Florida, or Idlewild, Michigan, where numerous luminaries of the Harlem Renaissance summered (though Morrison says her own family would never have had the money to vacation there). Morrison says she was interested in exploring the legacy of such resorts, which thrived during a time when a vibrant, independent black society existed before civil rights; the loss of this sort of establishment is one of many compromises that had to be made in exchange for integration. Morrison's elegiac remembrance of this era is designed to re-examine preconceptions about civil rights and the idea that "everyone got on board with it," as she puts it.

"It's not about the civil rights movement not being a good idea. It was absolutely necessary, particularly in terms of jobs and so on. It's just that there was a price, that's all," Morrison says. "There were these fabulous black schools, high schools, insurance companies, resorts, and the business class was very much involved. They had worked very hard to have their own resorts outside Detroit and New Jersey where they were all black and very upscale. Those stores are gone; those hotels are gone."

Though Morrison has received her share of criticism over the years for pursuing a particularly feminist or black nationalist agenda, one of the most striking aspects of the novel is how Morrison refuses to judge her characters, how they develop lives of their own, despite what even the author herself may have envisioned for them. The original title, *A Sporting Woman*, took its inspiration from a character whom Morrison originally saw as a personification of "free-floating malice," someone both "wanton" and "rootless." But as Morrison continued writing, she grew to understand her character more thoroughly. That character, Junior, still plays a significant role in *Love*, and the character's callousness and her particular brand of morality strongly impact the novel's outcome. But now, she's only one of a passel of memorable characters, nearly all of whom get equal attention as Morrison spins her tale.

"These are not people that I would go on a vacation with," Morrison says. "But they are fascinating to me, compelling to me, even the minor ones. And my eye is rather calm when I examine them because I can't do them justice if I'm judging and condemning."

Toni Morrison remembers Lorain, Ohio, the town where she was born, as an integrated place, where blacks and whites mingled freely. She set her first book, *The Bluest Eye*, here. Located on the shores of Lake Erie at the mouth of the Black River, Lorain now is, much like the seaside resort town at the heart of her new novel, a city in decay, its best years long since relegated to scrapbooks, its population slowly but inevitably dwindling. "The people we knew here, they're all dying," says Lois Brooks, Morrison's one surviving sibling.

Though Morrison doesn't get back to Lorain much, and hasn't called it home since her mother died in 1994 at the age of eighty-seven, her presence can still be felt here—on Elyria Avenue in the house where she first lived; at the public library in the Toni Morrison Reading Room; at Lorain County Community College, where an abstract sculpture entitled *The Gift* depicts three figures holding up a stone upon which appear quotations by both Aristotle and Morrison. "We die. That may be the meaning of life. But we do language. That may be the measure of our lives," Morrison's reads.

She was born here in 1931 as Chloe Anthony Wofford, the daughter of George Wofford, who worked in the construction, shipbuilding and steel industries, and Ella Ramah Wofford, who, when she wasn't staying at home with her children, worked at the American Stove Works and as a custodian in the Lorain Public Schools. Her childhood pal Rosemary DiFilippo, a retired schoolteacher, remembers the Woffords as being "a very warm family." DiFilippo used to play with Toni using home-made dolls that they fashioned out of hollyhocks and toothpicks, since neither family had the money to buy dolls. "It was a good Christian family where there was unity and love and very much compassion towards the people who lived near them," DiFilippo says. "My mother was very comfortable with me being next door knowing that Mrs. Wofford would take care of me. Everybody watched over everybody's kids."

Morrison had two brothers and had a tight relationship with her sister, Lois, with whom she still talks nearly every day. They were so close in age (Lois is a year and a half older) and they were together so often that Morrison says it took a while for her to recognize her own name: "People used to call out, 'Loisandchloe! Where's Loisandchloe?' And I wasn't sure which part of that was my name."

Morrison's earliest memories are filled with the sounds of her mother's singing. Mrs. Wofford was part of the choir at the Greater St. Matthew A.M.E. Church in Lorain. "She was amazing," recalls Morrison. "She sang *Carmen*, she sang what Ella Fitzgerald sang. . . . Her voice was beautiful; mine was nothing."

If she wasn't much of a singer, she was, by all accounts, a dedicated reader. Her first-grade teacher, Esther Hunt, remembers her fondness for reading, even in the first grade. "She was just a nice little girl from a good family with very cooperative parents. She and her brothers and sister were all bright and always clean and well-dressed," Hunt says. Morrison's sister, Lois Brooks, recalls that while the family moved all over the city, they were always near the library. "Our parents encouraged us," Brooks says. "We told stories a lot. There was always a lot of storytelling and that leads to books." Chloe even worked at the Lorain Public Library during high school, serving as secretary to the head librarian. Today, the library's reading room is named for Morrison. "I tried to detour them from something else they had in mind, which was either a statue or a street," Morrison says. "I said, you know what I would really like? I would like a room with books in it and comfortable chairs and nothing else and just call it the Toni Morrison Room."

The rest of the Morrison story is a tale of some personal trials interspersed with phenomenal professional artistic success. After graduating from Lorain High School, she attended Howard University, where she majored in English and toured the South with a drama troupe, the Howard University Players. She received her B.A. in 1953. Amiri Baraka, the author of the play *Dutchman* and the controversial former poet laureate of New Jersey, attended Howard with Morrison. He remembers her as "one of the most beautiful women I'd ever seen," but says he didn't have the nerve to say so, because she was a senior when he was a mere sophomore.

"I remember her running for queen of Alpha Kappa Alpha sorority and I remember her riding around on campus in an open limo just like the president," says Baraka. "I don't think she won, but as far as I was concerned she should have."

After Howard, she went on to Cornell, where she got her M.A. in English literature in 1955. Her thesis concerned William Faulkner and Virginia Woolf. She later returned to Howard to teach, and met her husband, Harold Morrison, a Jamaica-born architect, with whom she had two children, Slade and Harold Ford, also an architect; Morrison got divorced in 1964 and raised the boys on her own. She entered the publishing world as a textbook editor in Syracuse, New York, for L. W. Stringer, a subsidiary of Random House, and then in New York City at Random House itself. Morrison's first novel, *The Bluest Eye*, began as a short story she wrote while she was at Howard. Published in 1970, the novel used young Pecola Breedlove's tragic desire for blue eyes as a metaphor for the ravages inflicted by racism. Though not a major commercial success at the time, it is now seen as a landmark in American literature, signaling a shift away from the white male–dominated literary establishment.

"*The Bluest Eye* dealt with a lot of no-no's," says Adrienne Seward, a professor at Colorado College and the current president of the Toni Morrison Society, which is composed of about four hundred members and is dedicated to scholarship regarding Morrison's work. "Incest, self-hatred, those sorts of things that weren't supposed to be discussed in the black community. Incest was supposed to be a white problem."

"Morrison was trying to complicate the romantic notion that many black people subscribe to, that black is beautiful," says Marilyn Mobley McKenzie, associate provost at George Mason University and a former president of the society. "But there were parts of the country where black wasn't beautiful yet.

That book showed that there were pockets of self-loathing and racism that had not been confronted yet."

Morrison took the money she made from *The Bluest Eye* and took her parents and her children to Aruba. "That was hip," she says with a laugh. "That was fantastic. They'd never been outside of the country. They loved everything, even the little things."

Throughout the '70s and '80s, Morrison alternated between the lives of writer and editor; while she was working with such authors as Toni Cade Bambara, Angela Davis, and Muhammad Ali, she was also writing such novels as *Sula* (nominated for the 1975 National Book Award), *Song of Solomon* (a 1977 National Book Critics Circle winner), and *Tar Baby*. One of the reasons *Tar Baby* was so full of references to cooking and food, Morrison has said, was because she was editing a cookbook at the time. She left publishing in 1983, and a year later took a job as a professor at the State University of New York at Albany. In 1988 Morrison won the Pulitzer Prize for fiction for *Beloved*.

Though literary critics have described Morrison's work as transgressive, she prefers to call herself "a saboteur," an author who continually challenges her readers' and her own preconceptions about some of the defining issues of American culture: racism, civil rights, slavery, patriarchy. Emerging in an era when black writing was seen as a predominantly male endeavor and women writers were perceived as predominantly white, she redefined the role of a "black woman writer."

"I didn't want to be an honorary male or an honorary white person," Morrison says. "When people complimented me, saying, by implication, 'You're better than a black or a woman writer,' I would always counter with 'I am a black woman writer,' and that was not a narrow field. Because of those two modifiers ['black' and 'woman'], I felt my imaginative world was wider and deeper, that I had some access to and some sensibilities about worlds that may not have been available to white men."

"She wants to challenge what white people have taken for granted about race, and she's very interested in complicating what black folk have taken for granted about race," says Marilyn Mobley McKenzie.

Morrison's contribution to the world of literature was confirmed with the ultimate honor: After the publication of *Jazz*, she was awarded the Nobel Prize in literature. She was the first black woman ever to receive it.

"Ooohhhh, that was the height," Lois Brooks says with unbridled glee when recalling her sister's honor. "It was just incredible. I can't describe how much it meant for me for her to get it. We talked about it that morning and then my phone started ringing like crazy."

If Toni Morrison seems somewhat fatigued, that still doesn't mean she's getting ready to take a vacation any time soon. She has recently completed a libretto for *Margaret Garner*, an opera with music by American composer Richard Danielpour. Its eponymous heroine was the real-life inspiration for *Beloved*. The rest of Toni and Slade's sextet of children's books are on the way. A miniseries based on *Paradise*, produced by Oprah Winfrey's Harpo Productions, is currently being written by the Pulitzer Prize–winning playwright Suzan-Lori Parks. And Morrison is already at work on her next novel. It will be set in the eighteenth century, a period she says she is now researching. "It's scary stuff," she says. "But then, it's all scary to me." Most likely, Gottlieb says, he will be the editor. "We both hope to be together again," he says. "If it takes her eight years and we're both eighty, who knows? If it takes her two or three, actuarially we have a good shot at it." And Morrison is, of course, gearing up for the book tour for *Love*.

"I don't even know what it means to go on vacation," she says. "Work is pleasure for me."

Still, all the work and success have come at a price, and there is a sense that what often seems like weariness is also a yearning for what has passed. As conversation turns again to Lorain, Ohio, the author says she might, in fact, go on vacation if only she could be sure she'd see the stars at night. She says she's barely seen them in thirty years. If she knew where to find them, she might just take a vacation so she could see them again.

"They used to be up there in Lorain," she says. "As kids we saw the Milky Way. Seeing them was something you could count on. Life is different if you can look up and see the stars. I suppose if I were really an adventuresome person, I would just say, 'Look, I want to know where the stars are,' and I would go on a ship and I would just go follow the stars. I'd get a travel guide or something. I'd say, 'Where are the stars? Take me there.' There are probably generations that don't remember seeing the stars, and I think if somebody ripped away whatever it is that's blocking them, and the stars were out, there'd be a massive shift. All the kids would run out into the streets. Instead of fireworks, there would be this thing in your life, these stars."

"Oh, you've got me going now," she says with a laugh. "I'm going to go on a star trek. That's just what I'm going to do."

The Nature of Love: An Interview with Toni Morrison

Diane McKinney-Whetstone / 2003

From *Essence* (October 2003). Reprinted by permission of Diane McKinney-Whetstone.

I've got Toni Morrison's voice in my ear, her voice so textured and nuanced, with an ageless quality though she's in her seventies now. She laughs easily and often during our conversation, speaking in rivers of sentences that flow and deepen and then converge in ideas that are startlingly precise. I'm realizing more than ever the importance of that voice, which has defined the beauty and brutality of the human condition, from *The Bluest Eye* to *Paradise*, earning a Pulitzer Prize for *Beloved* in 1988 and the Nobel Prize in Literature in 1993. Now, in her eighth novel, *Love*, Toni Morrison locates us so sensually in the book's coastal setting that we actually feel the mist rise up from the sea as we become absorbed in the lives of the women who revolve around Bill Cosey, wealthy owner of Cosey's Hotel and Resort. Even after Cosey's death, the women struggle with having been obsessed with him, having been damaged and saved by him—having Loved him in some way. Following are portions of our conversation.

Diane Mckinney-Whetstone: You've said that in all your novels, you are answering a question. What question were you answering as you wrote *Love*?

Toni Morrison: I was interested in the way in which sexual love and other kinds of love lend themselves to betrayal. How do ordinary people end up ruining the thing they most want to protect? And obviously the heart of that is really the effort to love. The first thing I wrote was that gang-rape scene. I had this kid in mind, Romen, who is unable to participate in this male rite of passage and is ashamed of the fact that he is unable to do it. And to the contempt of his friends, he releases the girl.

DMW: You don't back off from the themes that some might find unsettling. Do you feel obligated as a novelist to disturb?

TM: Well, I get disturbed, I'm mindful of what disturbed means. I have some friends who tell me what they really think about what I write. One said, "You really take us to these terrible places, but the consequence of having been there and come out of it was a kind of cleansing." Another said, "Oh, my dear, I'm so glad that you're willing to talk about things that don't get talked about."

DMW: What do you say to people who find your books complicated or challenging?

TM: I find that a good thing. We're a very complicated people. I take my cue from music. Nothing is more complicated than jazz, or even the nuances of the blues. We're accustomed to very complicated art forms, we really are. It's only in literature that we think we're supposed to skim, probably because of the way in which we've been educated. So much popular literature takes the more convenient route to arouse emotions and satisfy rather than what I think is the more interesting, which is the provocation.

DMW: What's absorbing you these days?

TM: I've gotten myself into so much. I did some children's books with my son. We revised all of Aesop's tales, made them kind of hip. I was commissioned to write the libretto for an opera based on Margaret Garner, the woman whose life I sort of plundered for *Beloved*, and I finished that. Also some essays, and I'm still teaching at Princeton.

DMW: As a former book editor, what do you think of the current literary scene?

TM: I've been very pleased by some contributions, particularly from younger women. Some are African-American, some are Indian, Native American, Asian. There's such a wide variety now—people in their twenties and thirties really making that effort. And I'm delighted because I had had the feeling that most creative people were going into other genres, into theater or moviemaking, which is fine, but I had thought that the novel wasn't as seductive a calling as it used be. There is an enormous Black readership and their hunger is bottomless, and it is being beautifully, beautifully fed. I'm very optimistic.

Michael Silverblatt Talks with Toni Morrison about *Love*

Michael Silverblatt / 2004

From *Bookworm* on KCRW Radio (February 12, 2004). Reprinted by permission of Michael Silverblatt.

Silverblatt: From KCRW Santa Monica I'm Michael Silverblatt and this is *Bookworm*. Today I'm very pleased and honored to have as my guest Toni Morrison who has been on the show once before. Once again, we are speaking to her by phone to her home in New York and the occasion is the publication of her new novel *Love*. She's the author, of course, in reverse order of *Paradise, Jazz, Beloved, Tar Baby, Song of Solomon, Sula*, and the *Bluest Eye*. Those are her novels.

I wanted to begin by saying that it struck me that people are needing several years to read *Jazz*, to read *Paradise*, and now *Love* because the books seem to me to be extremely brilliant and complex in their organization. This book *Love* seems to me to be about time and place—the way in which, depending on who you are and when you were there, your experience changes who you are, what love is, and what you know. The setting of this place has once been a resort. The people in the resort have moved into a home on Monarch Street. They are in an area that has been once an Oceanside, but now there's a place called Oceanside, not by an ocean with very cheap government housing. Other places that people remember are covered now by water. The place that we're hearing about so vibrantly does not exist except in memory. And the book seems to be about the way love is a collection of the pieces that people can assemble even when they can't speak to one another, the reader assembles love. Is that correct?

Morrison: Very, very close. What came to mind as you were talking was the idea I had of the way crystal forms. You know you have a small piece and then it expands to another. And another layer comes on in a different shape, but it's all the same material. And when you get finished it's different facets, different light looking at one simple thing.

Silverblatt: Now how does one go about . . . I know that it is in a sense a presumptuous question because one never asks a magician about a particular trick. And it's even wrong to think of it as a trick, but the book seems to have been constructed in a very unusual way. That is to say, I don't know the words for it, but it seems that there are gists for each character, and in each section there's a passing of impulse almost so that one character reports on the previous one's experience and then extends it. Were there diagrams, how did you work? (Laughs)

Morrison: (Laughs) No, I had diagrams for groups of people and rooms and streets, but the structure basically was how to reveal this responsibility that this man Bill Cosey was given, all these roles. And how his life and his entrepreneurship affected, destroyed, helped, re-made a set of people who lived in that community. So he is sort of not really on stage. Everything has to accrue around him. And in order to describe how and whether and what was possible in terms of the range of kinds of love in the book, I had this collection of people who knew him and each other in different ways and had a terrible time trying to articulate this.

Silverblatt: Now you mentioned crystals, and I noticed that there were certain constellations that seem permanent in the book—but from group of characters to group of characters. We have a couple who are raising their [grandson], and also in a house, we have a very similar situation with a granddaughter who has come. Her grandfather is now dead; her mother has been put in a home—there is a sense of how generations mirror one another through layers of time and space.

Morrison: Well it's true. It's that the past of one is very much connected to the past of another and across generational lines. In the book, I wanted to stress what happens when you can't talk between those lines. I'm thinking a lot in this book about the connection between love and language, and I wanted to have the narrator, the woman who opens and closes the book, who intervenes in it, be a person who understands how precious language is. And it was interesting to me how she only says three or four things to the characters and styles herself as a woman who was always quiet. But she's talking constantly to the reader, constantly going on and on. And for her some things were unspeakable, I think. And for the others, theirs was not unspeakability; it's just a frozen language. They have no language to talk to one another. But the ability to speak . . . she says, "if they only understood how precious the tongue was . . . ," to be able to say, or to reveal, or to admit, which is a way of knowing. And they were never able to do that until they get rid of the hovering excuse they had for not coming together, which was Bill Cosey.

Silverblatt: Now the book seems to be arranged so that the narrator, Toni Morrison, or . . . how do I put this, so that Toni Morrison can be separate from several different narrators. And that the structure should emerge almost on its own. The author is in charge of charting a crystalline growth, say, or an accumulation. So for instance, we will watch a woman leave home on the way to her lawyer's office. She has an idea. By the time she reaches that office, a very brief scene, we've gone through several of her lives and marriages. And it's all been in a sense, immaculately stage managed. The amount of background that gets compressed into each scene—it's not just a matter of linkages; it's a matter of knowing how to manage the house so that the hotel at the center of the book is something really for a novelist. In a hotel, many people are living and it takes the efforts of an entire staff to chart who's on the dance floor, who's at the foyer, who's in the kitchen, who's cleaning, who's made up the menus for this day's special, who's hidden the will, who's hidden the deed, and where will this all go? And it's almost as if the Toni Morrison, implied by this book, is a vast staff of arrangers whose job is to get everything immaculately in place and then disappear! (Laughs)

Morrison: I hope I disappeared. I hope I did. Well, you know my feeling is that the plot, the lean plot, is information. This is *what* happened. But the *meaning* of a novel is in the structure. The question of when the information is given, at what time, what you want the reader to not just know, but feel about this character. And then to learn more and that's when the crystal begins to take its shape. Just writing the beginning, the middle, the end is one way to do it. It's not very interesting to me because it's not really life-like. I mean, we don't live lives in plots. We sometimes retell ourselves the narrative of our lives in a chronological way, but it doesn't happen to us that way. We learn something today that clarifies something ten years ago. Or, we think the most momentous thing that ever happened was something that happened yesterday or twenty years ago only to learn that it was part really of something else, or that it wasn't momentous at all. So that the way in which the mind takes in the varieties of experiences of life and other people, has to be reassembled for its meaning and that's where the structure, at least what I work very hard at, is the sort of deep structure, what is there underneath this activity. And then you see it from another person's point of view; not just one character but another's, and how and when that information becomes available to the reader seems to me to be the real adventure.

Silverblatt: It seems to me that we come to understand of this group as several others in your books: that their identities are dependent upon their relations to one another.
Morrison: Absolutely.

Silverblatt: And that they may often, for private reasons, want to conceal those relationships. They may be the subjects of scandal. And so truth is about what conceals identity in some strange way. And the working of this book, at least, is to watch—I thought of interconnected cogs—like a watch works. To watch these cogs turning until they turn so carefully with such jewel-like design that their arrangement allows the reader to see a whole beyond the purview of any single figure.
Morrison: Exactly. If you're careful, in the reading you get the whole sort of back of the clock as well as the face, as it were. And you see them working and depending on one another so completely for almost every movement, every thought, whether it's back and forth, or wordly, or whatever. I like that notion of the cogs. It gives me another way to think and talk about it. But there are no isolated people. They may feel separate, but everything they do and think is connected to the behavior, or what they think was the reason for the behavior of somebody else.

Silverblatt: We get the sense, really, that the only way to know, even within a single consciousness, is to assemble the whole. Now would you be willing to tell me in what way you think of the *whole* in this book. What are they reaching toward?
Morrison: The title.

Silverblatt: Love.
Morrison: Love. But not just carnal or the way we normally talk about it, reduced to its lowest common denominator, but that human instinct to care for somebody else. Whether it comes from Romen, as a teenager, who doesn't even know that he wants to rescue but he can't help it and is ashamed of it; or whether it's appetite, or whether it's parental love, or love of a father as Cosey

had for his son; or the love of the grandfather trying to explain in some comprehensible language and give advice to his grandson; or just that closeness of two children that is so close they're like invisible friends. And the sort of wide-spirited love that L has for them all, which is sort of unconditional but it has some certain conditions because she's perfectly willing to judge them very sternly, but she obviously is not going to abandon them. As a matter of fact, she takes steps to make sure that they are not abandoned no matter how silly or stupid they may at some point appear to her to be.

Silverblatt: Now I'm beginning to understand this. Is it possible, then, that for each of these characters there's a defining love? Cosey's for his son perhaps, Billy, Billy boy.
Morrison: And then his mistress.

Silverblatt: And then his mistress, and that other simulacra, other mirages of love.
Morrison: All kinds. May is just terrified of the revolution coming. She will lose her place, the property. Her move into another status; the girls are shattered not only because they had been separated, but they had been trained to hate one another, which is a little bit different from being split apart. And then there is an abiding love of the L character. And then there is the nice sort of companionship of the grandparents who are Romen's grandparents. And then there is this little broken girl, Junior, who had no opportunities, really, to experience it except for one tiny moment when Romen lifts her broken foot up and caresses it. And she feels this strange, alien thing that makes her giddy. She doesn't even know what it is. It's almost like trust. Not big enough to be called love. But it's the beginning of something. And then so that this urgency, this thing we want to be, someone should love us, and also we have to love somebody. And that's the simple way of saying it, but when you take it apart and look at it closely, that's what they were all yearning for and having difficulty achieving, responding to, and clarifying. So I did run through that manuscript carefully after I finished it and knew what the title would be and removed every word every time "love" appeared so that it would be raw when the first time those women say it, is the only time they could say it.

Silverblatt: Yes, and what happens is, ultimately, there are replacements for love that they try to use, and love's a hugely uncomfortable thing. And so in

one case that love between young girls becomes the hatred between those two women. And that hatred replaces their love, but binds them together.
Morrison: Right. They're still there. They can't live without one another.

Silverblatt: In the same house. Oh my goodness. So in other words, there is for each of these relationships, a spectrum of alternatives to love . . . in other words they desert love.
Morrison: Exactly. They abandon it and it morphs into this other thing. Junior, hers is hunger—she's just eating all the time, trying to fill up. Romen is embarrassed by the first one until he is able to claim himself with her. But it's something that doesn't go away. It might even be natural to him. It's true, appetite can take the place of that feeling he had when he was at that party. It's true that Junior can, knowing that it was all her, the only one she can trust is herself. So she's constantly looking for more things to eat. And the women are there in this frozen, clear silence together.

Silverblatt: The characters are going to replace love with something that feels stronger than love to them: envy, hatred, jealousy, wealth.
Morrison: Love is scary to them.

Silverblatt: And so now what, in relation to this, is that empty resort.
Morrison: Well, it is I suppose a culmination of something that started out with a certain kind of love on the part of Bill Cosey, which was to have this fabulous place that was for good times.

Silverblatt: The best good times.
Morrison: The best good times, this side of the law. And to see that slowly drain away for a number of reasons. You're right; it wasn't only that Black people didn't have to go there anymore. It wasn't only that he was distracted after his son died and married this little girl because he had the license to do it, he could act out a whim because his mistress left town. It wasn't only because May was so destructive in her terror. And it wasn't only because of his choice of a bride. It was a combination of things. But what sucked up all their ambition about loving one another was turning their attention to him. He was the one who authenticated them. He was the one whose legacy they would all fight over. He was the one who ruined their lives beyond repair. And they lied about it to themselves all the time. And he probably wasn't thinking about any

of them. But the point is that they were complicit in that movement of constantly making him the big daddy, the one who did it all. And everything was his fault and, therefore, *you* did this, and *you* did this, and *you* did this, until they finally exorcise him. But, in any case, they're at the point now where nothing but language can save them. And that's when you can say L-O-V-E.

Silverblatt: It seems to me, then, to go back to my observation at the beginning, that people are almost needing years to interrogate these novels, these more recent novels. (Morrison laughs) It seems as if a novel is something like a haunted house; that as we live with a novel longer, as it becomes older, as it is no longer new and populated with characters who are new to us, but rather as time goes on with ghosts, we start to know where the bodies are buried. We start to know what ghosts need: attention, need to be bombed. It's almost as if the time spent by a novel in its culture is about healing that novel. In other words, the problems are not solved in the novel, but are solved, in a sense, by time and the position of the reader who was asked to explore the haunted house until it can be free of its ghosts and re-inhabited. Yes?

Morrison: Yes, and then the epiphany. I mean, it's true. If you would just, as a reader, open the door or see an open door, step in, and look around. No, you don't know who this is right away, no, you don't know who that is, no, you may not know what that room is for. If you like it, you'll go further. If you're afraid of it, you'll step out. Maybe you'll go back in later in another time. And then maybe you'll run around the whole house and get the lay of the land. And then later you'll go back into that house, and now you can see something else, something different. Now you don't have to worry about what's going to happen. Now you can just enjoy the place where these things happened and understand far more than the characters ever did about what this place is. And the more familiar it becomes, my hope is that it doesn't become dross, that it's still interesting; to look in these nooks and crannies, to have that visceral response as well as this sort of cognitive, intellectual response to how this whole thing is put together.

Silverblatt: Ah, so in other words, for the book as for some of these characters, clarity brings resonance.

Morrison: Absolutely. You know for me that's the reason one reads, again. I mean I, and I'm sure you have, books that you read one year and later on you read them again, and it's a different book or it appears to be. It isn't. You've changed perhaps or you know more now, or you're looking for something else other than the obvious, other than the *what happens*. And the only other thing I know like that—well I'm sure they're many other things—but the one that comes closest to mind is, in addition to becoming familiar with and being interested in a house, is also music in which you hear a song when you're seventeen and then you have a powerful reaction in one way. And you hear it later, and you have another reaction. But what you're reacting to is the same piece of music, perhaps done in different hands, but your memories of it are of the first time you encountered it, as well as what you're thinking now, and so now it's worth listening to again.

Silverblatt: That is so interesting because one of these characters thinks to herself that "Mood Indigo" will help someone swim.
Morrison: It's seductive.

Silverblatt: It will set the rhythm. And one takes "Mood Indigo," if one's listening to its words, as a song that would impede passage. "You ain't been blue no no." And so yes, after you've lived with the words long enough you hear the force and the structure.
Morrison: Right. Exactly so.

Silverblatt: Well it's been a real pleasure to talk to you again. I've really enjoyed it.
Morrison: It's always a delight talking to you. You are a really, you're such a first-rate reader. I mean it's lovely.

Silverblatt: Well I'm grateful to have the work of a truly extraordinary novelist to read.
Morrison: Thank you so much.

Silverblatt: Thank you.

"I Want to Write like a Good Jazz Musician": Interview with Toni Morrison

Michael Saur / 2004

From *Rowohlt Revue* (Fall 2004). Reprinted by permission of Michael Saur.

Happiness, Pain, Obsession—the Nobel Prize–winning author writes of love and loss of love in her latest novel. Michael Saur spoke with her about the magic of power, Black bourgeoisie, and the advantages of being famous.

Saur: Your latest book *Love* appears at first to be a story of hate. Two old Black ladies, who live together under the same roof, hate each other's guts. One is the widow of a prosperous colored hotel owner, Bill Cosey, who in the sixties ran a successful holiday resort for well-heeled Blacks, the other is his granddaughter.

Morrison: The Civil Rights Movement of the sixties suddenly released Black people into their own class society. Before, they had all lived together. After apartheid, Blacks could go to other schools, move into neighborhoods in which whites lived. The unity was shattered. Today, the history of the Civil Rights Movement is glorified. The two women in my book represent this class difference. They live together in a house, but they are from different classes. And they, therefore, feel profound hatred for each other.

Saur: Are you criticizing the Civil Rights Movement of the sixties?

Morrison: We owe it to the Civil Rights Movement not to see it glorified. It deserves the meticulousness that any good idea deserves.

Saur: Why did you name your book *Love?*

Morrison: At first, I had another title, which was very useful to me during the writing of the book. I wanted to call the book "L." That is what the narrator of

224

the story is called. Only when I got to the end did I notice that her full name is really "love." I then replaced the word in the text each time with other words. It is only spoken by the narrator herself—and once in the last conversation between the two women, when they finally reconcile. They have earned the word for themselves.

Saur: Your two protagonists live for years together without speaking to each other.

Morrison: That's another reason why I like the title: We human beings distinguish ourselves from other beings through the fact that we have the power of speech, and that we can love. I wanted to give back to the worn-out word "love" the emotions that it has lost through eternal presence.

Saur: Did the idea for you begin with the women and their silence?

Morrison: The idea for this book began with the question of the entrepreneur Bill Cosey. He is a Black businessman, who does what he wants. He is unscrupulous. And I had to build up characters around him, who would look up to him, whom he would need in order to be successful. I wanted to show the Black bourgeoisie. The silence comes only later.

Saur: Were there really luxury holiday resorts for Blacks?

Morrison: Yes. These resorts existed everywhere in the country. I did not make the place in my novel a specific place, but there were at that time many Black resorts, in which the Black middle class, having separated itself from its poor brothers and sisters, would holiday. Some of these settlements survived and became Black communities. Many closed, because the Black bourgeoisie pushed its way into exclusive white clubs.

Saur: In *Love* Bill Cosey remains a powerful man even after his death. The women cower before his portrait. Are women more influenced by men in your books than the other way around?

Morrison: *Love* begins in the late forties. And at the time, women's identity was strongly tied to what men did. The identity of a woman was linked to the power of her men. And that continues to this day. But what interested me was that this man in my novel would not have all this power if the women had not given it to him. The women are his satellites, but they also nurture him.

Saur: What exactly is power?

Morrison: Power is life. Women know about the incredibly seductive potency of power, which has an effect not only on women, but also on men. Power possesses magic, and I have always wanted to demystify that power without taking away any of its potency. For power is vital.

Saur: Are power and love compatible?

Morrison: Power does not change. Love, on the other hand, always means something else. For the generation of my great-grandmother, love meant to make sure that my grandmother would not be a slave anymore. For my mother it meant providing me with an education. My love for my children consists of letting them be free.

Saur: What does love mean for the younger generation?

Morrison: I worry about the new generation, which only concerns itself with new toys. It worries me, too, that young parents are afraid of their children. They are afraid to set limits for their children. They fear giving their children orders. These people want to be their children's friend. The result is that children are growing up without adults. An infantilization of society is taking place. And this is true for all levels of society and races.

Saur: Do American Blacks have more power today than ten years ago?

Morrison: I think we're stagnating. Large corporations such as American Express or Time Warner are run by Black bosses. Some of those men are true philanthropists. They administer incredible amounts of money, and they give some of that back. One can really change things in that way. But it doesn't happen too often.

Saur: Do you distrust Black politicians?

Morrison: Nothing is to be expected from politicians like Condoleezza Rice or Colin Powell. They only have the power to negotiate, not to influence. They are a part of the great mass, they're not interested in those who do not belong to the mainstream. They believe people who have money can help, since only with money can one change things, can one achieve social improvements.

Saur: You don't sound optimistic in regard to the future of African-Americans.

Morrison: I am, I believe, as a matter of principle, not optimistically minded. Blacks are trying to become integrated into the great mass of American society. If the attempt is successful, it will bring not only the merits of that great mass, but also its horrors.

Saur: Where do these horrors lie?

Morrison: We live in a country in which middle-class independence is no longer encouraged. Our government sees in us only consumers. After every problem, we are told we need to buy more, as a way of solving, or at least diminishing the problem. What did the politicians advise us to do after September 11th? Consume, travel, take in a play, go to the mall. I can understand that nobody wants to see the economy collapse, but what was packed into that piece of news? We show the terrorists how strong we are, that we are, in spite of it all, on our way to Disney World.

Saur: What would you like to give your readers through your books?

Morrison: I want as an author to be like a good jazz musician. To make music that impresses people who really know something about music, and that all those who see music as pure entertainment can dance to it.

Saur: Has the Nobel Prize changed you?

Morrison: You get good tables at expensive restaurants. My son asked me recently: "The person who got the Nobel Prize, does she walk behind you or in front of you? Do you like her, or don't you?" I do like her, and she walks ahead of me, so that I can see her and warn her before she does anything foolish.

Pam Houston Talks with
Toni Morrison

Pam Houston / 2005

From *Other Voices* (Fall/Winter 2005, vol. 18, no. 42). Pam Houston originally conducted her interview with Toni Morrison on assignment from *O Magazine*, in which a short excerpt of their discussion first appeared. Reprinted by permission of Pam Houston.

We feel lucky if, during the course of our lives, we have a chance to sit and talk with one of our heroes. But when our hero not only lives up to, but overreaches our expectations, we feel something closer to chosen, even blessed. Such were my feelings a little over a year ago on a humid summer morning at Toni Morrison's apartment in lower Manhattan, where we began an extraordinary conversation that would—to my surprise and delight—last all day.

Ms. Morrison is a person who gives you her full attention, who wants, even in the context of an interview, to have a conversation, who is entirely self-possessed without being the least bit self-obsessed, who is at every minute teaching and at every minute eager to learn. The occasion was the publication of her eighth novel which, like many of her other novels bears a one-word title, *Love*. *Love* is built—"like a crystal," Ms. Morrison said— around two women, Christine and Heed, best childhood friends, whose relationship disintegrated because of the internal pressures of desegregation, and the sexual shenanigans of one powerful man named Bill Cosey.

Originally from Ohio, Ms. Morrison has perfect elocution, and speaks more precisely, more articulately than anyone I have spoken to in my life. She is soft-spoken and regal, except for the odd moment when she erupts into raucous laughter and throws herself sideways into an overstuffed chair. At seventy-three she is young in spirit, long in wisdom, as dedicated as ever to her craft. Her humor and authenticity put me so at ease it was hard to remember I was in the presence of a Nobel Prize winner.

"The award itself is fine," she said, "but it is not going to help you with the things that really challenge you. You have to deal with your children and your friends, and that is what makes life original and interesting. I grew up with a group of people who were unimpressed with books and all that goes with them, and my greatest fear is that they might think I wasted my life. I don't mean wasted it in the sense of not becoming a famous person, but that I just didn't live right, that they would suck their teeth at me about everyday things."

Ever since Ms. Morrison began her first novel, *The Bluest Eye*, in 1965, writing has always been her place of clarity, an "unsullied place of envisioning and imagining," a place she has been totally free. Right from the beginning she saw her own project as groundbreaking in its dedication to writing without what she calls the White Gaze. She was committed to writing like a Jazz or Blues musician, just for the people, an audience she knew would be demanding, honest and sophisticated, and once she got into that brand new space a whole world opened up for her. Out of that world has come *Sula*, *Song of Solomon*, *Tar Baby*, *Beloved*, *Jazz*, *Paradise* and *Love*, a body of work unequalled in American letters, the nearest thing America has to a national novelist, according to the *New York Times*.

Each of Ms. Morrison's novels rise to a greater narrative challenge. The identity of her narrators often remain elusive; sometimes they seem like no one in the book, sometimes they seem like everyone in the book, sometimes they are recently back from the dead, sometimes they seem to speak as the physical book you hold in your hand. Her novels are always complex, structurally demanding and ask for, but do not require a second reading. Reading her novels teaches us how to read her novels, teaches us to trust her narrators, teaches us that if we just keep reading, if we give ourselves over to her spyrographic style, all the truth we need will be revealed. And yet to read Ms. Morrison's novels more than once is to understand exactly what separates good literature from great literature, to see how on the third and fourth and fifth time through, these novels only intensify and deepen, offer up more of their secrets, remain true both structurally and thematically to themselves.

There are no villains in Toni Morrison's books and no heroes. The narrator of *Love* whose name is L., says of Bill Cosey, "you could call him a good bad man, or a bad good man, depends on what you hold dear . . . he was an ordinary man ripped like the rest of us by wrath and love." This ability is what makes Toni Morrison perhaps the greatest writer of our generation. For all her fluency in the English language, for all her breathtaking flights of lyricism and song, for all her ability to create one structural masterpiece after another, to redefine the phrase "narrative tour de force" with each subsequent book, the greatest of her gifts is her insistence on honoring the complexity, the multiplicity of the human spirit—it is the steady and unflinchingly honest observer's eye, combined with the unfaltering and deep compassion she brings to each of her characters, and by association each of her readers, and by association the whole world.

Please join me in welcoming to the pages of *Other Voices* . . . Toni Morrison.

PH: I was reading all the old books again, in preparation, and I couldn't help seeing the relationship between this book, *Love*, and *Sula*—with a different ending. You know, this time the women have the conversation at the end. Was that a conscious rewrite?

TM: I think the idea of a wanton woman is something that I may have inserted in almost all of the books. A kind of an outlaw figure who is disallowed in the community because of whatever reason—her imagination or her activity or her status, whatever. That kind of anarchic figure has always fascinated me. Even in *Paradise* there is such a woman. In spite of the fact that they are either dismissed or upbraided, something about their presence is constructive in the long run. Sula being someone they missed terribly when she was gone; they lacked a kind of focus in their community after she died—even though she was the pariah.

Then in *Love*, Junior is a poor, rootless, free-floating young woman, the narrative cuts her loose from the ground. And what you get is a survivor, a manipulator, a hungry person; but nevertheless, she does effect a space where people can come with their better selves—not just Romen, but the two women. So the consequences of that female figure are frequently distinct improvement or some kind of personal progress for the characters that surround them.

PH: I was thinking about how in *Sula*, Nell and Sula never reconnect. That seems to be the big regret of that book—and in this book Christine and Heed do, so I was wondering if you gave those two figures another chance to work it out.

TM: Yes, in life and in death they finally talk, when they are about to lose each other. They were so in love they didn't mind living together in pure hatred as long as they were entangled, and then when they were faced with the possibility of one of them not being there—then there is a clear, unpolluted stream; a real conversation, that has never taken place at all between them, not since they were—

PH: Eleven and twelve. Romen seems to be on the way to being the purest-hearted man in your work to date. Does he reflect a change you see in men at this point in history, or could he have come along in any era?

TM: Well, Paul D is a good man; and Romen's grandfather, Sandler, is a good man—caring and fussy and important—and he has something to say to [Romen], something to do with how he turned out. Part of my feeling is that contemporary young men don't . . . There is so much absence of real talk in this book. Missed opportunities to say what one means, so that Romen has the benefit of the generation—not his parent's generation—who still talk to teenagers.

There is a moment when Sandler remembers how his parents talked to him, how difficult it is now. Vida complains about that gap in the generations, and she says that it is speech that jumps the gap. Somebody's not telling somebody something. I don't mean history and like that. I mean, real conversations that could have taken place and should have taken place, don't.

There was a problem along that line in *Paradise* as well, when the old fathers talked about everything historical except their own lives. The contemporary notion of talking to offspring when one talks about one's life is to romanticize it almost. Not getting off the dime the way we talk about the '60s, the way we talk about the '70s, but with nostalgia—with real desire not to remember it with excitement or hatred or whatever, but to stay there; to stay in that place of permanent youth, which means that the youth don't get any youth.

That's what I meant; that's what I think. Well, that's not what I meant—I didn't say any of it—but the notion of using one's own experience to enable young people, rather than keeping them bound up in fantasies of what your own youth was, that's the difference between the fantasized past that some people keep (and it is a weight on the next generation) versus using one's own experience in order to move it along a little bit; giving the young person an opportunity to fail or to be whatever he is or to call forth that quality, like Romen does. He is a caring person, and it embarrasses him tremendously until he gets permission almost, from his grandfather.

PH: It seems like all of your books are about love. It seems like that's one of the things they are all about, and I wonder what it was about this book that led you to call it Love.

TM: I called it *The Sporting Woman* for years. After Celestial.

PH: Oh, I wondered also if she at one time had a larger presence in the novel than she does now.

TM: No, what I wanted was her undertow existence; but I was thinking of Christine and Heed as another kind of Sporting Woman. Not in the sense of a prostitute, but a woman of courage—a woman with game so to speak— another kind of figure that toughed it out in a sense. But that didn't seem to work, because in order to bring all those things together their behavior would have to be a little bit different, and they wouldn't go there. They would have to be—

PH: Stronger?

TM: They liked each other. I mean, it just didn't work; my plans for them didn't work out. They had some other agenda apparently. Then I decided to call it *L*.

PH: Just *L*, period?

TM: Yes. Because of the woman who tells the story and who knows everything and who is an active participant in the novel. Now her name is Love, and somebody suggested it as a title, and I felt very alarmed—but the fact of the alarm was more interesting to me then just saying, Oh, that's terrible. I began to think about why. I mean, I didn't just say, Oh, ridiculous. I said to this person, "That is easily the most empty cliché, the most useless word; and then of course it is, at the same time—because hatred is involved in it too— the most powerful human emotion." So then I mulled and thought, Is there another book with that title? He said *love* is used in millions of titles but never by itself, and I don't know if that is true, but I had a feeling that maybe it could carry its weight that way. And then I also thought if I removed the word from every other place in the manuscript, except by the woman named Love—nobody else ever uses that word, except at the very end when . . . somebody is dying.

PH: But we don't know who.

TM: [*laughs*] I do, but you don't. So then it becomes an earned word. If I could give the word, in my very modest way, its girth and its meaning and its terrible price and its clarity at the moment when that is all there is time for, then the title does work for me, and I will just put up with—

PH: Whatever they say.
TM: [*laughs*] But you know I have to tell you—I didn't use the word a lot, but when I went back to clean up and never say for instance, *I love the night*, just to take out all those *loves* and look for other words and other sentences, it was just the most amazing exercise, because now I know why everybody uses the word: because it works.

PH: It fills in.
TM: It fills in. So if you have to find a fresh way in the parlance, in the vernacular, whatever—it took some time.

PH: Love says, at the end of her first section, "a story that shows how brazen women can take a good man down." And the story turns out to be quite different from that. I mean, I get that Love is a brazen woman and she takes Bill Cosey down, but again the story seems to be so much more about all the things we do to avoid love, and about the real love that exists between the women.
TM: Real love between the women, and the generous love of Love for him. She just lets him be.

PH: Love's love, you mean, for Bill Cosey.
TM: And her generosity with other people. But her love for Bill Cosey is another level. I don't even know what to call it. It is slightly maternal, but not really. It is totally acceptable. It is Jesus at his best.

PH: In *Paradise* you call it "unmotivated respect."
TM: Yes, that's right. And Bill Cosey's love for Celestial makes him do all sorts of things: first his son, then Celestial, and the thing about his father. So it is a kind of exploration of exactly what you said; and the grandparent's relationship to Romen; and of course the teenager's notion of love, which is awful except that one moment of the kiss when Junior looks at him and starts getting this alien feeling. I thought it was more like trust, whatever it is— something she's never felt for a human being. Instead of feeding on him like

birthday cake, she gets to feel something slight and ripply and scary and pretty, so there is a possibility for her. And then of course he leaves on his mission, so when she is scooting around eating lamb and stuff, she gets to feel scared about feeling vulnerable in a way that she never has before. And I was hoping to suggest that the future for her is not clear. The women say, Yes well, she could be a criminal; but they may be keeping her—she doesn't have anyplace to go. Even L says, "Maybe a caring hand . . ." But I didn't want to close off Junior's possibilities.

PH: The order in which we learn things about Bill Cosey is very interesting. We start out believing that he is good for the community, good to others, and then little by little we learn things that make us distrust or dislike him. But then he is sort of redeemed in a way by Celestial's scar—because that connects him back to Romen, and the foot, and loving the injured thing.
TM: Well, that scar was from a fishhook that connected him back to *his* son, whom he loved and bragged about, but loved in a trophy way. And that connection back to the trophy son—although he admits later that he didn't really know him—makes him quite obsessed with Celestial, and she stays with him, but his real engine is his father.

PH: Dark.
TM: There is a Dark in every community—maybe in every family, as L thinks. There is someone who is not on your page, and who makes money by withholding the truth, and then sustains the role, so to speak, in an insidious way. And in trying to reverse that pattern Cosey may have ended up betraying everything around him. He has certainly betrayed Christine—he couldn't even look at her—and he doesn't even know that his wife, whom he loved . . . She can't stand it when she finds out all this stuff he had come from. The constant things in his life as far as women are concerned—in so far as he was a womanizing man—were Celestial and Love. He is a complicated figure. He does terrible things, causes people terrible pain that they can't get over. On the other hand, he was enabling to people in the community. And as L says, he was just an ordinary man, torn like the rest of us. Nevertheless she felt he had to be put away, fast.

PH: It is interesting that Love is the one—the one with the name Love—who takes that power of judgment over him in the end. Tell me a bit about the organization of this book. The nouns that divide the sections [represent] the things that he was, I'm guessing.

TM: All the things that he was or—well, he wasn't *all* of these things, but it was organizing according to the idea of maleness. What everyone is looking for in masculinity: that benevolent or hostile notion of maleness. The first part was originally called Image, which I liked better than Portrait, but it has a contemporary meaning— you know, image, imago—so I decided I would just say Portrait, because it was there.

PH: On the wall. It was interesting to me that *Paradise* was divided by the women's names, and that this man was subdivided in the book called *Love*.
TM: I heard a guy say, "Women. You can't live with them, and you can't shoot them." It is interesting what happens over time with our notions of male–female relationships. As father, as brother, they aren't just guys; they are all these other things. Especially women in their sixties who have had to escape—they have to manage the control men have in their imaginations as well as in their personal lives, ending up as they do with a ghost in the house.

I have lots of questions in the novels. I was very much interested, not in the male–female love relationship, which is ubiquitous, but in other relations of the women with the idea of what maleness is in their lives: father, husband, benefactor, friend.

PH: Benefactor. Can you tell me where the book began, or where books begin in general for you?
TM: The ideas were very dark and complicated, and focused not on Junior but on a kind of wanton loose spirit affecting . . . She has those boots and stuff.

PH: And a cloven hoof.
TM: She has all these sinister things, so it was important to give her a real context, so she's not, like, the Devil. She's a person. I just wanted to wander around and to have L think about that miasma of surveillance, which for her is just the dark side: things just happen and you have to worry about them. I didn't know it was that girl. I just wanted to place that evil—not in the pompous sense; sort of an everyday evil—but I didn't know who that person was. The first thing I wrote, before I knew anything else, which was a very compelling scene to me at the time, was Romen at that party. And I wrote the

whole thing out, and I liked it a lot. In fact when I was chatting up the book to the publisher, that's what I was talking about. Then, putting that in context, the crystal just kept adding little parts. I was able to make it work as an ur-text as well as a narrative: it was underneath, and all that was down there could either bubble up or not. It worked on several levels for me.

PH: Was there anything different about putting all these characters next to the ocean?

TM: Yes. Once I knew that I was going to talk about the very successful life of African American business before integration—a life that one saw in various places, [with] excellent black schools, property owners, and physicians; that whole pre-'60s era—I opted for what is generally not remembered or talked about: black vacation spots in New Jersey, Lake Erie, Sag Harbor . . . all those places where black people were very happy and content without integration.

PH: They had worked it out for themselves.

TM: They had worked it out. That was called racial uplift. It was the goal. And resorts like this one existed in the South. It was where the musicians went; it was where the people went. In comes, No no no, we want to assimilate completely. And that was a good move, but like all good moves, all those places—not all, but pretty much all the black stores disappeared, the black schools are desperate for money. That's what you pay if you want this other thing. That's the way the world works; it can't do two things at once.

So the collapse of these hotels and restaurants, and even neighborhoods, was a very significant and powerful shift, and I just wanted to track that with him, with Bill Cosey, who had built this business. And even people who didn't go there were delighted with the fact that it existed. African American life had both extremes. You had Christine over there passing out pamphlets and joining underground groups and screaming, and her mother—who is an exaggeration of another kind of fear—saying, "What are you doing?" She is terrified of revolutionaries, because they are going to ruin what she loves; which is all black and, for her, socially upward business and community. And I'm not at all sure that that debate—which did exist very powerfully during the '60s—now everyone was on the right side of the battle, to hear them say it. There was a big argument about what the consequences would be, and the conversation between young African Americans and their parents was over control.

I think those same seeds flower now in debates about Affirmative Action, about whether race is really impacting on people or not. And you have a maybe small but certainly very vocal group of Americans who are questioning the value of this liberal aggressive move that sweeps away everything and has its own agenda. So that tension still exists, and it is the consequence of this very extraordinary trajectory of what racism does to a whole people.

PH: Forever.

TM: Forever. It is, one more time: the reason for this is *this*; the reason for this, is *this*. I mean, you are trying to be a complex human being within the canvas of the fortune or misfortune of race—that has been an indelible mark on our history. It is not as though assimilation was easy, because of the powerful physical difference that is skin color. Any other group can make it through a little bit. So racial assimilation seemed to me to be a current—and maybe permanent—well, certainly a current theme that harks back to the same questions and confusion about him.

PH: Bill Cosey.

TM: Because even Sandler says, "I don't know I sort of liked him." But he was more of an education than anything else. [Sandler] was trying to figure out who this guy was, what he was really like. And loving how Cosey could speak to a cop, pay somebody off, pay for somebody's education, do these things that were generous and large. And he liked fun. So there was a positive side to him, but there was this other personal story underneath that was just conflict and selfishness.

PH: Well, I think that is one of the things about your work that is so powerful. The women are black women, but they are also women, and they are also black people. So much of the sexual abuse and the histories of sexual abuse and the cycles of abuse that goes on and on—there is so much of that that has to do with race and so much of it that is apart from race, that is just about men and women.

TM: That's right. Precisely so. And when you push it all into one area, you get this flat, to me very boring story. If you push it off into the other, where race is of no consequence, it is not accurate. There *are* real consequences, so if you can butt those two together, it is richer. And it may be unsatisfying in a sense, because I don't tend to [lead] people . . . But, if you know something really

important at the end of a book—if the characters do and the reader does—
then that is a happy ending, even though . . .

PH: Sure.
TM: [*laughs*] She says *sure*. It's about what you can say.

PH: Well, you can't tell anyone how to think in fiction, or you'll get the exact
opposite response.
TM: Right [*laughs*]. But if you can just lay it out a little bit and have this dramatic talk—conversations in a book that move the story along but are also
revelatory for the people who have them. I can't remember what L says about
it; if they had only known how precious the tongue is, or the uses of it. You
know, all this time—

PH: You could have been speaking.
TM: What you could say instead of the silences and the evasions—or just to
keep from turning one's life around into some terrible thing.

PH: But that is interesting too, because she herself was so silent, she gave
everybody permission with her silence. That's what so great about your work:
the opposite is always contained in every assertion. That's why it is so true. In
this novel, and in all the novels, women have so much power—but they don't
always know it, and they don't always act like it.
TM: It is a question of exercising power. Not just dominating people. *How*
you exercise it. Sometimes you have to shut up and let people do what they
do, and sometimes you intervene. It is a very complicated process, and in
a funny way we were not trained for it.

PH: We being women, or we being black women?
TM: We being women were not trained for it. On the other hand, in a funny
way African American women *were* trained for it, because the social circumstances were such that—you know, I always knew I had to work. It never
occurred to me that I wouldn't. And there was a time when black families who
could afford to send one child [to school] always sent the girl; as opposed to
I think what is true for most white families, where they would educate the boy,
and the girl would have to scrape or beg or maybe if they had enough, maybe
she could go too. But [blacks] always educated the girls rather than the boys.

And the boys agreed. They weren't made to feel lesser, because the girls could go into nurturing professions—teacher, nurse, you know, something caring—whereas if you educated your sons back then, they, being men, would want to compete, take over. And they would have difficulty.

PH: With the father, you mean, or with the white people?
TM: With white men.

PH: So you could sort of sneak your girls in.
TM: That was an organism that was trying to survive. I know so many black families in which there are, like, five women doctors. I have heard stories from white friends of mine who talk about the difficulty of being taken seriously as an educated person; and I always think of it in a way like sending one daughter to the convent—sort of a protective thing. Like in Catholic families, the family does something that is going to help. You can't do all of it, but you could do something. So black women had a certain kind of power, even though it was limited. They couldn't be CEOs, I don't mean that, but they could go to college. That ability may have seemed to some of them like a burden. I mean, not the education but now I have to work *and* raise the family. On the other hand, for some it was a road to power and they exercised it that way.

I don't know what the training is now. I can't imagine how professional women who are thirty or forty years younger than I am train their girls. Do they take their daughters to the office? It doesn't mean that you necessarily get a better job; it's what you do with it when you get it. When I was working for a company in which women had positions of some power—they didn't own it but they were close to it—I was just amazed at how violent—

PH: Like in academia?
TM: Oh, they just stand at the gate and chop off every feminine head that comes their way. It was just stunning. And even when a woman was treated badly by a male boss and we chatted about it, she just went on and repeated and repeated that cycle. I gave a commencement address in New York called "Cinderella's Stepsisters," and I said that it was an interesting story because there were these women whose sole purpose in life was to destroy another woman, and they did—what held them together was the destruction of other women—and that there were such stepsisters throughout the professional world, and I was appalled. Well not that theatrical, but I was trying to

suggest to the graduating class that when you go out of this school and off this campus and get these jobs that you have been so brilliantly trained for— just remember that that's not your job. *Your* job, you know, is that if you are free, you need to free somebody else. If you have some power then it's your job to empower somebody else; it's not a grab bag candy game.

PH: Don't you think . . . Well, I think, here at forty—
TM: Are you? You look like a little girl.

PH: I mean, I have come to understand that the only thing that consistently makes me happy is service, is acting on behalf of others with generosity. I mean, I write books, and I've had some success and that's been great, but the thrill of that lasts about fifteen minutes.
TM: Right.

PH: And everybody likes you for the wrong reasons then; there is all of that. But the thing that is immediately satisfying and consistently satisfying is when I act with generosity toward another person. And it is so insane that we are not trained that way, because it is so easy and natural. It is the easiest way to be.
TM: It is instinctive. Romen doesn't do it because of—

PH: Peer pressure?
TM: Yes. Guy stuff. And weakness. It is regarded as weakness. We are sup-posed to be dog-eat-dog and sweep everyone out—and that is a sad, sad, no-win idea: that we mark our success by how many people we don't have to pay attention to anymore.

PH: How have you managed your own power? You know, with all the awards you've received. I mean, you have become a very powerful person. I'm not asking [whether] you managed it badly. I just mean, what do you tell yourself to make sure you stay in touch; or does that just come naturally to you?
TM: You know, I didn't start writing until I was your age—publishing any-way. I mean, I was thirty something when I started *The Bluest Eye*, thirty-nine when it was published. I never had youthful—

PH: Stupidity?
TM: Accolades. And people weren't paying a lot of attention anyway. So I grew up with these other responsibilities. And another group of people who

I regarded as people who approved of me—these people were unimpressed with the book and all the stuff, and they are still sort of out there. And my greatest fear is that they might think I wasted my life. I don't mean wasted it in the sense of not becoming a [successful] person, but that I just didn't live right. That they would suck their teeth at me about, you know, everyday things. So that is where I live.

PH: Still. . .
TM: Oh yes. And there have been some nice things that have happened since I have won awards and things. The award itself is fine, but it is not going to help you with the things that really challenge you. You have to deal with your children and your friends and family, which is really where it *is*—and that is what makes life original and interesting to me. The other stuff is not so interesting. And the down sides are, you mentioned one, people are not looking at me—

PH: As you.
TM: No.

PH: As a human being.
TM: No [*laughs*]. And so I am clinging desperately to the friends I have who knew me before. And I sent this manuscript off to people who have no interest in flattering me at all, who read books but who are not in the literary world, they just are insightful; and people I trust to be who they are. I wanted to see what their response was before I showed it to anybody whose job it was to—

PH: Like it.
TM: Yes. I had a moment after I won the Nobel Prize where I thought—well, I thought, Whoopee! This is the biggest party and I am going to enjoy it. And then there was the after thing, about going back to work. I was already working on a book, *Paradise*, when it happened, so I didn't have to think up something, but it took a little while for me to shut the door, clear my head; and I never had to do that before. I never had to think about critics. I was never *there*; I was always *here*. Having worked in publishing, I was always aware how such things could happen or not happen, but I was never very dependent on outside people's evaluations.

It was a little naive, but it helped clarify and keep unsullied the place where my imagination lives. That's where I am free—it was the only place where I was always totally free. And I could not have that penetration coming into that place, because in every other aspect of my life I am beholden to somebody else; teaching, for example. I mean, I don't mean you don't have solitary fun, but this is how I feel: *that* is about other people; *this* is about what I think, and what I can envision and imagine, and my glory in manipulating language. I could write every one of those books again. You know what I mean? Sometimes when I am standing up there giving readings in public . . .

PH: Do you edit on the fly?
TM: I just think, That's not right—*now* I know what that word ought to be!

PH: I always find when I come home from a book tour—I actually like touring, because I like the conversation in general, but then I find I have to make such a huge change to stop being the kind of politician I have to be on a book tour and start being a writer again.
TM: Yes, yes. I like signing books in bookstores. And maybe it is not the best use of my time. Publishers would rather have me with television or press for two hours—which maybe is cost effective, but I would spend two hours in a bookstore any day, because that is when I get to meet readers, and also being there helps independent bookstores, but that part of it I like. *This* part—I mean, you are easier because you are a writer, because you are asking more intelligent questions. Television is hard, but I feel obliged to do it, to garner readers and to make myself available as much as I can since I am around. And I have a nice readership in universities, which is a big benefit because I speak in ways there that I couldn't on television. And to have future generations reading my books—*The Bluest Eye* they read in junior high school.

PH: And *Sula*.
TM: And *Sula*. My sister wouldn't let her daughters read *The Bluest Eye* until they were eighteen, and I wonder, why do they want them to read it so young? It is not a children's book. It is scary. I've changed my mind about that a little bit now because I have heard teachers and students talk about it, and it was not at all what I thought. And also I like to think the books can be read again later, when it is not an assignment. I think you are the second or third person—there haven't been many before—who talk about my work from a writer's point of view.

PH: Well, since you said that, I'll go back for a minute. One of the things about your work that makes it interesting to read multiple times is that you leave so much space in your work for the reader to enter. And I try to do that in my work too; that is the way I talk about fiction with my own students.
TM: I get so many questions about what happened, or complaints that it is difficult, [the students] don't know what is going on—I decided that maybe no one is reading anymore. Maybe they are just skimming and not reading. I don't know, maybe it is, you know, turning off the show at the end of the half hour. The other day I was talking to somebody about pornography. I was saying that I had seen two pornographic films. I was trying to say why I didn't like pornography, having very little experience with it, but the two occasions I had were very instructive. One was, well, some people had a live eel. Black and white, grainy, a graduate student film. There was a girl in there and some other people . . . I mean, abuse to the eels you wouldn't think would be the most—anyway, you are just screaming for this eel, so we just shut it off. But then later, in Germany, we turned on the television and this spot kept coming up with these two very beautiful, surgically perfect women having sex—

PH: With each other?
TM: With each other. Repetitive, repetitive, repetitive. The same two or three actions, and I'm sure there are much more interesting ones. This has something to do with leaving space, I promise [*laughs*]. If you don't have an imagination . . . I just invite you to think about it. When I do sexual scenes—which I hope are very sensual—but the reason they are is because the metaphors come from some other place, so you can place your own sensuality, your own sexuality in that place, which is always the sexiest. I mean, after all, it *is* yours. So watching somebody else seems to be like watching somebody in love, or on an operating table—very clinical. But I think it is useful, maybe, because people don't think in images anymore. They may have frail imaginations, and this kind of film fills it out for them. But in text, if everything is out there for you, all the information is given, then you don't have any work to do.

I was raised on radio where you listened and you had to pick it up—the action, the scene—and the books I like are those that don't shut me out by giving me everything there is. So (a) that is the kind of writing I like, and (b) I think it is good for the active imagination. It is not just being fed information; it is producing it, along with the author. It is harder too, and I like that.

PH: Me too. One of the things that your books do for me—and always have since I started reading them twenty-five years ago—is, I finish one of your books and I notice myself looking at the world differently. Especially coming to New York. I live in Colorado. I live in a very white place. I teach at the University of California; actually I am running the program there.

TM: Oh my goodness!

PH: Yes, but these are my Colorado months. And having reread a lot of the books that I had read before, and reading the new book, and then getting off the plane in New York and being immersed in such a different world . . . I find myself looking at people the way—back in the days when I was afraid of people—I used to look at landscape: mountains and rivers and things that I could get next to comfortably. I look at them with such fascination. Your books do that for me; they make me look at everyone and think that they are these absolute miracles walking around—complicated and impossible to fathom. And it seems to me that that is a very hopeful thing right now, in a time when it is easy to get bogged down in hopelessness.

There is a lot of cause for alarm right now, and fear. In fact I was noticing this one part in *Paradise* when Sargeant sounds just like Bush to me. [*flipping through book*] There it is, page 308. I wrote Bush on the bottom of the page [*laughs*]. The question here boils down to a pretty generic one, I guess, which is, What is the role of the literary artist in times of insanity and distress?

TM: You have to go to work. I was feeling aghast. I kept saying, *What?* for the last couple weeks. I kept going around with my mouth open, disbelieving, and I realized that was, for me, a form of paralysis; just being shocked. Saying, *It couldn't be. No one . . . Impossible.* I had this last story that had come through on the desk—the transcript of our president's visit to Israel, talking to the prime minister of Palestine. And *Haaretz*, which is a very respectable Israeli newspaper, translated the minutes of the meeting in which George Bush said that God told him—did you hear this? Well, he said—I mean, I know he is righteous [*laughs*]—God told him to bomb Afghanistan; and that God told him to bomb Iraq; and that now God told him to fix what was going on in the Middle East between Israel and Palestine, but they had to concentrate on it, they had to get it together soon, because he [Bush] would have to go pay attention to the election. And I said, This is Room Nine information; this is straight-jacket stuff.

But I have to give him credit, because last year—because I was in that position of frozen apprehension, shock, despair and amazement—I said, I can't live like this. So I finished *Love* earlier than I thought, because I just went to work and said, This is what I do and this is what artists should be doing. It was like all those people in occupied France who just wrote—you know, Sartre, all those people. I think this is the time for artists. Yes, this is the time for every artist in every genre to do what he or she does, loudly and consistently. It doesn't matter to me what their position is, it just has to be overwhelming.

PH: And honest.

TM: Absolutely. When those poets [were] asked to gather at the White House, and then [the administration] called it off, you think, *Really?* They really *do* believe the poets are the legislators of the world, and they really are the philosophers, and they really control—you always thought that, but now you see they are frightened of what the poets might say. It is as clear a test as anything. So with that feeling of necessity for clarity and for the power of imagination to do the work, I sank into that work—and I am still feeling it for any project I undertake. This is no time for anything else than the best that you've got.

PH: I was thinking of how many books I've read since 9/11, or since Bush got elected. I was thinking about *The Hours*, and how in *The Hours* all the characters are doing their best, and in a way that is true about *Love*. I mean, even Bill Cosey is doing his best—that's what they always say about abusers— but he is doing his best to break the cycle of abuse, and not succeeding in a lot of ways. I just finished a novel of my own where that was my unspoken goal: I wanted all the characters, even the ones that are motivated by evil, to be sympathetic, and to be understood and human; and I wanted the narrative to be sympathetic to them, in as much as it could be. And I wonder if now the world, or Bush—or whatever you want to call this Genghis-Khan-losing-his-perspective moment in time—is supplying us with so much evil, and that presence is so ubiquitous that we don't have to identify it in our books anymore.

TM: It is that; plus, that kind of evil is so anti-human.

PH: It has no place in a novel.

TM: You've got to keep asserting the complexity and the originality of life; and the multiplicity of it, and the facets of it. And this is about being a complex human being in the world—not about having a villain to blame. And not about *God* telling you . . . I thought maybe I'd write him a letter and say, *Dear George, I changed my mind. Signed, God.*

PH: *Dear George, This is God; call off your dogs.*
TM: [*laughs*] I wish—I hope—I should do that. I have thousands and thousands of letters unwritten in my head; well, written in my head, but there should just be this onslaught of artists from all over the world just pouring letters into those offices.

PH: Everyone signing them *God.*
TM: I'll be the first. Peter Sellers and I had this conversation not too long ago; he came here for an award that Sundance was giving to artists who take risks. He asked if I was available, and I said yes. But the question was, This is a singular separate little category of artists who take risks—versus what? The norm? I said I thought it went with the word, artist—that the two words went together. But anyway, we were talking, and he always makes me feel a little bit better whenever I talk to him about the necessity of the contradiction; the undermining of conscience; the reassertion of what we know about the world, its treatise, its grand gestures and everything. And I was feeling highly cheerful after that for some reason, because I had been just seething. I was just sitting around seething with everyone I knew, feeling so helpless and powerless, because this is ruthlessness at a level I have not witnessed—and ignorance.

PH: I've been amazed at how I have been censored, even in women's magazines. I'm not allowed to say *Bush.* I am only allowed to say *the current administration.*
TM: I heard a funny joke about Bush and the French: Bush says, *The trouble with the French is that they don't have a word for entrepreneur.* It is seeping down. It is so Gestapo; it is like saying *The War Between the States* instead of *The Civil War.*

PH: Who are you reading now?
TM: Well, I've just gotten back to reading. I can't read anybody when I am working.

PH: And you haven't started a new book.
TM: In my head I have. But I can't read anybody I like when I am writing.

PH: I will tell you this just very briefly. I turned in my novel in May and have just gotten it back from my editor. I am going to spend August and September doing my rewrite, and I thought, well, what great timing, to read all of your books again. Could I have picked a better role model to read in the break?
TM: In that little section. When I was writing, I was reading old books; old Dickens. I think I just graduated to a better level of mystery. I read a book called *The Bookman's Wake*. It is a detective writer who is a rare-book collector, so here was a detective story set in the milieu of somebody who deals in rare books, talks about how terrible his publisher is because he doesn't put the first edition on the first page, that kind of thing. I want to read Marquez's autobiography. Those I haven't read [*indicates a pile of books on the coffee table*], I just had them on the table. I moved them because of my flowers; they aren't there to impress you [*laughs*]. When I come up here I swear I am going to read, but those are still a little crisp. I started reading reviews again, book reviews. I hadn't done that either—I didn't want to know—but now I am back.

PH: Can you talk about how you feel things have changed over the course of your writing career? How things have changed for women, or for black women? The things you say in your books are very clear to me—I don't mean simple in any way—but the way you are empowering human beings in your books is very clear to me. But what do you have to say, if anything, to young women? How is their situation different from yours, or do you think things have mostly stayed the same?
TM: No, they have changed, I think. There is a lot of data that makes me happy; one being the number of African American and Latina and Asian women writers. I read an interesting galley, *A Warm December*, and then I read *Bruised Hibiscus*. They were just young opening novels, but so mature. And the readership is everywhere; you can really and truly see the difference. I can remember when I couldn't, as an editor, publish two black authors in the same season, because no matter what they were doing they were going to be reviewed together. It could be, you know, Ishmael Reed and—

PH: Walter Mosley.
TM: Exactly. And so I would have to space them. But obviously that has changed. There is a demanding readership. That's the heartening thing, as well as the writers. Professionally I live in an academic world, so I am more aware of those changes. I am always startled in the entertainment industry

to see what is going on. So there are huge changes, job related. And there is some enormous amnesia, always at the same time. Nobody remembers anything. Recycling? I thought we did that. I thought we had gotten past that; what are you doing that for?

The hip hop world has some of that quality, of total a-historical nuttiness and powerful edgy insight; it combines those two things. It has a kind of glorification of the underworld—that's its cache I guess—and apparently it makes a lot of money. It is a phenomenon. If you go to Germany, Turkey, France—everywhere you go you hear rap, and it's the ruling vernacular, but something else is going on, I feel. I don't know quite what it is, I am struggling to define the useful, powerful part of it, which is coupled with the part that is so consumer-oriented—*the give me!* and the daring; that quality which is bad—but it is opening up something. And evolving quickly, too—probably more outside the industry than inside it, because it is dominantly designed for white kids in Long Island who want to hear gangster rap.

PH: Or Beloit, Wisconsin, by the way. I taught there last fall—the visiting whatever there—and these corn-fed, freckled, fat-faced farm kids, driving around: *pu-pump pu-pump*, their whole car is vibrating.
TM: I love it. So there is that, but I insist there is something going on in there that is interesting, and not just superficial stuff. I think I can probably get it. One of the reasons I like to hear the Frankfurt German rap is that I don't understand what they are saying.

PH: What they are saying about women.
TM: Right [*laughs*]. And then you have the women's rap. I mean, I don't know, I have to go read some good deconstruction, some postmodern analysis of it, because there are people who are seriously into it. All I know is that it is stripped language. It is stripped down, and it also pulls in interesting ways from this outrageous consumer society—you know, it has a kind of irony in it. I don't want to belabor the point. How did I get to that? You were asking me what the changes were.

I suppose this is simple, but you know, there are eras in African American life in this country that are marked by the musical style—spirituals or gospel or blues or jazz or bop or variations—and when I hear that word, I think of the language of that period. I think of the aspirations, the sounds; the way people looked, how fabulous the '30s look was—I mean, even poor people looked good in those clothes. You know, black and white were . . . So now I am thinking in terms of rap. It is not clear to me yet, but it seems to be defining a particular moment in African American life, whatever else happens to it; and how it got started was quite simple: black kids trying to tell somebody in Detroit what it was like to live in Brooklyn. That's the only way they could really talk about the cops and what was going on, and the evolution it took was quite different and got very murky with the money that became available to everybody.

It is kind of a defining moment. The music is defining something about the so-called progress, the good part and the bad part, and I'm not sure what that is. I am just sort of inching up on contemporary life as I do these books. You know, 1996 was about all I could do for *Love*, because that was as far as I could see. What happened after that, you know, I'm not quite sure about until I get the next book out—but I am going to have to match it with 1730 or something in order to make sure they have these bookends. You know: This is now, but don't forget, don't forget.

There is a lot of ugliness; I feel it. I don't know if the population feels it, and maybe most of it has to do with the tension between the street and the office—maybe it is just that, and that is true of every group you ever encountered—maybe it is just that simple, but these are really critical times. I was just, again, aghast at what the current administration said in Africa the other day—this sort of "slavery was terrible" and disdain—and I said, Why is he telling *them* that? He should be over here saying [it] to black leaders—or whoever wrote that for him. That kind of dialogue should be held here. The consequences of slavery are such that—blah blah blah—instead of going way over there and talking to them about . . . I mean, they are dealing with the consequences of Colonialism, really.

This is all to say that I feel uneasy about describing a timeline of progress in racial matters—even though you can see how different things are even from when I was a kid; extremely different. But at the same time [I am] trying to peel away things that I hate: resistance to common cause—between the races and between the classes; because the class thing is surfacing so powerfully now, just poor people versus anybody else.

It is so marked to me because I grew up in a little industrial town in Ohio where everybody came for work—Mexicans, East Europeans, Greeks, and first generation Italian—and I never lived in a black neighborhood, we were all just poor. One high school to which we all went. I didn't know the

Southern thing; I didn't know the big city or eastern thing, so I am aware of how easy it is to share common aspirations. Also I was born in a period where rich people had to explain themselves. You know, it wasn't so much about getting money, it was nobody believes you can get that rich without thieving. And I was born in a time when you could be a poor person and an adult at the same time. You can't anymore. You saw men who did menial work, but they could build a house or make a garden or raise a family—they could do something that made them adult. Now, if you are poor, you are a child. You have to be fed. They tell you where you can live. You are at the mercy of the society, which may be beneficial or not, but you are an infant; you are treated like a child, and that wasn't true when I was young. It wasn't true for my father or my grandfathers, and all those uncles I had who were poor men; they had these other avenues to adulthood, and I think it was true for men in general, people in general perhaps: they could do things that allowed them to enter an adult world.

Now the differences in economics seem to be more profound and more problematic, so that you get a kind of romance of the street by some people. Do you remember when hobos were not homeless men? When Hemingway could write about hobos as if they were heroes: anarchic, solitary, and not embarrassed about it? I can remember them making *X*s on our doors. A shift has taken place so completely that it has engulfed everyone in the whole country and how one views oneself—and of course for minorities in particular it is more complicated than the media lets us, or encourages us, to believe.

However, the kids who graduate now from college have what can only be called an embarrassment of riches. It is true the job market is a little low, but while they are in college they can think up all these different things to do. When I went to college I just wanted to go where the books were; I just majored in English. You come out, you major in more English, in graduate school. And now women, particularly, have just as many academic choices of interest—even though they say the market is narrower than it has been in some time—almost the same that men do, and they are sometimes liberated by the fact that they have so many choices and sometimes just wiped out by it.

PH: What is your favorite class to teach?
TM: I don't teach it anymore, but I used to teach a class called "Studies in American Africanism," which was interesting for me, out of which came a

book I wrote called *Playing in the Dark*. I was looking at canonical American fiction just to see, you know, writers—I mean what are they doing about race? This is a big question in their minds, how to handle a democratic country that lives on slaves, or post-slavery. What are they doing about it in literature? It is not about whether they are racist or not—it is not about what they thought—it is about what Twain was really doing, or what Poe was really doing, that kind of thing.

I would really like to teach a course about nineteenth-century African American writers and what their response to the *white gaze* really was, how it shows up in their work. That look that is always there, and that you have to shed if you are—well, that you want to shed.

But now I do something else. I taught that course for about six years, and I was hoping somebody else would take it up. I was teaching creative writing also, and I stopped that because I had this sudden epiphany, which was: I'm tired of artists going around always saying nobody treats us right; nobody gives us this; we don't have this, we don't have that. I thought, Well, then we have to do it ourselves. I don't want to ask the government for another dime. I don't want any foundation scraping around telling me why can't we do it. We used to do it. It used to be the great translators were the great poets, the great critics were the great writers. What is all this chopping up into little bits, and now we are on the dole all of a sudden? So I went from that idea and pure annoyance to, How can I do what I do in an academic world, that has something to do with the work I do? In creative writing, I never brought my work in. I mean, it wasn't about my work; it was about the students' work.

I had an interesting experience writing lyrics for Andre Previn and Kathleen Battle. They were experts at what they did, and I was an expert at what I did; but I was a novice in what they did. I didn't know anything about it, so working with them was just amazing. So I started to shape language to do other things. Not to *be* the music, but to just sit there and hold it, so that somebody else could do what they did. That was the first new thing since novel writing that I had done creatively, and I wanted to duplicate that experience at Princeton, so I got some seed money and inaugurated a program called Princeton Atelier. I would bring in artists from all genres, and they would work on what the artist wanted to do. The artists wouldn't make up work for the students; they would do what he or she was doing, and we would get the Princeton students to work with them, or for them. And it's ten years now; I've been doing it ten years.

PH: That's what drives me so crazy about academia—that this is what happens here, but there is no relationship to what is happening out there—and I avoided academia for a decade because of it.

TM: That was exactly my problem. And the question for me was, can the academy—they love art, they love us, but they don't like the process. They can only give fail/pass. They want it to be like Play-Doh. I wanted students to understand how hard this stuff is. It is really hard stuff. We can't grade it that way; it is not a measuring thing. That doesn't mean that it is not powerfully intellectual work—as well as the heartbeat, the inspiration, and your muse. It is really hard, and I thought that if someone came in and worked [the students] to death then they would figure it out, and they do.

PH: I want to go back to something you said earlier. You said when you are writing, it is the only time you don't listen to any of those other voices. I'm tempted to ask: is that really true? Like, are they really gone? Can you make it so they are really gone, all of them?

TM: Oh, yes.

PH: Why? How?

TM: Well they didn't exist in the beginning. When I began to write they weren't there.

PH: Well, some of them must have been.

TM: Oh, no.

PH: I don't mean like the *New York Times*, or the Nobel people or whatever, but all the self-defeating voices.

TM: You mean other people?

PH: The ones you internalize. I mean, it could be a reviewer, or it could be the Nobel people, or it could be whoever hurt you—the hurtful people in your life that you hang on to.

TM: No, no they are gone; they were never there. I mean, they are there in my life [*laughs*]—Oh, the right word to say to him now! But in the work, from the very beginning there was no *them* there, if I can paraphrase, because I was just that arrogant. I just didn't think anybody was ever going to do what I was doing. They couldn't judge me. Nobody was going to judge me, because they didn't know what I knew, and they weren't going to do it. No African

American writer has ever done what I did, which was to write without the *white gaze*. This wasn't about *them*.

Everybody I knew, the ones I admired—Ralph Ellison, *Invisible Man*—invisible to whom? Not me. They are confronting the enemy; the enemy is a white guy, or the white establishment or something. No one was going to write only like a jazz musician or a blues musician, just for the people. And they were going to be very demanding, very honest, unwilling to be flim-flammed—very sophisticated, that reader. That was me, as it turned out. So I couldn't abide the notion that there was anybody else in this world that I was reading or reviewing, recollecting, inventing, who was going to make the center of a story the most helpless creature in the world: a little black girl who doesn't know anything, and who believes all that racist stuff, so *vulnerable*, so *nuts*. And who was going to say she wasn't like that but some other little black girls—because they had never been center stage; this was brand new space.

And of course once I got them into it, it was like the whole world opened up, and I was never going to give that up. I didn't know if I was going to write another book when I got through, of course. But I'm hooked now. This is where I want to live. So I am sitting on the subway going to work and all I see and hear is *Sula*, and what is that really about? And I thought, Nobody is going to like this, and black people are going to be furious because they want, you know, everybody's grandmother and how you can eat off their floor or whatever, the best foot forward. I didn't care what white people thought—they didn't know anything anyway, about this—and my writing was different. I didn't think it was as good as it—

PH: Turns out to be.

TM: [*laughs*] No, I was going to say, as good as it *ought* to be. I thought there was room—that place—nobody was coming in there. I really felt original, I really did. I hate to admit that because it sounds so self-regarding. I didn't feel like an original human being, but that was original space for me.

PH: And that must have been freeing.

TM: Absolutely. That was it. So, when I told you that after the Nobel Prize I had to struggle—that was a mighty battle for me, because All right now you've won this money, and you've won this prize, and that word will never leave my name. It will always be Toni Morrison Nobel, forever, forever. It is not a bad thing. There was something before that prize and presumably something after. Nevertheless, I had to work at it then. I had to work at getting them out of my head. And it took a while, even though I was already clear about what the work was going to be.

PH: Meaning *Paradise*?
TM: *Paradise*. But that struggle was there, and I think I did it well because I went into a place I had never gone before, which was into religion and into the Bible. I am a Catholic; some of my family is Catholic, some of them are Protestant, some of them are all sorts of things. And what saved me was, I think—what helped me at any rate—was knowing that I was going to take religion seriously, I mean belief.

PH: Faith.
TM: Faith. Seriously. It wasn't going to be ironic. I wasn't going to be—these are people who see things, who envision things, who act on things that come, and I wasn't going to disparage it, and I wasn't going to comment on it.

PH: Be sarcastic.
TM: Right. And that was a new space for me, and also I didn't have a lot of contemporary literature to look at. I mean nobody really good does that. Reynolds Price does that, and a guy I used to publish named Leon Forrest did it, but more in a cultural sense. For me it was going to be somebody who takes literally "What a Friend I Have In Jesus." I mean, he walks with me and he talks with me. I mean, my mother had this very intimate relationship with her maker, so that is what I wanted to re-create—and then to take varieties of belief systems and put them in a pot and see what happens with a New Age self-involved woman who learns the spiritual quality of herself, versus [in] the traditional Catholic [sense]. And I thought that was wonderful and new.

PH: And risky.
TM: And risky, and a lot of danger, and the notion of being able to ruin it entirely was there. So I fight like everything for that. It is the only place I have. It doesn't exist anywhere else; I mean, I don't ski.

PH: And to get back in it you had to take the bigger risk. Tell me about the relationship between that and language. I find tremendous freedom in metaphor, personally.
TM: Oh, yes.

PH: For me that is the place of faith and that is the place of freedom.
TM: You are right about that.

PH: And obviously writing is what you do, so that is not the question I am asking. I believed in the transformative power of language before I believed in God, and now I believe in God because of that. That's how I got to God, through the transformative power of language.
TM: Right, right. I have these semi-mystical experiences. I don't remember myself being in the world before I could read. I just don't remember what that was like.

PH: Me either. I was taught at two in West Trenton.
TM: Yes, see, I was about three, because my sister was four and a half, and I remember writing on the cement sidewalks with her; it was an early thing. And I don't remember myself before forming and understanding language, so that is the way I entered the world. I also had this thing about black language, and there was something going on with that kind of speech that I revered that was funny, that was powerfully metamor—full of metaphors. It just pulled at me, you know. It is the way that one hears one's own family talk; you are always interested.

PH: It is funny that you [were about to say] *metamorphic.*
TM: It is metamorphic and metaphoric both. And then I liked the levels. English has something I don't know if other languages have. It is full of everybody's language; it is a polyglot. It has slang, it has standard, it has sermonic, it has lyric, it has all these things that you can pull from—and the point is to make it simple and powerful at the same time. Well, you know what the point is, why am I telling you?

PH: It's O.K. I love hearing it.
TM: So that's what I was trying to do. It was a quality of speech that I was trying to get: if I couldn't hear it, I couldn't write it. Like *The Bluest Eye* began some way, I don't know, and it wasn't working. But then when I got "Quiet as it's kept," and I could just hear those women talking over the fence, gossiping, *quiet as it's kept* . . . So there was that quality of hearing as well as it being accessible and appreciable quietly on the page; trying to do two things at once. So then I thought, the myths and the tales and the lore within the culture had

for so long been enough for the average black person—because we had the music that was the form—and then the music suddenly belonged to anybody. Now, anybody can play great jazz; it's in Japan. I mean, you know, it may be identified as culturally black, but it is not *within* anymore—and I thought, Now is the time for novels.

PH: Because [black people] gave the music away.
TM: We needed something else to go with. We didn't really need novels before; but back in 1965, when I started to write, I said, We need novels. I don't know who needs novels—cultures need different things at different times. The English got their little novel when they needed it: with the classes converging, they needed a way to explain how to get married, or how to get a husband, or what a bad girl was.

PH: Yes. Do you know that essay "Mr. Bennett and Mrs. Brown"? Virginia Woolf's essay [about] the necessity of the change in the literature; that humanity changed forever in 1910?
TM: Yes, that's it exactly. And I felt that we, being deprived literacy—I mean, white people paid a fine if they taught a black person to read, and all that nonsense—and then of course literacy being the escape route . . . Slave narratives had so many jobs to do: they had to encourage abolitionists, and make money, and not call people names but say [slavery was] a terrible thing. I thought, Things are going too fast in 1965; I am going to write a novel that's like this: It's not going to be explaining anything to white people. It is not going to be warning—I'm not into that—it is just going to be literature, and it is going to be about a real girl, and how it hurts, and how we are [accomplices] in that hurt.

I thought, This is the age of Black is Beautiful—and well, yes, that is certainly the case [*laughs*]; however, let us not forget why that became a necessary statement. Because of self-loathing. So that is what made me think it was terribly, terribly important, and no one was going to do that. You know that feeling—isn't that the greatest feeling? That if you don't write it, it will never be written. This thing is never going to happen if you don't [do it]. Eudora Welty can't do it, only you. It felt daring to me, risky; a forbidden book. As a matter of fact, there were lots of people to tell me that: admirers, young black women who said, You know, I really—nice nice nice—but I was really furious with you for exposing it, for saying it.

PH: For not playing the party line.

TM: Exactly so. And I said if I didn't expose it, how would you ever know? I mean, you have to go out there with the public secret. Same thing with *Love*. No one wants to hear that everybody didn't love Martin Luther King, but I remember when many blacks thought he was out of his mind, *What is he doing?*

PH: He's going to make it worse.

TM: Right. It was like during the Resistance in France—now *everybody* was part of the Resistance. Now *everybody* was for the Civil Rights movement. There is a lot to do; that's what's good. There is a lot to write. It just takes so long. I can't do it fast.

PH: Do you go to the computer easily?

TM: I don't go there at all. I mean, I go there eventually, but I can't start there. I have to start with the old legal pads and pencils, because I don't like the act of writing—you know, the formation of letters—so I tend to be crisper and more economical. The computer . . . I'm a good typist, I could go on forever.

PH: And write bad stuff?

TM: And write bad stuff. So if I write it and cross it out and then put it on the computer—

PH: The pressure is greater.

TM: Yes. Then the printout I mark up again, but the beginnings of everything are written with pencil. I let it steep. If you've got it, you got it. If you don't, you don't. There is something called *novel time*. If you lay it down too clearly then you are just following a map and you are not letting it—you just have to let it go, wait for it to be there. Do you get that question, *Do you write everyday?*

PH: What amazes me is that some people say yes.

TM: Well, some people I think apparently do. That's what a friend told me: Toni, what are you talking about? If you write two pages a day, at the end of the year you'll have . . .

PH: I want to write an essay about how writing is completely impossible, and then it is completely possible, and there is no middle ground.

TM: That's true. You can't do it.

PH: You can't do it. And then you can. And that miracle of being able to do it, and you are sitting there thinking, God, I'm the luckiest person on the face of the earth.

TM: But you can't *get* there. All through *Beloved* I said, Well, now I know why nobody wrote this—because you can't do this; this is not a thing that is to be done. But you are right. Somehow, you need a trick. I mean, you need all kinds of little tricks, or little things you do, because I learned in *Song of Solomon*—I thought, Why did I say I was going to do this? And then my father died, and I was really out of it for a long time, thinking, What is that town doing there if he's not in it? Why does it exist? I remember thinking, I wonder what my father thought about those men? And for some reason I knew then that even though I didn't know [what it was], that I was going to get it—that he was going to let me have it—and instead of scratching for it, I went concave. And I thought maybe that is why writers are so self-destructive or melancholy—because they need to be flat, out of it sort of restful; and sometimes they can't get there unless someone punches them, or they're—

PH: Drunk.

TM: Drunk. Then they are exhausted, and then an idea arrives. So the point for me was how to get there without going through the grief. Does someone have to drop dead for me to—? So then another thing happened; I wouldn't tell anybody but you this. When I was really on it and really on it, and really close to it, I would get so sleepy I couldn't stand it, so I would go to bed, and the rest of it would come. So I knew from the *Song of Solomon* experience that you really had to go down, and stop fighting—

PH: Well, your body will do anything to keep you away from the trauma.

TM: That's right. Suddenly, two o'clock in the afternoon, and of course sleep wouldn't come, but it is just knowing. I tell my students: This is all very mysterious, and we all do it differently, but you figure out when is your best time; and when you are really on pace—whether it's dog, music, sandwiches, darkness, whatever it is—find it, and know how your body or mind is either trying to get you there or keep you from the truth. Going to sleep in the middle of a thrilling idea: sabotage all the way. Even so, it is such a good thing to do, to have language to go to.

PH: That's my trick. When I'm just avoiding, I say, O.K., just one concrete sentence about the physical world is all you have to write right now.
TM: That's right, can you do this?

PH: No emotion, just one concrete sentence about the physical world.
TM: That's right. Describe the table!

PH: Look out the window! [*pause*] So, what would you like to do that you haven't done?
TM: Other than write other things? [*laughs*] Nothing.

PH: That's good!
TM: I bought a house in Princeton and I'm fixing it up. And I thought, What are you doing, buying houses? My real house is on the Hudson. My sister says it's because we were born in the Depression and we kept moving every minute from one dump to the other, and I thought yes, maybe that's why; and then I thought no, my ultimate goal in life is to read and play house [*laughs*]. Have a little garden and play house—and if there is nothing to read then I'll write it, so that I have something to read when I am finished.

PH: I'd like to be able to speak French fluently, and I'd like to go to cooking school in Europe. I try to make sure I have a couple of goals that aren't related to writing. I love to cook, and I'm a good cook, but I would love to be able to study cooking in the spare time that I imagine one day having.
TM: You could do them both in France.

PH: I could multitask.
TM: Listen, do you want to—what do you have to do today?

PH: Nothing.
TM: Do you want to go to lunch?

PH: I would love that.

Index

261